THE HUMAN
PARADOX

THE HUMAN PARADOX

It's Time to Think and Act as a Species

Gilbert E. Mulley

To order additional copies of this book, contact:
Xlibris
844-714-8691
www.Xlibris.com
Orders@Xlibris.com
837687

CONTENTS

QUICK-READ OPTION

For a quick overview of this book, read the
Introduction, **boldface text**, and Chapter 6.

INTRODUCTION

The human paradox: we human beings are all the same, yet each one is unique. This is life's continuum—always has been, always will be.

At one end of this enormous spectrum is you, the unique individual. At the other end is our collective species, the soon-to-be eight billion of us alive on this rocky and wet planet. All social interaction from our earliest existence has occurred within the bounds of this huge range. No human activity, ever, has happened outside this paradox, and none ever will. The human paradox will persist as long as we *Homo sapiens* dominate planet Earth.

We, as civilized human beings, have come a long way in improving individual lives and our me/us cultures, but we haven't paid much attention to our species. Why? Because we haven't given the human paradox much thought. We're delinquent here because our energies, for millennia, have focused on smaller social entities such as families, clans, tribes, city-states, and nations. For practically all of human existence, we didn't know we were one species, but now we do.

If the earth belongs to the living, as Thomas Jefferson said, then we, the living, need to acknowledge the human paradox and upgrade the political importance of our species. Our planet can no longer accommodate the overabundance of me/us cultures that deny our species sameness. Earth cannot endure our worn-out social orders, our mindless adoration of strongman leaders, and our religious sanctimonies that separate rather than unite. Our finite planet is pleading with us to think and act at the species level because this may be the only social order left that can meet its potential.

This book presents ideas about how we can accept the human paradox and gestate a species-wide mentality. A few preliminary thoughts:

1. Our species makes a century-long (at minimum) transition away from the predominant themes of nationalism, voracious materialism, and fractious religiosity that undergird hierarchical politics. In their place, we move toward a path of human fulfillment based on global themes of species survival and planetary integrity. Impossible? Naive? Crazy? For living human beings, nothing should rise above the positive goals of species survival and planetary integrity working in tandem—*nothing*.

2. We humans have no choice but to concede that nature will prevail over our own and the planet's future, so why not admit that fact and adapt to it? The COVID-19 pandemic proved how vulnerable we are and how nature can, with little warning, bring us to our knees. Creeping climate change is already kicking our derrieres and upsetting economies well ahead of predictions. Overpopulation may push us to eating our seed corn if we're not careful. We love fantasies, utopias, lottery wins, "technology that will save us at the last minute," and every other dream that fulfills our egotistical selves and our me/us identities, but this self-absorption and limited focus preclude action at the species level—that's been our species' Achilles' heel up to now.

3. Of course, we can continue to laud national sovereignty and kill one another in the name of some ideology or savior politician, or we can believe that some deity will save us because our brand of faith is better than others, and we can wallow in our wealth/achievements/comforts and enjoy some schadenfreude for those below us. In other words, we can keep doing what we're doing now and feel helpless in the face of power perversions, discrimination, and huge income gaps, or we can accept the human paradox, understand it, teach it, and base political power on it.

Question: how often do you say out loud or just to yourself, "I am a *Homo sapiens*"? Not part of your daily routine, is it? Odds are you have never said anything like this.

We don't think of ourselves as members of one species because we've got dozens of other identity options available. Every day our personal identity grows away from species identity, not toward it. For most of us, species identity is just a taxonomic designation taught in biology class—and a rather boring one at that. Being a social media personality or a red-state republican individualist, a humanistic democratic #MeToo liberal, a Black Lives Matter activist—now that's what's important!

Hey, I get it. All around the world, it's the same. You, the individual, love being a prideful American, Chinese, Christian, Muslim, Jew, or whatever core identities make you feel unique. These distinctions seem infinitely more notable than being a member of a species. Being just one of billions is ego diluting, not uplifting—almost every healthy ego will say that, and there are all kinds of emotional and spiritual reasons to feel gratified about who you are, your heritage, your culture. That is not going to change, but that's no longer all that's important for you and our planet.

The first time I got a scent of species identity was in Cu Chi, South Vietnam, 1969. Rockets were stepping across the base camp early one morning, and I could tell they were headed my way. I thought about sprinting to a nearby bunker, but my gut said I wouldn't make it, so I hit the floor instead. A rocket blew up my hooch, filling it with dirt and debris—I had a new skylight courtesy of the Viet Cong; my door was blown off its hinges. Shrapnel passed through my little wooden hut, wounding two men nearby, but I was not hit—a small miracle.

Traditional flag-waving, "Pledge of Allegiance" patriotism was a big part of my life as I was growing up in the 1950s and 1960s. I completely fell under the spell of emotional nationalism. I added two semesters to my college career so I could get a commission in the U.S. Army. All the movies, TV programs, and World War II–hero worship of this era created a deep curiosity within me about "defending" my country. I was not then nor am now a warrior and was not a fan of the Vietnam War, but I was quietly infected with patriotic fervor. Experiencing war firsthand would affirm my duty-honor-country beliefs, satisfy myriad curiosities, and be one of life's great adventures—I was sure of that.

When my service Bronze Star tour in Vietnam ended, I realized that I had been—and there is no other way to say it—conned. My disillusionment did not stem from the discipline and maturity the military provided (I was grateful for that) but from the bungled political leadership that created and sustained such a wasteful war. Upon reflection, I had risked my life for no great purpose—no purpose at all, really. I had no burning interest in purging the earth of communism. I never felt I was doing that in Vietnam. I had nothing personal against the Vietnamese people.

The fact that we human beings all share the same biology, psychology, needs, wants, and sensibilities plays little role in the political debate that generated the Vietnam fubar (or Afghanistan and Iraq). Species similarities are hardly ever publicly considered by leaders. Instead, it's the power competition, the one-sided contest that was so important at the time and still is oh so important. Us versus them, win or lose, democracy versus communism —binary fixations like these are still today's power imperatives, and to hell with the rest. Leaders and most citizens don't seem to understand or care how this ultra-competitive form of geopolitics undermines our species and the planet's future.

Our ancestors' legacies of wars, ever-upward economic growth, and massive accumulations of capital in few hands, along with a continuous drawdown of natural resources, simply cannot be maintained on a finite planet. Earth cannot sustain our current behaviors much longer; it cannot carry us to the growth ends we've set as defaults. History suggests that we can set the future based on the past, but does that still work? Is that still the way forward? We're stuck in a wheel-spinning, backward-looking, conservative rut that defies the species' and planet's best interests. Loyalty to tradition needs to become a quaint legacy of the expiring generation, not a continuing mandate for the living. Vladimir Putin's recent unprovoked and barbaric invasion of Ukraine is a prime example of me/us leadership that values history-driven obsessions over living human beings. A sustainable future for humans and the planet will come about only when there is a stepping away from defunct values of the past. Let the dead teach us lessons, not lead us.

Politics now needs to go the other way around. Leaders everywhere need to use species survival and planetary integrity as the starting points for forming and modifying governing and business organizations, policies, justice, and diplomacy. To living human beings and their progeny, what's more important than species survival and planetary integrity?

Citizens and leaders need to take charge of history by declaring that our species is now in a "sustainability age" that will consume and reward human energies for decades to come. Everyone on the planet can have a role in this transition. Sustaining the species and planet is where the economic opportunity is and will be for decades to come; savvy capitalists know this and are already moving their money in eco-friendly directions. Human fulfillment on a whole planet—that's the guiding principle of a new political ethos, a new tagline for our species, and yes, this extremely challenging goal can be realized with species-focused effort, sound leadership, and patience.

We must now acknowledge that planet Earth is all we have; we must accept this simple fact and demand that acceptance from our leaders. Our weakness as individuals and nations is fantasy, brain garbage, "alternate facts"— beliefs that some leader/savior/genius will save me/us, that some distant planet is a realistic refuge, or that some ethereal deity will validate our religious faith with eternal life. First things first: the species and planet need to be the animating principle for us, the living. Nationalism, religion, and all other culture and religious markers are secondary or tertiary concerns.

Leaders and followers must now face the seemingly contradictory and incredibly challenging ends involving sustainable species survival and planetary integrity. Finding common ground between the demands of these seemingly opposing poles will keep our species busy with every aspect of civilization (politics, business, commerce, agriculture, science, engineering, law, community, health, education) for many generations. These are the emerging markets, the fertile ground for change; this is where human fulfillment and a whole planet reside. Continued denial of human commonalities in favor of local/regional/national uniqueness and special interests just subsidizes political rancor and brings more rockets to young men's doors.

Simply put, governance in almost any form that exalts species survival and planetary integrity has the greatest potential for our species' future, whereas tradition-bound, nostalgia-driven, exceptionalism politics does not. Tribal/ethnic/nationalist/religious identities must cede ground to species identity if our planet and species are to survive—that is everyone's bottom line and everyone's individual responsibility. It is time for us to mature as a species. Nothing less will do.

A few of this book's main point include:

- Everyone needs to recognize and accept the human paradox: we human beings are all the same, yet each one is unique.
- We humans live in three worlds our entire lives: the natural world, the human-made world, and the ethereal "me" world. These tri-worlds are our species' common bond.
- Old models of leading and following no longer apply.
- Planet Earth does not have enough untapped resources to support ever-upward economic growth.
- Democracy and capitalism need to accept planetary limitations, or both will be replaced by systems that do.
- Sustainable development, peace, natural integrity, health, and education have more value for living human beings than historically differentiated national, ideological, or religious prides.
- Men need to share leadership with women and find ways to dampen their innate bellicosity.
- No God or gods will solve problems we created for ourselves or forgive our ignorance, greed, and stupidity.

America can be the leader in making the needed transitions to a more stable and peaceful planet; it can be the planet's visionary if it so chooses. However, this will only happen when it becomes a vocal and sincere advocate for species homeostasis—that is, an expounder of a species-wide vision of life. A new American destiny will never come about if dualism, exceptionalism, hate-inspired politics, racism, wars, and a balance-sheet mentality dominate—all traits of America's wasteful red/blue, snake-pit politics.

American public and private sector leaders have been riding on the backs of tradition and momentum long enough—they're coasting, not leading. Their decisions legitimize public and private interests yet often betray the species and planet in the process. Leaders now need to address the big questions facing the twenty-first century before they get citizens' allegiance.

We living human beings need a more inspiring pallet of political hues than the monochromes of so-called conservatism that service the past or the rainbow illusions of liberal idealists who promise more than they can possibly deliver. A sane middle polity based on provable facts, science, education, planetary integrity, and species-wide progress is the path forward to a survivable and peaceful future.

This book was written to begin a debate that can lead to a purposeful transition toward the sovereignty of species survival and natural integrity— yes, sovereignty above nationhood, private interests, and religious righteousness. This change will not happen quickly or easily, but the discussion about it must start sometime, and now seems as good a time as any to stir the pot.

Let's start by looking at things that all humans have in common.

CHAPTER 1

Everyone's Three Worlds

Gilbert, out of bed! It's time for Sunday
school and church! Get up, NOW!
— Martha J. Mulley

When I was a teenager, my mother made me go to church every Sunday . . .
and I mean *every* Sunday. I had to have the bubonic plague, rabies, and a
stroke at the same time to get a sick day from her. I attended Sunday school
at 9:30 a.m. and church services at 11:00 a.m. at the First Presbyterian
Church in Shreveport, Louisiana.

I was the only person in my age group to show up every Sunday, so I got
elected by default to preside over the junior-high fellowship. I was president
of the senior-high fellowship too, but I was a bit craftier by then. The
preacher's son and I would occasionally slip out before the eleven-o'clock
service. We'd cruise around in his Impala convertible, smoke cigarettes,
and amp up the radio. Little Richard would wail and Sam Cooke would
croon as we blew smoke rings that dissolved in the moist morning air. We
had the timing down perfectly—we would sneak back into the sanctuary
before the doxology was sung. A faint odor of tobacco on our Sunday best
was the only thing that might have given us away.

Leading began young for me, and I have held numerous management
positions in my seventy-plus years—nothing big, no elected positions,

except for professional organizations—but I have had enough management challenges and headaches to gain the perspective of being a small-scale leader. Follower? Sure. I am a citizen, father, veteran, voter, little brother, volunteer, and so on. Like most Americans, I've played different roles in different circumstances at different times in my life. I don't think of myself as anything special, just normal and happy.

What proved most interesting about my youthful church years wasn't my faith but the questions that hovered in my mind that never got answered— the Holy Trinity, for instance. Why does God need three manifestations of himself: Father, Son, and Holy Ghost? Isn't being God powerful enough? Okay, God and Son—that seems like a dream team; why add the Holy Ghost (and what exactly does the Holy Ghost do?). Perhaps, it occurred to me, the mystique of the Holy Trinity isn't so much the cast of characters but the number itself.

Observe your daily life, and you will find triads of one sort or another everywhere; the number three has its own allure for us humans. Most TV advertisers mention the name of their product or show the product at least three times in their commercials. Other trines include the following: executive, legislative, judicial; id, ego, superego; duty, honor, country; faith, hope, charity; means, motive, opportunity; gold, silver, bronze; blood, sweat, tears; life, liberty, the pursuit of happiness. Triads are common because we humans begin to trust one another when there are at least three reasons to do so.

Reality

Perhaps the greatest reason we gravitate to threes is that reality happens to be a trinity too. **We human beings occupy three worlds concurrently every second of our lives: the natural world, the human-made world, and the ethereal "me" world.** We all know this somehow, but we don't think about life this way. This book suggests that we should. Every thought we have and every action we take involves these three worlds and nowhere else. While we are alive on this planet, there *is* nowhere else. What varies is how much of each world we inhabit at any moment.

This state of being—a continuous but changing presence in all three worlds—constitutes reality for everyone alive on this planet. It doesn't matter if you're the president of the United States or a beggar in Bangkok; we all share these three worlds in common all the time. We are all hardwired to function in these three worlds, so we might as well accept them as reality, try to understand them, and try to find the most rewards we can in each world.

We suffer when we fail to understand these worlds because we end up denying reality. Our lives get confused or warped; a few of us go off the deep end, and we hurt ourselves or others. Alternatively, when we accept tri-worlds reality, we empower ourselves, we become mature (finally), and we may even feel fulfilled and actualized about our lives.

Because this book deals with reality's essentials rather than its particulars, let's define our terms *very, very* simply:

Natural World — If a human being didn't make it, it's natural. Plants, trees, soil, water, wind, clouds, air, mountains, animals, stars, space—all result from natural processes.

Human-Made World — If a human being created or produced it, it's human-made. Buildings, houses, roads, airplanes, automobiles, language, mathematics, law, art, economics, music—all result from human-made curiosities and actions.

Ethereal World — If "it" can't be defined as either natural or human-made, then it's ethereal. This is the world of human thought, emotions, memory, and faith, the world of visions and dreams, streams of consciousness, the world of the mental and righteous "me." This world takes in and processes information from the other two worlds and itself and tries to make sense of it all. Intelligence, stupidity, determination, ambition, bravery, cowardice, talent, fear, arrogance, love, hate, creativity, genius, sanity/insanity—all human intellect, emotion, and behavior stem from this three- to four-pound world that resides within the human skull.

Can you think of anything that falls outside these three categories? I can't.

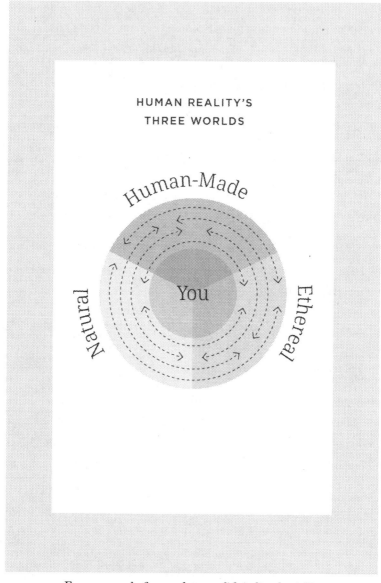

HUMAN REALITY'S
THREE WORLDS

Human-Made

Natural

You

Ethereal

*Every second of every human life is lived within
these three dynamic worlds. No exceptions.*

**Your lifetime assignment includes knowing where you are in each world
at any moment, being aware that overlaps exist among these worlds,
and enjoying the challenge of clarifying the significance of the worlds**

in which you find yourself. This state of being constitutes tri-worlds reality, a key to understanding the human paradox.

There will be times when you lead or follow. There will be times of confusion and despair. There will be periods of love and enlightenment. Each of the three worlds is where you reside physically and/or mentally at a particular point in time. One world will probably be more relevant than the other two at any given moment. Most of us have to focus on the human-made world for most of our lives because we all need to make a living, we all need food and shelter, and we all have responsibilities to ourselves and others.

The main thing to remember is that one world will not provide you a fulfilled and actualized life, and neither will two; you live in all three worlds all the time, so that's your baseline. Salvation in the form of self-reliance, independence, and sanity for individuals comes from all three worlds, not just one or two. Acceptance and understanding of and involvement in all three worlds form the basis for self-love and caring for others.

It's important to keep in mind that while you live in your own three worlds, the other billions of us have our own perspectives of each world. Seemingly endless viewpoints of the same three worlds make for the serious, ridiculous, and sublime experiences we have every day. It's difficult enough for two individuals to make a success of a monogamous relationship in modern society, much less for the billions of us of different nationalities, cultures, and religions to get along peacefully. Ultimately, humanity's common ground is the species and planet. If perception is reality, then broadening our perspective to the species and planet becomes a shared goal for everyone.

Human beings with varying points of view and beliefs bring innumerable factors into play each day that complement or conflict with your own points of view. **Tri-worlds realists are people who understand and accept that they live in three worlds all the time.** They can cope and thrive within a world of biases, confusion, and stress because they function within tri-worlds reality; they accept its basics, and they accept, even enjoy, its potential for endless permutation.

In addition to an appreciation for the human paradox, this book develops these three worlds as the underpinnings of reality and, thereby, of human life on this planet. That's presumptuous, I know—and why bother? Because we humans have way too many belief systems that want to override our basic humanity and to usurp undeserved power for their particular points of view. We all become prisoners of our mental programming/experiences and their resultant beliefs and attitudes. We overvalue the me/us end of the human paradox. That seems inescapable, but it is not. Accepting tri-worlds reality makes understanding the species end of the human paradox sharper by emphasizing human sameness.

It should surprise no one that we humans repeat the same problems over and over, as individuals and as nations, in part because we restrict ourselves as to how we think about them. For example, instead of accepting the human paradox and tri-worlds reality, many aspects of today's societies teach dualism: right versus wrong; us versus them; good versus evil. Dualistic thinking has an evaluative place within each of the three worlds, yet binary evaluations like these reject the tri-worlds. Why? Because dualism is only partial to the three worlds of reality that exist deep within every human being. **Your three worlds are innate; binary choices are learned.**

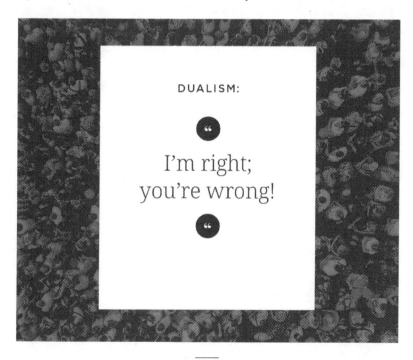

DUALISM:

" I'm right; you're wrong! "

We humans run hot or cold depending on the situation at hand and who is pulling our strings. That's dualism at work. Most of our daily stress comes from having to make yes–no, either–or choices all the time, having to meet deadlines or quotas, having to put on a happy face to meet the demands of our workday lives. Regrettably, that's not going to change anytime soon because of the intransigence of the status quo. We will continue to live with this behavior because dualistic thinking resides and is so deeply entrenched in today's human-made and ethereal worlds and because decisions and choices, once made, usually require commitment and action.

For most of us, the "real" world consists of the human-made world of making money, raising a family, being a responsible adult, and being a good Christian, Jew, Muslim, or whatever. Nature, on the other hand, doesn't wear a watch. We humans enjoy going into nature to refresh ourselves because we know our stresses and strains are unnatural and nature can usually decompress us. Nature obeys its laws in its own time and pays no attention to what happens in the other two worlds.

You, the *individual*, manage which worlds are the foreground and which are the background in your life, which take center stage, and which wait in the wings. People who live full lives realize that you cannot choose to be exclusively in the ethereal world on Sunday, the human-made world Monday through Friday, and the natural world on Saturday. You live in all three worlds all the time; that point isn't negotiable. Of course, you can and will consciously manage the time spent in each world, but you will always be in all three worlds to some degree *all the time*. That's good news in that you don't always have to think in dualistic ways, as many others would have you believe. **When you feel trapped in one world, there are two others for refuge and new insights. The core trinity of reality can always trump dualism if you let it.** This is true for everyone alive on this planet.

To offset any doubts you may have about the existence of the tri-worlds, let's address the premise that every human being lives in all three worlds every moment of their lives. Common sense proves the point. Are you breathing air right now? Did a human being make the air or did nature? A human-made air conditioner or furnace may cool or warm the air, but these machines did not make the air itself (nitrogen, oxygen, argon). Every moment you are alive, you need air to breathe, so you are in the natural world.

Are you sitting in a chair right now? Standing in a subway? Flying on an airplane? Wearing clothes? All are human-made. Virtually every moment of every day, you are in touch with something made by humans.

Are you thinking right now? Daydreaming? Having romantic fantasies about someone in your subway car? Praying? All the self-talk and content that rumbles around in your mind is abstract, not-real-until-you-make-it-real-by-doing-something ethereal activity. Even when you sleep, the ethereal world kicks in when you dream.

If you are alive and conscious, you're in all three worlds all the time; each world affects you, and you, in turn, affect each world, however slightly or profoundly.

A major premise of this book is that we human beings live in three worlds concurrently our entire lives. We are in a constant tri-worlds flux, and we travel through these worlds at our own speed and level of understanding. Because the variables in each world are so incomprehensibly large, every human being lives and dies as a unique individual with a distinctive collection of natural, human-made, and ethereal experiences.

Life's Basics

We humans spend our lives pursuing sustenance, security, and comfort, primarily in that order. These have been and will continue to be the drivers of human existence throughout time; these are life's basics. Obtaining these things is why we spend most waking hours in the human-made world. In democracies, the leaders most able to advance these goals usually get voters' support. Issues judged excessive or irrelevant to life's basics usually do not get majority support.

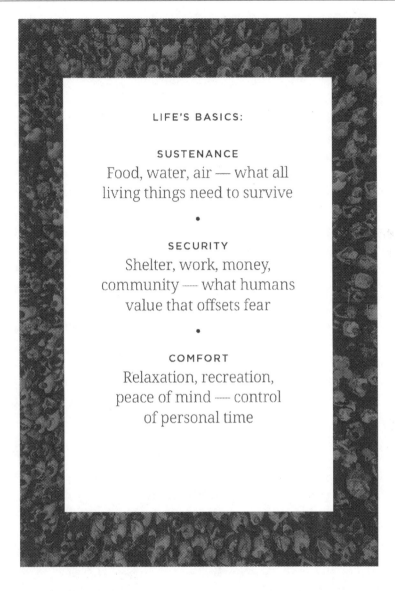

LIFE'S BASICS:

SUSTENANCE
Food, water, air — what all
living things need to survive

•

SECURITY
Shelter, work, money,
community — what humans
value that offsets fear

•

COMFORT
Relaxation, recreation,
peace of mind — control
of personal time

One threat to the universal goals of sustenance, security, and comfort is fear because we humans tend to be fearful creatures. We do not want to die of hunger or exposure, we do not like feeling insecure, and we do not want to give up our comforts. We dread the unknown; we fear the loss of life, face, or status.

Individuals who understand that reality consists of three worlds are less fearful because they more readily anticipate and accept reality's ups and downs. Striving to understand all three worlds and broadening thought processes helps allay fears so fear itself becomes less of a factor in establishing one's beliefs/values/morals and when evaluating and selecting those who want to lead us. Leaders who exploit citizen fears usually do so for dualistic reasons that benefit the few rather than the many; they tend to be mono- or bi-world idealists rather than tri-worlds realists.

All nations commit to a guiding precept like a constitution, conventions, or leadership dictates that provide a framework for subsequent decision making and governance. Some countries value freedom and law; others value autocracy/monarchy/religious or tribal-clan values. The language in these guiding documents, pronouncements, and traditions tends to be grandiose and general in nature.

American politicians translate wording in the constitution to have one dualistic meaning or another, to support or not support their own or their voting district's needs and dispositions, or to leverage these words to their political power for factional advantage. Friction results from competitive dualism; time and energy get expended advocating political leadership ego positions. Average citizens' and the planet's real problems linger, and their resolution gets delayed because the political process and political posturing become more important than resolving the problems themselves. Contrived political complications hinder action. American politics, so far in the twenty-first century, leans to the splintering of means and ends rather than the unification thereof.

Representative democracy has served Americans well so far because life's basics have been achieved for most citizens, but it is slow, sloppy, and contentious because those with governmental power tend to lead in dualistic, highly differentiated ways. Most are lawyers and other political types for whom winning or losing political battles, for whom identity as a good Republican or Democrat, and for whom retentions of power are usually more important than balanced tri-worlds considerations. That mindset needs to change because species-wide and planetary issues can no longer be procrastinated. Species-wide and planetary issues are now the utmost political agenda for every citizen in every nation.

Paradox and Politics

Each of the three worlds has currents and countercurrents within it. Nature can be beautiful and peaceful when you walk along a tree-lined path on a sunny day, but walking that same path at night in freezing rain makes nature less endearing. Human-made comfort and a sense of career security embrace you when you sit in a plush corner office in Manhattan unless that office was in the World Trade Center on September 11, 2001. Ethereal beliefs can bring you peace of mind and comfort, yet it was religious fanatics who flew the planes into New York City's Twin Towers that day.

No matter how much we humans try to organize and sanctify our lives, there always seems to be a counterpoise that weighs against our efforts, some thing or someone that thwarts or dilutes our best hopes and intentions. We all have periods when everything seems to come together just as we had hoped and planned; these are movie moments, and they are wonderful, but they don't last. There's always a Monday morning that brings us back to daily responsibilities and unceasing routines. Reality's opposing weight to our desires comes from us all being finite beings and from the relentless persistence of paradox, contradiction, and irony that reside resolutely within all three worlds. Reality's countervailing forces never let up, and they never will.

Variables, change, and information dearth make reality a persistent contrarian to our personal wants and dreams. One human being cannot possibly think of or anticipate all the variables that may impact a plan or decision that he or she makes. There are usually too many factors and too many unknowns to consider, and collecting sufficient information about every variable always comes up short because of all the endless details and the changes that come with time. Perhaps artificial intelligence will one day improve our options here, but that's more conjecture than fact. The problem with making any choice or decision is the limiting nature of the action itself—picking one thing or action over another leaves many other options behind.

One reason we humans come together in teams, businesses, and governments is to consider as many variables as possible, to commit to a plan, and then to deal with problems as the plan gets implemented. Risk for individuals and groups results in large part from information shortfalls and from factors not considered. Also, the world outside the individual or group changes constantly, so even optimum decisions made at one moment change for reasons beyond individual or group control. Trite but true—change is the only constant.

Every individual human being, every business, and every nation collects as much information as possible, weighs variables, anticipates change, make choices, and then lives with and mid-course corrects as plans get implemented. That is essentially what all law-abiding, moral, and ethical individuals, pods of self-interest, and units of common interest are about in modern civilization. Complexity is the rule, not the exception. Someone has to decide, adjust, motivate. That's why we have leaders—they are supposedly guides to the future.

Once decisions are made and life continues under their umbrella, individuals, businesses, and nations evidence various levels of commitment to their chosen paths. Cultures and identities stem from these commitments. Every individual and interest pod has political tendencies because we human beings are social creatures who identify with more than ourselves; we all have multiple identities because we all play multiple roles in life. We are all competitive and political to some degree because we all have opinions and emotions that affirm or question our choices We all want to verify that our decisions, beliefs, and choices are optimum, at least for ourselves. Individual identities stem from our beliefs, values, and commitments.

In today's world of predominantly dualistic thought, individuals who lock into a fixed set of beliefs and principles are usually labeled conservative, while those who are more amenable to change are called moderate, liberal, or progressive. In truth, most individuals are a mix of conservative, moderate, and liberal tendencies; every label depends on the issue involved and how self-interest, values, and personal attitudes toward change affect one's views. Also, in modern societies, most life choices tend to draw us away from our commonly shared core of species traits. The tugs of dualistic gravity usually out-pull the attraction of human commonalities because of individual and pod self-interests. The species and planet are usually way down the list of personal concerns; they seem just too big and too remote for individuals to do much about, if they are even considered at all.

Theorists, politicians, and pundits love the expansive conservative-to-liberal political range because it provides fertile ground for sowing seeds that appeal to believers predisposed to one position or another, for seducing the uncommitted to a particular point of view, or for proselytizing contrarians. Swaying or affirming others to think a particular way about an issue defines what politics is all about. Dualism loves to act on this political stage, as do self-serving advocates of mono- and bi-world stances.

Politicians constantly draw lines in the sand and define one side as good and the other side as bad. Dualism reigns supreme in American politics because it supposedly keeps complicated issues simple for most voters who usually do not have the time, interest, or patience to consider the details. In turn, dualism sanctions shallow leadership because issue details and complexities get buried beneath simplistic and manipulative labels that politicians use to protect their dualistic positions and careers.

Politics supposedly rolls up the hopes and fears of individual citizens into laws and policies that reflect the integrity and morality of those individuals. In America, it took a revolution and a civil war for the United States to establish a national identity that could evidence to itself and the rest of the world that a heterogeneous population could make democracy work—an endeavor that will continue to evolve as long as the country exists.

America's political challenge now is to decide how it will move forward in an inter-connected digital world, a world of global economic interdependencies, and a natural world that does not have the capacity to accommodate consumers' ever-growing appetites. For us as a species, there is apparently more complication ahead of us than behind us, which raises the question of why we rely on outdated thought and decision-making models that now appear severely flawed—can't we living, thinking human beings do better?

Reality Deniers

We modern human beings spend a tremendous amount of time avoiding the full scope of reality—that is, all three worlds. Many of us seek refuge in one world at the expense of the other two. My mother, who died in

1991, thought constant exposure to religion (the ethereal world) would make me a good person. I appreciate her intentions, but my memories of church life lean as much to outdoor adventures at church camp (the natural world) and the magnificence of the church architecture and the music (the human-made world) than to unquestioning religious faith. Any goodness within me comes from understanding the need to attend to all three worlds rather than depending on one world to make me happy.

People with a bias to one world often become defensive or hostile when others question their uni-world outlook. This is especially true of mono-world humans, whose economic well-being depends upon their singular view—they sell their world as the be-all and end-all to adherents, they eschew the other two worlds by ignoring them or minimizing their importance, and they appear shocked and offended when anyone questions their whole-hearted resolve and beliefs. Zealots of any stripe fit this mono-world mold: evangelical preachers, radical mullahs, money-mad tycoons, militarists, tree-hugging environmentalists. Any mono-worlder who claims to have the panacea for your problems or the globe's problems often creates more problems than he or she solves because their singular passion denies tri-worlds reality.

Ultimately, a prescribed mono-world lifestyle does not work for most of us because we know intuitively that we live in three worlds constantly; **in truth, no single world can provide the content, challenge, and reward of the other two.** Instinctively, we recognize the pull of all three worlds, and without attending to all three, we know something is missing in our lives. Mono-world views and systems may make a few individuals rich and famous, but it doesn't work for the rest of humanity because one-world life recipes just don't taste right; we know some ingredients have been left out.

Even a bias to two worlds cannot provide enough substance for a fulfilled life, but it gets us closer. I spent many years working in the private industry and the public sector writing and editing magazines about engineers, economists, scientists, politicians, academics, government officials, contractors, planners, and business leaders. My job in the trade and corporate press was to tell their story, to give them and their work exposure, to position them to succeed in the human-made world. The overwhelming majority of these people have a bias to the natural and human-made worlds.

They are pragmatic bi-worlders, the ones who understand the "real" world and how it operates. They build things, they change things, and they make things happen through their decisions and actions. Ethereal claims and concerns are not within their professional purview.

At the other end of the human behavioral spectrum are criminals who also tend to live in two worlds: the human-made and ethereal worlds. They believe an easy score against a bank or harming another human being will fulfill a fantasy or impulse they have or satisfy their dreams of easy money, notoriety, or revenge. Criminals don't spend much time thinking about the natural world because most of them lack the intellectual curiosity and self-discipline needed to think beyond their flawed childhoods, their impulsive needs, their ignorance, or their drugged, psychotic, or machismo fantasies; their only link to the natural world seems to be their defective instincts. Criminals can "do the crime and pay the time" because they value the act and the result, the instant payback, and the rush more than their freedom; they are inordinate egotists. Some criminals are clever and get away with their crimes; most are just arrogant, narcissistic, or stupid and think they will never get caught. Almost all criminals continue along the path of least resistance until they are killed or jailed, go underground, or reform. Locked-up criminals only begin to appreciate the natural world when they are deprived of it, but even then, many don't change their addictions to bi-world behaviors.

How will you know when you are in tune with all three worlds? Self-confidence, self-esteem, respect for others, inner peace, physical integrity, and love of self and others become real and personal. These aspects of maturity and happiness are no longer abstract concepts or self-help phrases; you can define them about yourself.

You stop lying to yourself; you stop kidding yourself about who you are and where you are in life. Reality tempers dreams and aspirations, but even with a solid tri-worlds grasp on reality, you will still have fears and worries, all the stresses that come with just being alive in a modern society. These aspects of life, however, will not dominate your thoughts and actions as they may have in the past. Understanding and accepting all three worlds will simply make you a more fulfilled person to yourself and to others; you will finally "get" what life is all about (responsibility, moderation, balance, and love).

Sovereign nations, which rarely recognize any earthly authority higher than themselves, will benefit from more consciously and openly using these three worlds as the baseline for leadership, diplomacy, and policymaking. At present, the world relies on various governmental structures and leadership that often overreach or under-reach their intended purpose. Their aims become misdirected; they lose perspective. Money and power concentrated in the hands of a few usually yield decisions that benefit the few and the friends of the few rather than the average citizen. In some countries, this situation is so egregious that citizens suffer and die at the hands of their own leaders. **The era of following political leaders whose actions do not provide for the sustenance, security, and comfort of their citizenry needs to end.**

CHAPTER 2

Sameness and Difference

The mounting challenges we face in society
are going to require strength and scale that
none of us can accomplish on our own.[1]
— Heather McGhee, *The Sum of Us*

Think of yourself as a one-man army. You're not only
the commander-in-chief; you're the soldier as well.
You must plan and execute your plan alone.[2]
— Donald J. Trump, *Think Like a Billionaire*

The main premise of understanding the human paradox and accepting tri-worlds reality is that we human beings are more alike than different and that acceptance of human sameness has irrefutable worth for species survival. Well-entrenched dualistic thought tries to overshadow these truths by focusing on our apparent physical, intellectual, social, cultural, and religious differences. **Differentiating one person from another has become habituated into human ways of thinking because it sells better than sameness in a dualistic and competitive world and because differentiating messages get constant reinforcement through mass/ social media and mono- and bi-world advocates.** We humans emphasize our differences *way* out of proportion to our basic human sameness.

You may ask, "What sameness?"

Let's look at our shared physical traits. Every human body contains billions of cells. Within each cell resides a complete set of forty-six inherited chromosomes, half from Mom and half from Dad. The DNA in the chromosomes of any individual averages more than 99.9 percent the same as that found in all other human beings on the planet—that's what makes us a species.[3] Genetic mutation involving the 0.1 percent difference in our DNA allow variations in our individual physical attributes. All of our unique features come from the blending of our parental heritage and that tiny percentage difference in our genes. Paradox: nature made all human beings out of the same material, yet each one is unique.

Medicine and other sciences depend on our basic physical sameness. A surgeon knows where to incise a patient for a heart operation because that organ resides in the same location in virtually all human beings; it performs the same functions and is constructed the same basic way. An orthopedist knows how to set a broken femur because the anatomy of a human thigh is essentially the same in all patients, and the bone will usually take the same amount of time to heal. The liver in one healthy individual performs the same function as in all other healthy individuals, as do the brain, lungs, and kidneys.

The normal physical design, content, and function of our bodies are the same species wide no matter what our race, nationality, or faith. **Bottom line: we human beings are all biologically the same no matter how different we may be in looks, color, ethnicity, language, tradition, or religion. In biology, there is no such thing as race.** Skin color, the source of so much social pain for centuries, is, at most, two millimeters (.078 of an inch) thick.

Nature also guarantees our limitations. We all must eat, we all have to drink water, and we're all going to die. No human can flap her arms and fly; no man can grow ten feet tall. Productive human beings use their talents and drive to obtain life's basics and, by so doing, contribute to personal and overall social/economic well-being. Those among us unable or unwilling to contribute to society survive through charity or exist in psychic, drugged, or physical incarceration. Some humans are smarter than others, some more clever, some more devious. We come in all flavors.

Most humans get enthused by the possibilities that this life or an afterlife offers, yet we all get bored with life's routines, with the same faces and the same places day in and day out. Ironically, daily routine also defines what is "normal" for us. It becomes the basis for well-being; it's what we missed most during COVID-19 pandemic restrictions. We are all inescapably human, all members of one species—we are all individuals with something akin to free will, yet we are concomitantly restrained by the margins of our species' physical, mental, and "local" social/communal/religious confines.

Religion brings people closer together by allowing individuals and families to identify and share some human qualities through common beliefs. Religion also provides fellowship and its own form of comfort and security. No matter what religion an individual follows, the same basic human needs are being served. The need to give and receive love, a welcoming community of fellow human beings, adulation of a greater power, humility, devotion, social structure, sharing—whatever specific mix of spiritual fulfillment or order an individual seeks, some religious milieu will inculcate them.

Even if you're distrustful of natural sameness or religion, just look around at your neighbors, your coworkers, even your children—are they not more like you than different? What do you see? Do they not have two arms, two legs, two eyes, two ears (most of them anyway)? Aren't they better off with love than without it, just like you? Is it not apparent that we are, in fact, members of the same species? These obvious, common-sense similarities are just as strong a basis for believing in human sameness as science or faith.

At present, natural human sameness carries little weight in a world of diverse human-made societies because of familial, cultural, and political mental programming. We are all physically, instinctively, and emotionally similar—well, so what? Genes aren't destiny. The geographic environments we live in, our different cultures, our individual levels of intelligence and drive, our work, and other life choices have just as much or more to do with who we are than our genome.

Because we human beings have as our first identity our individual self and then our family, our tribe, clan, ethnicity, religion, work, or nation, all these identities tend to be a higher priority than our common genetic heritage. Why is that? Are we missing an opportunity here? Why don't we think about our sameness as human beings, one species? Why don't we identify ourselves through species sameness? We don't think this way because virtually every aspect of our individual lives emphasizes our *differences*, not our sameness. Human commonalities are dull; human differences (looks, cultures, nationalities, languages) are interesting—or so we've been taught to believe.

In addition to physical sameness, we humans share similar sensibilities. Each of the three worlds gives us a sense about ourselves that becomes a portal for understanding our lives and the worlds in and around us.

Natural Sense — Nature gives us a *natural sense* from which we behave instinctively and develop an understanding and appreciation of nature's beauty, power, and limits.

Common Sense — The human-made world gives us a *common sense* to help preserve our individual selves and to help us value one another, to work together to achieve mutual goals, and to attain life's basics of sustenance, security, and comfort.

Exceptional Sense — The ethereal world gives us an *exceptional sense* that helps us separate ourselves from species commonalities, customizes our personal identities, makes us curious, and gives us individual ambitions, dreams, and faiths.

Rather than acknowledging the existence and influence of all three senses, however, we let some sensibilities dominate and others recede. We get out of phase; we create mono- and bi-worlds upon which we focus our energies and talents to the exclusion of other sensibilities. We become less than fully human because of our misunderstandings, emotionalism, ignorance, greed, or feelings of power or lack thereof. Sensibility imbalances keep us apart from ourselves and from one another; they generate rationales for denying our human sameness and the importance of that sameness to species survival. Such imbalances are markers of our species' immaturity.

Exceptionalism's Traps

The act of differentiation has become the most powerful tool of success and persuasion in the human-made and ethereal worlds because of its strong appeal to humans' exceptional sense. Politicians and religionists pull our ideological/emotional strings to get us to follow their limited or glorified versions of the truth or their outright lies and distortions. We voluntarily give our strings to these puppeteers because they make us feel special as individuals or as social pods, and differentiation is the key tool used by economic entities that profit from making people feel privileged and exceptional, somehow different from and better than the unwashed masses.

Individual feelings of exceptionalism may be deeply held, such as religious affiliation or nationality, or they may be superficial, like brand loyalty to a cola or a shampoo. We humans tend to want the things we lack or lust for. The more things we know about and don't have, the greater our feelings of inadequacy and desire for them. We are in constant pursuit of more stuff, being "cool," getting the right partner, or getting recognition for being unique—all to not feel meager or alone.

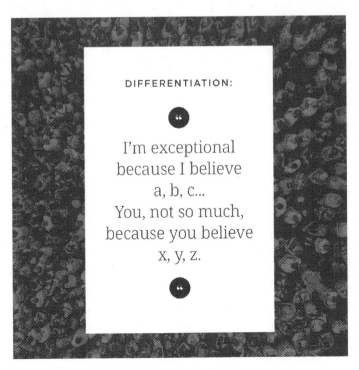

DIFFERENTIATION:

"

I'm exceptional
because I believe
a, b, c...
You, not so much,
because you believe
x, y, z.

"

At its most extreme, differentiation reduces human beings into individual units of loyalty, faith, or some other identifier that tries to supplant species-wide natural and common senses with feelings or thoughts of being extraordinary, righteous, and accepted. For example, patriotism plays to loyalties within a nation's citizenry by making individuals feel special about their dedication to a nation's goals and values (the flag-waving patriotism I bought into in my youth). Religious zealots make followers feel exceptional in the eyes of God and then route them to the zealot's ends. Every TV ad presents overt and subliminal corollaries that appeal to the exceptional sense: "If you use our product you will be a winner! Beautiful! One of a kind!"

Today's human-made world expends virtually all of its time and attention emphasizing differences among individuals, among pods of human interests, and among products and services that attend to life's basics. Comparatively little emphasis within the human-made world goes to our basic human sameness. Every interest pod we associate ourselves with provides a basis from which we can claim uniqueness of one sort or another, some type of separation from the crowd, a feeling of worth, and a sense of acknowledgment that we're unique in some way. We're addicted to competition, picking a side, cheering on me/us.

Nationalities, heritage, automobiles, clothes, sports teams, housing, job titles, salaries, social status—virtually everything within the human-made world tends toward differentiation, toward individual and pod otherness. The idea of universal human sameness makes most modern-day people yawn; it just won't sell. "Sameness yields mediocrity," say the differentiators, all of whom stand to gain by playing differentiating games. However, human sameness doesn't go away. It is always quietly omnipresent; it's right in front of our eyes.

We are all suckers for exceptional strategies that establish and then reinforce our individuality because we are all vain and envious to some degree. Everyone wants to feel special and to be recognized as such by others within their life circles; we all want to feel vital and cared for. At present, we have little counterweight in our minds to offset this bias; we simply don't give species sameness much credence because hardly anyone talks about it or gives it currency. Paradox: we humans share the same physical and psychological needs, sensibilities, wants, and limitations, yet **we focus exponentially more time and attention on our differences than on our similarities.**

When Americans talk about the "real" world, it's the dog-eat-dog, human-made world of competitive differentiation being referred to, not the natural world that made all humans 99.9 percent the same. It's the highly stratified human-made world that depletes our energy banks on a day-to-day basis and stresses us out—our emotional highs and lows come mostly from the human-made world of differentiating and competing in business, politics, romance, possessions, and status. Add to all that the fantasies and ego dreams of the ethereal world, which give us carte blanche to bounce off the walls of our imaginations or to sanction rootless self-empowerment—it's not hard to see why many Americans are wired tighter than banjo strings and why we suffer so many real and psychosomatic ailments. The ubiquity of differentiation in our lives replaces natural rhythms and common sensibilities with human-made stresses, strains, and ethereal escapist expectations that can overwhelm and destroy a single individual.

Politicians and private-sector dualists rely heavily on differentiation to justify their stances or to sell their products, especially political conservatives. These advocates claim that Americans are especially unique among all peoples on the planet—it is no accident that America is the only superpower, they say. American exceptionalism becomes the tap root for virtually all conservative beliefs and actions. What American conservatives have difficulty seeing is that like-minded people elsewhere share the same exceptionalism toward their own nation, religion, culture. Osama bin Laden was a conservative, as is Kim Jong Un of North Korea and Vladimir Putin of the Russian Federation; Adolf Hitler was a right-wing politician. Conservative doctrines tend toward hard-core dualism, autocracy, and sanctimony rather than to a more universalistic posture of human sameness, mutual respect, and the peaceful/sustainable pursuit of life's basics. There is not much reward for a conservative leader to pay other than minimal lip service to human sameness.

Differentiation in the forms of pride and righteousness are common threads in the belief systems of virtually all tribes, nations, and religions because these systems work well in a "local" environment.

These values provide individuals identities that can be as deeply held as any American conservative's sense of patriotic pride and nationhood. Individuals everywhere identify with something larger than themselves, and they do that through pods of like interests, which yield true patriots, hardline capitalists/socialists, and devout religionists—everyone wants to feel exceptional about their belief systems and their identity pods because that, in their minds, yields personal worth and prideful local identities.

Up to this point in history, identifying with the human species has never been a worthwhile option. Think about it. **Doesn't it make sense that our species identity needs to be a primary identifier now because the issues human beings face (climate change, nature's debasement, overpopulation, resource depletion) are approaching the level of species survival?** From a living-species perspective, what's more important than survival? As we focus so much energy and attention on our differentiated parts, our planet and our humanity are slowly crumbling; we are destroying the earth and ourselves through our own devices. There is nothing conservative about that. That's simply self-destruction in the name of lesser gods.

So-called political liberals, the left, aren't much more sensible than right-wing conservatives from a tri-worlds point of view, but at least they are amenable to change. There are probably just as many descriptive adjectives for liberals as there are for conservatives, ranging from "progressive" to "socialist" to "communist." Where conservatives see the worst in "other" people, liberals often see the best. We are all one big happy family where those who work the hardest gladly support those in need. Large and impersonal government bureaucracies enforce the compromises and sacrifices individuals must make to serve the greater good. An ethereal naiveté pervades this liberality by projecting goodness and light onto pods and individuals whose motives are often not pure at all; they are more likely instinctual and selfish—realities liberals tend to gloss over.

Liberal elites foresee the functioning of a perfect governing and private-sector model that satisfies the needs, wants, and desires of happy individuals, each living a life of utopian contentment and bliss—a vision that, ironically, conservatives see for their own interest pods. **Liberal political extremes, conservative political extremes—neither are desirable or achievable**

within tri-worlds reality because they separate rather than unite the species and because most are based on ideological myths rather than current, provable realities.

For centuries, the pulling and tugging of conservative and liberal mentalities has polarized humanity's intellect and actions into dualistic advocacy—autocracy versus democracy, capitalism versus communism, fascism versus liberalism. Competitive human beings have chosen sides on the teeter-totter of dualistic political inclination because they never gave credence to human sameness or had to acknowledge nature's limits. Through some type of nationalism, racism, or other separating and elevating credo, political elites have conditioned citizens to accept stances and causes that seem worth fighting for, a high-mindedness worth dying for, a holy mission that assures eternal acceptance . . . and millions of followers have dutifully followed these callings (I among them). Can humanity, our species, afford to keep acting this way? Are our dualistic habits and differentiating traditions worth the species' collective future? Can the planet survive this old-fashioned modus operandi? Perhaps it is time to examine some alternative thinking.

Accepting the Human Paradox

"Human beings are all the same, yet each one is unique." That paradox needs to be emblazoned over the portals of every school, church, mosque, synagogue, building, legislature, and home in the world. If we spend time thinking about our commonalities as human beings and explaining it to our children, then maybe the idea of human sameness will find its way into our daily lives. Who knows? It might even become normal. Right now, we humans are not even close to acknowledging our essential species commonalities; the closest we get is tolerance of "others" who are not like "us." Wars, discrimination, and endless varieties of self-righteousness and exceptional status attest to this reality. As history has shown repeatedly, differentiation can lead to intolerance and eventually to disdain, hate, and genocide. The fact of our sameness, our acceptance of being one species, has yet to become part of our humanity and our daily dialogue—as a species, we are not even close to thinking this way because our fractions deny the importance of the whole.

Why? Why do we deny our sameness? We deny it because we're so deeply programmed to differentiate and to value our exceptional individual and local pod beliefs. We believe our differences somehow assure our survival; our myths and strident pod rhetoric seem to inspire us and fire us up much more than reality and its considerable demands (yet another indicator of our species' immaturity). We often need "enemies" or "others" to justify our pod logic, so we create "them."

Struggling and fighting to achieve idealized goals in the human-made and ethereal worlds seems much more exciting and rewarding than responsibly attaining life's basics and planning to enhance the species' survival and natural integrity. This seems especially true for leaders and differentiators who know they will benefit from a dualistic struggle, yet they know they will personally shed no blood in the process. Advocates of dualistic and differentiated ideals always seem liberal with other peoples' blood while they conveniently conserve their own (a personal grudge of mine).

The human-made world thrives on differentiation, as do many promises made by the ethereal world. While we Americans may feel some connection with other individuals or groups outside our private lives, teachings of both the human-made and ethereal worlds require us to develop an opinion, a comfort zone, some terms of proximity and endearment to legitimize that outside connection with our closely held value structure and political leanings. Humans compromise with other factions, not the species. This occurs because of a lack of species identity within highly differentiated "us" communities. **Compromising up to the species level is a foreign concept for most people—a considerable barrier to accepting the human paradox.**

People beyond our own personal/local community are considered strangers (and potential threats) until we mentally process them and allow them into our lives, marginalize them, or exclude them. Considerations of outsiders have to be filtered through our mental sieves of culture, religion, class, education, emotion, looks, age, social status, tradition, and sexual preference before we befriend or love anyone who is unlike "me" or "us."

As individuals, we are constantly qualifying and evaluating others as potential friends, lovers, or enemies. We're like a bouncer at a velvet-rope club; some in the queue get into our personal lives, but most don't because of some arbitrary criteria or temporized mood. Our general tendency is to give the benefit of the doubt to others who are like us (in background, interests, age) rather than to people who are apparently different. This filtering process seems natural to us when, in fact, it is not; it is most assuredly a function of deep-seated conditioning from the dualistic and differentiating human-made and ethereal worlds to which we are constantly exposed. We all become advocates yet prisoners of our highly differentiated and discriminating personal beliefs. There's little room for species identity here.

Rationalizations justifying differentiation and denying human sameness are rooted in mono- or bi-world biases, loyalties, and fears that dominate personal mindsets, social and religious cultures, and nations' politics. By going through the mental sifting and qualifying evaluation of others, we reinforce our differentiating tendencies much more than we question them.

Basic human sameness has little value in our lives at present. We are predisposed to making others fit into our molds, our view of the world, our tolerances, and our own differentiated personal community. This is the downside to individuality. We only include in our lives those whom we trust, who are fun/interesting/attractive/useful, whom we like or feel we can care about. If they do not measure up, they are excluded and, therefore, not our concern. This process of exclusion distances us from the species along with the ideas of human sameness and the collective will needed to address species-level and natural challenges.

Considering this prevailing mode of socialization, accepting a sense of commonality with everyone else on Earth will require giant steps away from considerations of race, religion, social class, economic status, education, culture, nationality, and sexual orientation—areas where we most commonly differentiate ourselves from one another. While evidence in the natural world proves that any individual is 99.9 percent physically the same as everyone else on the planet, that is usually not enough proof to override the convictions, cautions, and doubts programmed into individual minds that so heavily emphasize differences.

Human Sameness

For the sake of our species' survival, it's time to make more room in our lives for human sameness. It's time to admit that "others" also belong to the same species we do, and it's time to begin thinking about survival issues at the species level. **It's time to start rerouting the ship of humanity away from dualism (right/wrong, black/white) and differentiation (me/us, you/them) by accepting our basic human sameness and by giving that acceptance more heft in our thinking and political action.** We are all more alike than different in so many ways, especially when it comes to life's basics (sustenance, security, comfort) and our shared sensibilities (natural, common, exceptional). This simple act of inclusion will help our species mature, develop new attitudes, and provide an expanding platform for peaceful and sustainable survival.

For you, as an individual, this act of inclusion can broaden your view to that of humankind and can help displace some personal fears with a sense of commonality, decency, and kinship, all factors that can help de-stress an individual life, broaden it, and give it more purpose. Also, let's be honest— the human-made and ethereal worlds, which thrive on differentiation, are as they are because we humans need to feel special about ourselves. Everyone wants to be a unique and exceptional individual, especially to those closest to them.

To better understand the human paradox, we need to step back from our tendencies of labeling and stratification to recognize an extremely basic fact: we human beings are all the same in our physical makeup, our sensibilities, and our needs and wants. Stripped of all our differentiated status and finery, we are all the same ingestors, digesters, and excretors, all members of the same physical species. We all want to survive, be safe, and live as comfortably as possible. We all have instincts, values, and spiritual curiosities. We all have emotional and psychological needs. We are all built the same way, so let's quit kidding ourselves that we are not. There's nothing elevating or demeaning about this basic fact; it's just baseline truth for every human being on the planet.

To propagate and assure the longevity of this truth, we need to approach human sameness more as a matter of undeniable fact rather than as some do-gooder, kumbaya sentimentality that might dilute its immutability. Human sameness needs to be taught, repeated, and reinforced every day, everywhere. **Recognition and acceptance of human sameness are the primary countervailing points available to argue down differentiating claims that divide, exploit, and minimize the importance of species survival.** Without a strong and sensible counterargument to differentiating and dualistic exceptionalism, humankind will slowly destroy itself along with the natural world upon which our survival depends. Our destructive habits and the value we give them will continue to subsidize our crass and hateful tendencies.

Ethnicities, religions, races, political parties, and social classes—these are all ways we segregate and divide ourselves from species commonalities. Nations, cultures, and religions are all built upon these divisions and the self-perpetuating values they have created for themselves. Virtually all these segregations are considered more important than being *Homo sapiens*, one species. Many of these divisions have become primary or even exclusive in the minds of those in each differentiated pod. Attachments to these segregations can be so strong that people die for them. How many millions of lives have been cut short by warfare to satisfy megalomaniac/paranoid/narcissistic leaders who promised utopias for the select, pure, or blessed few? How many millions have died over the centuries in the name of Christ, Allah, or Yahweh? How many millions were killed through genocide because they were identified as Jew, Armenian, Tutsi, or some other "them" identity?

The tug-of-war between haves and have-nots, haters and hated continues because we have not applied the concept of sameness to the species rather than to local groups, nations, religions, or other "us" identities. Because we do not feel unity as a species, our preferred modes for survival and prosperity are primarily geared to benefit the various divisions within the species, not to the species itself. We adore our fractions at the expense of the whole. As a species, we are modern yet primitive, so grown-up but still so juvenile.

Where will the future take us if we continue repeating the same tired, differentiated themes? Greed, power, hate, lying, deceit, hypocrisy, arrogance, ignorance, bellicosity—themes found throughout history—will obviously take us to the same places they have taken us before: war, backwardness, depravity, misery, poverty, and early death for the many as well as wealth, power, and elite status for the few.

Of course, there are many beautiful and wondrous things about life that deserve recognition and elucidation, but the spread of these things has been diminished by human forces that overwhelm our ability to tolerate and accept "them." We seem trapped on this planet by our own self-destructive devices and by limited loyalties to which we automatically default, especially when fear and demagoguery gain a foothold. The mono- or bi-world boxes we cannot think outside of have completely inhibited our thoughts and actions.

Ironically, mono-world religionists (evangelical preachers, radical imams, elitist rabbis) paint a picture of just the opposite of earthly strife by promoting heaven, earthly utopias, mansions in the sky, and other blissful alternatives. By separating and glorifying the blessed few from the rest of humanity, these faith advocates deny human sameness for living beings; the only time sameness gets recognition is when we die, and even that fate may lead to a dualistic end (heaven/hell). These purveyors' views of reality discount the other two-thirds of what reality is. They give little credence to the natural world and the human-made worlds; it is their idealism and mythologies that drive them rather than planetary reality and concern for the living species.

Human-made-world differentiators who claim that consumerism, success, or wealth will fill an individual's cup are no more helpful for the species than religious proselytizers. Every mono-world life devoted to entrepreneurship, career building, or conspicuous consumption eventually seeks to include in it the natural and ethereal worlds for no other reason than exhaustion from or boredom with having achieved human-made-world objectives.

The contradiction of success in the human-made world is that it can be fulfilling yet hollowing at the same time. Aging helps quell human greed in most of us; acquiring lots of money and power turns into giving and sharing at some point because human-made world possessions and excess comforts don't have much meaning anymore. Maturity and self-esteem ask questions that cannot be answered through endless hedonism or by sitting alone in a mansion on a hill. Achievement in the human-made world can provide ultra-high comfort but often at the expense of spiritual sustenance, feelings of personal security, or the sentience of natural peace.

Being a mono-world naturalist won't work either. Even Thoreau left Walden Pond. Survivalist prescriptions of reverting to nature will wear a human body down and subject it to diseases and stress that can usually be avoided in the modern world. Aspiring to live in a log cabin in the woods or a thatched hut on a tropical island makes for great escapism but lousy reality. Nature will be harsh and uncaring even for humans with a deep understanding and affinity for it. Radicalism in the name of natural purity makes no more sense for our species than mono-world pursuits of spiritual perfection or overflowing pots of gold.

Isn't it time for us, as a species, to acknowledge our sameness? Isn't our species a primary identity? Why can't it be? Aren't life's basics (sustenance, security, comfort) our species' main concerns? Isn't saving the planet we all depend on more important than a parsed political or religious ideology? Aren't we due for a sea change away from the same old thinking and decision-making models that have proven their limitations and faults time after time? Why can't we admit that we all live in three worlds all the time? Why can't we acknowledge that lives dedicated to one world or two are lives incomplete? Why can't we accept the reality of the human paradox? By not openly accepting the primacy of our human sameness, we have little left to focus on but our differences.

Hold on. Let's slow down a minute. As long as you and I are alive on this planet, we will continue to compete in our day-to-day existence for resources that improve our lives and those of our families. We will still have local identities and all their demands. We will still rely on our individual intelligence, ambition, and skills to achieve personal ends. There is too much momentum and equity built into the human-made status quo to make overnight changes in social, cultural, and economic systems quickly, and in some instances, we don't have better ideas to replace them yet. We will continue to proudly identify ourselves in different ways, as Americans, Europeans, capitalists, socialists, Christians, Muslims, rich, middle class, and so on.

BUT, think of where humankind could be if our starting point in dealing with one another got elevated to that of the species—we could open new ways to eliminate distinctions and enmities among ourselves. Our default mentality, our most basic premise about life, is that we are all members of one humanity and that we respect others of our kind. All competitions occur within the boundaries of recognized human sameness, not in some superiority fantasy. Species survival and planetary integrity come first on every agenda.

By placing the species first, the rules change. Like doctors, our motto would be "Do no harm." Decisions made by world leaders would be held to account by the species, not just members of a nation, sect, or other local pod, and this accountability could be in real time and not conditioned to some past event or a promised future one. Religious leaders of all stripes could reference our inarguable species sameness as a platform for good deeds/empathy/love rather than emphasizing ethereal claims of exclusivity for a chosen few who follow a narrow doctrine. The denigration of others who are not in "our" pod would be recognized for what it is: the denigration of ourselves, our species. Political power would not be concentrated exclusively within the ranks of leadership but dispersed throughout the citizenry, where it should be in a species-centric world. Dualism's grasp on the human ethos would be replaced with the realization that we need to consistently consider all three worlds when dealing with one another and in decision making. Genocide would cease to exist because our primary identity would be that of our species, not some pod subset. On and on, the hopeful possibilities go. Premise: there is only *us*, no *them*; there is no higher identity for living human beings than ourselves as a species.

Idealism? Yes, of the highest order, but idealism founded on reality and what most individual human beings aspire for the species and the planet. We common citizens, we voters have grown tired of the senseless strutting and machismo of ego-maniacal leaders, the exploitation of power in many forms for a narrow ideology, self-aggrandizement, or political party gain that lead to conflict, racism, and suffering. We respect our patriots and past leaders, but we are not interested in repeating their mistakes, those that differentiate rather than unite.

We are also not happy with ourselves, with our ties to traditions, loyalties, and customs that keep us separated from one another, with our fears that make us so defensive, and with our vanities and fortunes that seem to advance only at the expense of others. No successful political or business leader ever gained his or her grandeur alone. They all stand on the shoulders of others; they all owe as well as own. We know we can do better for nature and ourselves as a species.

The beauty of being alive today comes from all the information available to cut through the ignorance, disease, and haze that engulfed our forbearers. We are better educated and have more options than our ancestors. We understand more thoroughly the potential and limitations of the worlds in which we live. We are making tremendous progress in medicine, science, technology, and sustainable economic alternatives. We are much more sensitive to environmental impacts and the need to remedy them than our Industrial Age predecessors. We have much less incentive to make decisions based on fear than they did. We can apply lessons learned from the past, and we do, but often we do not because of dualistic and differentiated thinking. We have many more resources available to break the debilitating habits of the past, yet poverty, illiteracy, conflicts, indifference, and poor leadership still plague us.

Ironically, because a democratic nation's policies spring primarily from its citizenry, the recognition of species sameness will come about only as *individual* human beings acknowledge and state an understanding of the human paradox and a commitment to three-worlds reality. This is the first step of many to empower species survival and planetary integrity. This change at the root level, the local level, will migrate up through human-interest pods into a nation's spiritual and policy structure. Regrettably, the pessimist within me believes this transition will probably take centuries, if it ever happens at all.

Individuals have to recognize that the human paradox is manageable, that we do, in fact, occupy three worlds concurrently, and that we (me/us) are more alike than unalike other *Homo sapiens* on the planet. This is the essence of a survivable reality, along with a recognition that the planet's problems will not be solved through dualism and differentiation. This transition is a very tall order and one that will catch on very slowly.

Why? Because of the innumerable differentiating forces cemented into our thinking and the countless vestiges of self-interest, tradition, and culture that this view of reality challenges as well as because many people will support their biased beliefs no matter how much information and logic exists to argue them down. Self-righteousness, stubbornness, and defaulting to the past are mentalities extraordinarily difficult to overcome and grow more rigid with age.

Short of one or more global mega-disasters, it will probably take a die-off of several generations and their highly differentiated and dualistic modes of thought for species sameness to be appreciated and acculturated throughout the planet. Hopefully, I'm wrong about that, and individuals, especially young people, will see the value of this concept, grasp onto it quickly, and make it a global norm.

Differentiation's Grasp

There is no doubt that differentiators have a huge thrust of momentum behind them and a powerful grip on individual minds. The differentiation of species-wide values and behaviors probably began the day we left our caves. Our predecessors' fear of the unknown, harsh climates, the survival instinct, and a host of other factors created the need for family, gods, and aggressive and defensive behaviors.

Today, paradoxically, it is the excess of divisions within the species that threatens our survival. Seemingly endless problems stem from the historically drawn lines of distinction that separate us, one from one another. **Too much differentiation, and our affinity for these divisions may be our species' undoing if we are not careful.** Our species can no longer afford self-serving ideologies that appeal to exceptional ego or pod fantasies at the expense of species-survival and planetary integrity.

The most exceptional differentiation can be placed on the laps of pod heritage and pride—that is, our tendency to value what we know and trust about our "us" community. One of the greatest burdens one generation has willed to its successor has been the perpetuation of its indomitable status as the sine qua non for that generation's actions, along with the expectation that the youth will honor this status. Parents, kings, and patriarchs in the past validated their individual and communal lives by passing on dualistic and highly differentiated beliefs to their successors; they relayed the same prideful hierarchy of instincts, values, and faiths they had learned from their parentage, blended with their own life lessons. The youth were expected to absorb and treat these differentiations with respect and to continue their propagation because they had unique "us" worth.

This seemingly endless cycle of exceptional differentiation sequenced history into one power struggle after another, with each victor dominating and exploiting the defeated "other." Virtually all victories were obtained on the backs of male fighters indoctrinated to believe in human-made world benefits (booty, a piece of land, slaves) and glorious ethereal outcomes intrinsic to their dualistic mental programming. Countless generations offered up the lives of its young people to the illusions, drives, and psychoses of pod leaders who did not questioned their own sanctimony or sanity. Hasn't humankind had enough of this? Neither our species nor our planet can afford to continue this type of conduct because we now have the capability to completely eradicate ourselves with weapons of mass destruction, which, ironically, we made to protect "us" from "them."

Regrettably, because human behavior changes only gradually and grudgingly, the will of differentiators will continue to have great sway. Islamists want to establish their own version of a perfect Islamic caliphate throughout the world. Militant Palestinians fight to get their land back, while the Israelis claim national sanctity for their biblical geographic birthright. Neo-con, know-it-all Americans want to force democracy onto countries not interested or ready for it. Muslim sects fight one another for regional dominance in the Middle East. Tribes compete in Africa for little reason other than old hatreds or strongman-inspired missions. Nuclear-armed India and Pakistan continue to shake their mailed fists at each other as they quibble over Kashmir. Russia destabilizes Eastern Europe in hopes of establishing a Eurasian counterpart to the EU. Donald Trump tried to become America's all-seeing, all-knowing autocrat at the expense of democracy, but he failed. From a species and planetary perspective, this is all wasted energy, time and resources.

On and on, pod-centric, narrow, dualistic, and differentiated arguments go. I doubt anyone involved in these differentiating missions has given much thought to their sameness with other human beings. To suggest human sameness to fanatics and diehards is laughable; they are too caught up in their own self-righteousness and intensity to see its worth. World political leaders never openly consider human sameness except at United Nations conclaves, with most of that for show. Emphasizing human sameness dilutes their form of dualistic/nationalistic/theocratic advocacy that they see as their raison d'être. Media do not cover human sameness because it is not contentious or scary; there's no headline-grabbing hook in the "human sameness" storyline except during natural disasters.

Human sameness has a hard time gaining a foothold on the world stage because it gets no acknowledgment or weight from those committed to the certitude of national, ethnic, ideological, or religious divisions. Human sameness, when it is even mentioned at all, remains nothing but a wisp of good intention that has no bearing on a politician's "real" world or the media's coverage of it. There is no human sameness army, no sameness nuclear arsenal. There does not seem to be much popular thrust behind the idea that all humans are the same yet each one is unique—at least, not yet.

A Species Focus

A tip of the hat to species sameness came in 1955 in the depths of the Cold War. Bertrand Russell, Albert Einstein, and various other scientific and intellectual cohorts published the Russell–Einstein manifesto, which outlined the realities of a global nuclear war. Everyone on the planet would lose in such a war, they believed; the earth would cease to be habitable (a regrettable but enduring truth). Their bottom line to avoid this catastrophe was to "remember your humanity and forget the rest." The principle of human sameness this book advocates extends this sentiment down to day-to-day living and all wars, not just nuclear conflicts.

Why is human sameness important? Because like a potential nuclear Armageddon, the species now faces serious problems with global warming, climate change, overpopulation, outsized prosperity expectations, and natural resource depletion, which no individual or nation can solve on its own. The entire species faces these challenges; we cannot hide from them or rationalize them away with mono- or bi-world arguments.

Bertrand Russell and Albert Einstein warned the world in 1955 about nuclear weapons—"Remember your humanity, forget the rest."

Denying their existence will not help any nation prosper but will ironically contribute to that nation's and the planet's demise. **Species-wide and planetary issues are infinitely bigger than any individual or pod agenda, even bigger than nation-states, and they will require a new level of focus, commitment, and effort to resolve.**

What about human sameness beyond physical and psychological traits? This is a world made up of differences manifest in language, culture, ethnicity, philosophies, religions, education, work, and recreation; virtually everything on which we expend our energy each day falls into this human-made world domain. Sameness here is limited mostly to the generic categories—we all have a language, come from a culture, have an ethnicity, and so on, but beyond these commonalities, it is all a jumble of differences. Again, so what? What difference do all these differences make if we are all made of the same stuff and we are all trying to reach similar physical, psychological, and emotional ends and we are all facing the same global challenges? Aren't age-old political prides simply different avenues headed toward the same hubris-infected cul-de-sacs we've arrived at in the past? Why can't we think bigger, broader? Doesn't differentiation and its claims of unique worth become the issue? Can't we, the living, eventually tame our divisive mentalities for the sake of species survival and planetary integrity?

The nature of the highly differentiated human-made and ethereal worlds is just that—an emphasis on differences. This emphasis manifests itself in numerous ways, many of which are hierarchical. Societies, governments, corporations, families—most pods still follow the well-known pyramid metaphor: workers at the base, managers and professionals in the middle, empowered figures at the top. In this organizational model, those who occupy the lower levels depend on decisions made above them (or pretend to). Those at the upper levels depend on information for decision making from the lower levels (or pretend to). The largest rewards go to the decision makers and others who supposedly take the biggest risks. Those who live smaller lives, have limited skills, or minimize risks are rewarded commensurately.

Nowhere in this pyramid model does species sameness appear or is it acknowledged as the background, a footnote, or any other relation to the model; all the pyramid model does is reinforce differentiation as it pretends to be the natural order of things. Species sameness in this analogy should be represented as the template upon which the pyramid rests because sameness underlies all human existence.

If we continue to deny human sameness, then old themes will simply replay themselves within the power pyramid. Those inside the pyramid will continue to play their dualistic and differentiating games; those at the bottom will continue to struggle to achieve life's basics, while those at the top will continue to believe that wealth, power, and high comfort make them happier/better/more worthy than the rest of us. For its own sake and the planet's, our species needs to develop higher priorities than these.

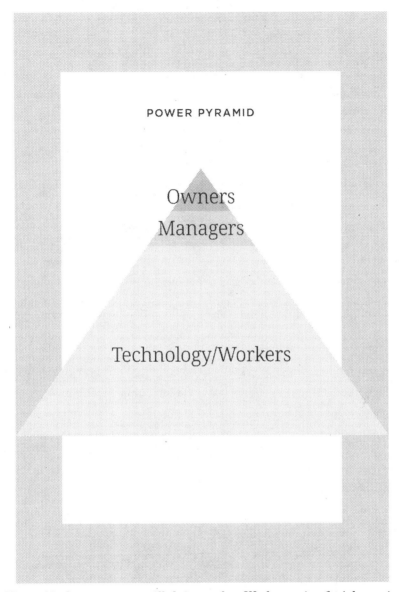

POWER PYRAMID

Owners

Managers

Technology/Workers

Hierarchical management still thrives today. Workers strive for job security, managers seek financial security, and owners want profits/power.

Is recognizing human sameness the same thing as socialism or communism? Please! Not no but hell no! It's human reality! There is no way that differentiators can prove they are something other than human; any claims to the contrary are pure deception, pure fiction, lies. Every one of us exists within the domain of natural laws, and that is never going to change. Sameness as a moral value can work well within democracy and capitalism and can strengthen them both. For national governments, it is the guts to argue human sameness with die-hards and ego-puffs who are still locked into greed-driven, dualistic, and vain self-concepts. It is a way to short-circuit mono- and bi-world arguments that recommend actions based on fear, fantasies, and limited/inaccurate information. It is a way to get leaders to consider the values, instincts, and faiths of all parties.

Advocating human sameness is a way to insert species morality into national differentiations. It is a way to slow down a rush to arms. For businesses, it is a way to broaden markets as the primacy of life's basics get acknowledged and emphasized species wide. For individuals, it is a belief that others of our species deserve mutual respect no matter what their station in life. It is helping others when you can. It is not putting others down because of some bias your parents/relations/friends brandish. It is applying the best parts of religion (love, family, social harmony), not those that promise exclusive eternal outcomes for true believers. It is employing these ideals within government and capitalism daily. It is providing an uplifting model to nations that do not function under the democratic-capitalistic aegis. It is acknowledging that race/language/culture does not matter as much as sustenance, security, and comfort for all those in the species. It is a way to acknowledge the need for individual dignity for all human beings. It is about sustaining human life now on this planet and nurturing the planet itself for those already here and for those on the way.

American democracy recognizes sameness through its founding documents, through "we the people." Capitalism recognizes life's basics through markets, mass production, and a prosperous middle class. Is it not clear that more interest in democracy and more revenue will come with a sustainable economic pie that emphasizes a growing global middle class and a whole planet? Economic progress needs to move ahead intelligently by respecting and working with nature. Inherent therein are tremendous developmental opportunities because many current economic processes exploit and abuse nature, not emulate and complement it. The potential for invention and reinvention within a greener human-made world is monumental. Smarter, eco-friendly development is the only sensible option for a human-made world that focuses on species survival and planetary integrity. Remember our motto: Human Fulfillment on a Whole Planet.

If basic human sameness is true, then why do human beings continue to act as if we don't have anything in common? Three possible reasons: (1) people have not thought about human sameness; (2) they don't believe it; or (3) they don't care—they've got their own piece of the economic/social/religious pie, and everyone else can go jump in the lake.

One reason for everyone to give thought to human sameness is that it may be just the pearl humanity has been looking for to achieve a more peaceful planet. If we are all basically the same, then why are we killing one another? A superior race, class, nationality, polity, or ethnicity—all these rationales for past wars (hot or cold) simply don't survive scrutiny. We have tried numerous better-than-thou themes (empire, Nazism, apartheid), and none of them endured because they denied human sameness and could not provide life's basics widely enough. Even so-called collectivist societies like Stalin's USSR and Mao's China failed because they were brutal dictatorships in disguise. China only got prosperous after Dung Cho Ping opened China's economy to capitalist ideas. The Soviet Union rotted from the inside out, and Russia still can't shake its paternalism fetish, so it remains an autocratic/dictatorial trouble-making backwater.

Therein rests a problem with past political leadership. Who can claim that the wisest and most intelligent leaders available have led city-states, empires, and nations? Who can argue that corporations have been led by the most experienced and well-balanced minds around? Who can argue convincingly that clergy have succeeded at bringing humankind up to the aspirations of their espoused theologies? Dualism and differentiation have never been identified as hobblers of species progress before because the species has never been thought of as a viable social and political entity and because the natural world has always been shoved into the background. It's time for a species-focused reorientation of politics that works outward from the basic reality of human sameness and natural integrity.

Without some universally shared obligations and goals, current leaders under any political system will continue their differentiated ways without giving nature or other facets of humankind a second thought, and as long as empowered sycophant loyalists are around to do their leaders' bidding, to salve their egos, and to mute boisterous contrarians, leaders will stay happy and will think "we the people" are happy too. **Leadership everywhere needs to be homogenized around human sameness, life's basics, peace, sustainable development, and the preservation/reestablishment of natural integrity.** Leaders need to "forget the rest" until they have at least achieved these basics.

Naiveté?

Let's examine the idea of human sameness being naive. "Ah yes, species sameness—what a great sentiment! What a crock! You, Mr. Author, are an idiot to think this will fly! Every aggressive politician, businessman, and conman on the planet would love to link up with a sameness softy like you," this argument goes. "They would take you for every cent you've got! And exactly how can the idea of human sameness gain traction in a cutthroat, competitive world where money, advantage, and differentiated power dominate?"

The idea of human sameness empowers the *individual* who believes in it, even when he or she must compete in the human-made world of specialization and contentiousness. Why? How? When you, a tri-worlds realist, believe in human sameness, you assume the broadest identity possible. You understand the human paradox, the three worlds, life's basics, and human sensibilities/motivations. Data is your friend. Truth/reality is your baseline. Your way of thinking and acting makes others think that there is more to life than their own biases and limitations. You don't feel little or unfulfilled, and you do not allow others to make you feel that way. Confidence comes with being fully human and recognizing yourself as such.

When you have beliefs built solidly around acknowledging the human paradox, when you understand and accept each of the three worlds, when you accept that everyone has essentially the same needs and wants as everyone else, and when you accept yourself and your specialized, human-made-world career, then your self-esteem and self-love become steadfast and evident to others; you personify self-assurance, and you usually read others accurately.

You have more in common with other human beings than those who have only mono- or bi-world biases, those who are ignorant of the human paradox and the three worlds. You become someone who knows your limits. You know when your own work specialty applies and when it does not. You become someone who knows that morality, ethics, and spirituality are more than academic course titles. You exude to others unpretentious intelligence, honesty, and self-esteem. You easily acknowledge your shortfalls and kinked armor and how your life lessons can benefit others. You personify integrity even as you tactfully question mono- and bi-world biases, and you maintain a sense of humor. Knowledge, honesty, and sincerity replace hustling and deception. You act realistically because ethics and morality make sense and are part of your personal principles. Your baseline is data-driven reality and sound principles founded on species and planetary needs.

Opportunists and manipulators will not have much luck overcoming a tri-worlder's integrity and savviness, which can see right through their pretenses and games. Human-paradox believers and tri-worlders aren't Aryans or Nietzsche-like supermen; they're simply people grounded in all three worlds and who accept and emphasize human sameness, peace, sustainability, and natural integrity. They understand today's reality and are trying their best to help themselves, our species, and the planet survive. They have developed a personal conscience centered on species survival and planetary integrity, their indefatigable sources of inspiration.

Also, by recognizing the basic sameness of others, these advocates can see past the facades that mono- and bi-worlders construct to impress, belittle, or subjugate others. Sameness serves as a personal center of gravity that can be universally shared. Issues become more important than personalities. You become more of a team member in life than a fan or admirer. What you look like and your accent don't matter compared to what you're trying to achieve in life with your skills and experience. You feel a lot more comfortable in your own skin when you know that those above you in the hierarchical pyramid are just as human as you are; you are not intimidated by them. Powerful people usually have good intentions, but they make mistakes; they need accurate input to make sound decisions. You aren't afraid to state the truth as you see it and to provide the facts that back up those truths.

Status quo elites may be more intelligent or have more money and power than you do, but they share many of the same basic concerns, priorities, and fears you do. The same goes for those lower in the power pyramid; they need sustenance, security, and comfort just like you do. Whatever you can do to help them helps humanity and gives you a sense of personal fulfillment. Being this kind of person is not easy. Complexity stimulates but exhausts; applied perseverance replaces empty hope.

Theoretically, individual citizens matter most in a democracy. What you think and feel as an individual is important, but powerful people cannot read your mind; you must tell them and show them what you think. Forget being shy; that does you, the planet, and the species no good whatsoever. Conscientious and caring leaders are always looking for good ideas. If common citizens do not share thoughts and ideas with the powerful, at least in a representative democracy, the powerful will gravitate to peers, elites, lobbyists, and other squeaky wheels. In America, our elected representatives want to know what you think and believe. They cannot hear what you do not say.

The U.S. Capitol, the White House, Buckingham Palace, the Kremlin, the Vatican, and so on—all these architectural gems were established to house powerful figures who control and influence human affairs. Well, guess what? The people who lead and guide our societies depend on these structures and other vestiges of authority to reinforce the idea of their differentiated special status and power. They love having their exceptional sense attended to. If you can look past all the glitz and glamour, however, you will find a fellow human being who operates in a stressful world of differentiation and dualism just as you do. They operate at a different level than you do, and most should be respected for the responsibilities they have assumed, but all of them are basically the same as you. All these famous places have offices, water fountains, and bathrooms just like your human-made world. You may be wearing Kohl's fashion, while they are wearing Armani or a bejeweled frock, but everyone is wearing clothes.

These symbols of power now need to house leaders who mutually focus on acceptance of the human paradox, species survival, and planetary integrity.

Recognizing human sameness helps strip away the pretense and the feeling of lower status and awe that power figures depend on for their differentiated superiority. You do not know as much as these leaders do about their particular responsibilities, but you know that your core values are human sameness, sustaining life's basics, natural integrity, peace, and caring for all three worlds. Ultimately, which is more important—the narrow interests of a specific pod or those of the species? Thinking at the species level leads to new questions. What is the leader recommending, and how would it affect the species under his/her control? Does the leader acknowledge human sameness? Who benefits from the leader's position, and why should they benefit? Who is included and why? Who is left out and why?

Americans have made some progress, however slowly, in acknowledging human sameness. Civil rights are one example. I was born in New Orleans in 1945. I grew up there in the 1950s. Everything was segregated. As I was a white kid, a fun thing to do in the summertime was ride public transit. For seven cents, you could ride one way and get a transfer with four stubs. My pals and I would ride around the city all day, transferring from one form of public transit to another as we explored the city. It was fun to stick my head out the St. Charles Avenue streetcar window and feel the warm, humid air blowing through my hair. It was also interesting to study the faces seated around me, to see what people were carrying and how they looked at or ignored one another. Black citizens were not having as much fun as I was, however. They had to sit behind signs that read "Reserved for Colored Patronage Only." White people moved these signs at will, sometimes generating tension between races even a ten-year-old could sense.

A lot of that racial tension has disappeared, but a lot still remains. Progress with civil rights so far has helped citizens discover that blacks and whites are not so different. Differences that remain are usually inherited prejudices. If you are programmed as a kid to hate others of a different race, you will be predisposed to think and act that way. That just makes them different and hated in your mind; it has nothing to do with what is real. The argument that African Americans are inherently inferior to Caucasian Americans has no basis in fact; it is a cultural lie, a nasty legacy from a distant but stubborn past. The same goes for denigrating other races and ethnicities. Sure, there are cultural differences among people, but at the root, we're all the same. Life is a lot more interesting and fun when you can appreciate both the sameness and the uniqueness in people.

The point is that both states of mind can and do exist at the same time: sameness and differentiation. You don't have to choose between the two, just accept that both exist concurrently. It is a paradox of reality we simply must accept, get used to, and teach to our children as soon as they can understand it: we human beings are all the same, yet each one is unique.

Species-Wide Issues

The most immediate reason human sameness gains importance is that there are problems differentiated pods cannot solve on their own no matter how big and powerful they are. We human beings now face the first wall of nature's limits, global warming/climate change, a problem human technology and politics helped create and that human technology and politics will have to help solve.

Individuals and their pods can each contribute what they can to help downsize or eliminate their carbon footprint, but it will be as a species—working together, learning together, sharing with one another—that we can reverse global warming and greenhouse gas threats. No individual, interest group, or nation can pull this off alone. Why can't we also come together to eliminate war, poverty, disease, and eco-destruction in a like manner? "Utopian nonsense," you say. Possibly, but these are much nobler and species-sustaining goals than fawning over ego-maniacal leaders, militarism, fear, nationalistic hubris, greed, and religious exceptionalism. We citizens need to quit being suckers for these old political games that lead nowhere but to a hallway of cracked mirrors.

Within reality rests another paradox: differentiation can benefit humankind, as can sameness. We won't escape differentiation anytime soon. Actually, we never will because we really don't want to. Life would be pretty flat without it. Differentiation helps determine so many aspects of our individual lives: what to buy, where to live, where to go to school, where to travel, how to make a living, who to love, and what to believe. Differentiation is the basis for each person's unique taste, style, and other aspects of life that make us feel special; it is what makes learning fun, the act of discovering new things, processes, places, and people we never knew about before. Realistically, if we live in a modern society, differentiation will continue to be a fact of life; it's impossible to avoid and should be welcomed.

However, too much differentiation and the importance put upon it ill-serves the long-term survival of human life on this planet. Continued denial of human sameness in the name of differentiation has ever-direr consequences. Human vanity, envy, and greed that feed off differentiation depend on anti-species behaviors to survive through arguments of pod superiority, exclusivity, or purity—behaviors that could destroy us all in the long run if our survival instincts, long-term values, and unifying faiths cannot offset them.

So what is our option? We can advance civilization best by accepting the human paradox and human sameness as well as focusing on the survival of the species and planetary integrity, which are common goals for all of humanity. To attain these goals, we must identify current political arguments that do not serve the species' long-term interests and then counter them with arguments and actions that do. Yes, there really are common goals for humanity that are more important than national pride or individual/pod self-interest, more important than ever-upward economic growth and extreme personal comforts. Acknowledging and acting on these macro issues needs to take priority over dualistic and differentiated priorities that do not serve the species and planet. Also, ironically, this reorientation will have to occur locally for it to become global. Human paradox understanding and three-worlds thinking must begin at the grassroots level before they can affect the pinnacles of power, at least in America.

What are things that divide human beings, one from another? Politics, language, religion, culture, economic competition, money, social status, race, hatred, war, and so forth. Of course, every one of these categories also brings people together; each one provides a basis for belonging to like-minded groups and provides some form of peerage and camaraderie. However, most of these groupings are based on dualism and differentiation rather than a principle of species sameness and natural integrity.

What are species-wide issues that can bring human beings together?

- **Sustaining planet Earth.** Without sustaining natural integrity, we humans cannot sustain ourselves. To believe that our species can ignore or overcome natural laws is pure anthropocentric fantasy. To think that we can delay action on natural issues so we can keep consuming more and more stuff without incurring increased costs and ecological consequences is self-deluding folly. To deny global problems of global warming, climate change, resource crises (water, soil, forests, overfishing), and animal species depletion is suicidal. To keep dumping our wastes in the ground, rivers, and oceans is to poison our own wells. To believe that nature is here only to serve us is the beginning of the end of civilization. Our epitaph will read, "Here Lies Humanity — Shortsighted and Avaricious to the End."

- **Defusing the nuclear threat.** While I am not an advocate of scaring people, fear of nuclear annihilation is still real. We all need to take it to heart and make the nonproliferation of nuclear weapons (and, ideally, the elimination of nuclear weapons) a key element in the agenda of every country, every year, under every leader. No leader anywhere has the right to push the red button; nothing from a species-wide perspective could ever justify such an action. No terrorist should have access to materials that can wreak nuclear havoc and destruction.

- **Universal responsibilities of government and individuals.** The government in every nation needs to serve as the counterpoise to private sector greed, to militant mono- and bi-world fanatics, and to irresponsible resource management. A government dedicated to the common good, one that sanctions ways for individuals to responsibly pursue life's basics and that gives the natural world a voice, has the greatest chance of survival because that is what citizens want over the long term. Governments are not money troughs established for the private sector to come get its fill; they are not just another market to be exploited. Governance is not a business like a corporation. Governments exist to establish and enforce laws, to collect taxes, to provide services and products that the private sector cannot provide, and to secure an environment where citizens can healthfully pursue their sustenance, security, and comfort. Wherever you live, however good or corrupt your government is, there are some basic services you should be receiving from it. Whether you agree or disagree with your government's right to tax you, the fact that some things (defense, social safety nets, large-scale public works projects) require government-level direction and oversight cannot be rationally countered. Private enterprise should continue to be the primary provider of life's basics and hopefully, someday, the source of the drive and inspiration to position nature as co-equal or superior in importance to financial growth and profits. The government will have to provide rules and oversight over the private sector until that day arrives. The government has to provide the systems/means/methods for its citizens to attain life's basics. Individuals in modern societies must depend on their own endeavors to improve their personal sustenance, security, and comfort; even within paradox understanding and tri-worlds reality, there is no free lunch. Learn to pull your own weight or get crushed by it.

- **Political activism.** Nothing is going to change if you and I don't get off our apathetic butts and start moving. In democratic America, elected politicians represent *us!* They work for *us!* Narrow-minded right-wing conservatives, self-righteous evangelicals, and left-wing idealists have been whispering in leaders' ears long enough. It's time for human-paradox realists to step up and howl. If we have a representative government, we'll always have to deal with egocentric politicians; they might as well get gratification doing something positive for the species and planet rather than the tired old practices of partisanship, special interests, and reelection obsessions. Globally, we need to hold all local, state, and national leaders to common performance standards. Can they provide ways to attain shelter, nutrition, and some comfort for their citizens? If not, why not? Many leaders can't even meet these basic needs and keep the peace. What are they doing that's more important than serving their citizenry? Why can't politicians say no to special interests that do not serve the common good or the long-term interests of the species and planet?

- **Universal demands on ethereal ideologies.** Isn't it interesting that none of the holy books (Bible/Torah, Koran) have been updated recently? Powerful tools for social control over the ages, these books are more divisive now than helpful for the human species. They provide spiritual comfort for individuals, but when religious groupthink takes over, human beings turn into sheep and suicide bombers. Why hasn't God updated his holy word? Why does he allow wars and terrorism to be conducted in his name? Why not just clear up all the confusion and say what is expected of the human species today? God, you used to talk to human beings during the Bible/Koran-writing days—what's the problem now? Speak up, God! We need to hear what you've got to say! Louder, please—we can't hear you! If you think that kind of talk is blasphemous, that is your right, but look in the mirror when you think that because you've got to admit that God hasn't been attending to his human creations lately, or barring such divine updates, perhaps it's time to respectfully step away from *all* holy books and focus on human self-care for our species. Holy books should not be the basis upon which infidels (people who are not like you) can be murdered in their name. Holy books should not be so out of step with science that they are laughed at. Holy books should bring humans together, not be bulwarks of divisiveness and recalcitrance. Undoubtedly, these books in their present form will continue to bring personal solace to millions of the faithful, but as persuasive documents that affect social, economic, and governmental policy, they are obsolete and irrelevant. They will continue to retain a high place in the ethereal world, but they have no practical value in the human-made or natural worlds.

- **Mutual interdependence.** When was the last time you farmed your own groceries, cobbled your own shoes, or assembled your own car? We individual humans are hugely dependent on one another for our daily sustenance, our jobs, our well-being—we're all glued to the economic web in one way or another. This will not change because the human-made world establishment doesn't modify itself quickly; it evolves slowly and reluctantly because it took so much effort to get it working effectively in the first place. New systems, new technologies, new jobs don't usually come about overnight; they emerge slowly and imperfectly in the form of a new piece of equipment, new computer hardware/software, an intern hired full-time, a new subsidiary—all aimed at ratcheting up a business operation's productivity and profitability. Getting an edge over the competition or at least staying up with them is the name of the game in the human-made business world. Success goes to those who provide the best product or service in the shortest amount of time at the most reasonable cost. If you live on this planet, this simple formula will be the basic economic motivator for virtually everyone who works, each of us doing our own thing, one dependent on another, all of us interlocked and interdependent, all of us bobbing up and down together on the economic tides.

- **Alternative thinking.** If you are an individual uncomfortable with life's dizzying palette of grays, labeling modes of thought as black or white may be helpful for you. Traditional thinking includes categorizing information into one pigeonhole or another and then evaluating and judging that information based on personal or pod beliefs and experiences. No matter who you are or how hard you try, you will, like the rest of us, continue with old lines of thought in some areas of your life. You just need to be sensitive to the fact that dualistic and differentiated thinking often leads to regression and troubles in a changing world. Whenever possible, tri-worlds thinking avoids dualistic either/or, win/lose choices for an evaluation of an issue based on understanding the human paradox and three-worlds reality: how will the issue affect the natural, human-made, and ethereal worlds? Likewise, how will the three worlds affect the issue? Whose values, instincts, and faiths are involved in the issue, and how do they matter? Who benefits, who suffers, and who is ignored? The goal here is to get beyond black-and-white thinking to consider more deeply, more conscientiously, the issue itself, its implications and complications on yourself, your loved ones, the species, and the planet.

- **Individual perspective.** Every human being has feelings of personal smallness at one time or another. The massive social, governmental, economic, legal, and cultural institutions that comprise modern civilization seem so huge and impregnable, so intimidating and monolithic that they overshadow the individual. Most of us stick to our knitting and do not get involved in big issues that we don't know or care much about. Behavior is one thing, mindset another. Everyone needs to develop a generalist view about life because it provides a basic context for living—an identity that is larger than your personal job specialty and your specific instincts, values, and faith, an outlook that goes beyond conservatism or liberalism—and this endeavor to become more generalist is important simply because forming a personal worldview is an amazing intellectual and emotional journey in itself. It keeps you interested in all phases of life.

- **World government?** The species isn't ready for this, if ever. Rather, more cooperation among nations that follow species-survival and natural-integrity agendas seems the most hopeful governance mode in the future. This allows us to retain our uniqueness while we acknowledge our sameness. It is entirely possible that the recognition of human sameness will lead to less government overall because humans will have fewer differences and need less arbitration and fewer resources to resolve them, but the throw weight of different cultures will continue to move societies in different directions for decades to come. That's fine as long as leadership hubris, arrogance, and belligerence can be checked and we all recognize our sameness and shared responsibilities. If a society's unique characteristics become appliquéd on a quilt of universal understanding of human sameness and planetary needs, then that society can make no arguments strong enough to overcome species survival and planetary integrity—ergo, no need for world government.

Love/understanding/peace and personal fulfillment of life's basics come more from acknowledging human sameness than from emphasizing differences. Relying on human-made status or ethereal beliefs to justify your basic superiority over another human being is a self-induced hoax. You may be smarter, stronger, or richer, but you're made from the same basic stuff as the one you demean. They have attributes you do not; they have skills you do not. We are all dependent on one another in so many ways—no one is as exceptional as they think they are.

Human smugness transmogrifies into self-inflicted wounds at some point as time and reality expose personal or pod exceptionalism as having limited benefit and, oftentimes, as largely a waste of time and resources. **If every individual can accept their sameness as readily as their individuality, then there's hope for the future of the species, and if individuals can acknowledge and openly value their basic sameness, so can nations and religions.**

CHAPTER 3

Natural World

*I went to the woods because I wished to live deliberately . . .
and not, when I came to die, discover I had not lived.*[4]
— Henry David Thoreau, *Walden*

We modern-era citizens get so busy with our daily concerns that we don't give much thought to nature's primacy in our lives, how dependent we are on it, and how dead we are without it. We pay attention to nature in passing—when we catch a beautiful sunrise on the commute to work or when the weather person says a new system moving through the area: "Thundershowers this afternoon. Keep that umbrella handy!" How nature interferes with our daily lives usually gets more top-of-mind attention than thoughts of nature's bounty and our total reliance on it. We are in awe of nature, but we take it for granted.

We do pay attention to nature when we hunger for it, when we need to vacate the realms of outside control and stress in our lives. Nature as therapy helps alleviate tensions and brings our bodies and minds into improved homeostasis. Nature's ability to pacify us comes from laws that are independent of human-made or ethereal influences; they are the stuff of what we humans call biology, physics, chemistry, and geology. However, we don't think about these sciences as we hike along a verdant forest trail or stroll along the shore with waves washing over our feet; we just enjoy communing with nature, of which we humans are so much a part.

Of the three worlds, only the natural world can survive on its own; human arrogance and political bluster oftentimes obscure this fact. All human beings—along with our aspirations, hopes, and dreams—exist at the generosity of nature. Our dependence on nature will never change because we are natural beings made from the same basic materials found in all living things. We exist at the largesse of the natural world's atmosphere, biosphere, and geology, which maintain, destroy, and renew themselves as natural laws determine.

Our simple working definition of the natural world includes our solar system, our galaxy, and the entire cosmos, including all its unknowns. All sciences and agriculture stem from nature. Virtually every aspect of business and commerce exploits resources that nature has provided at no charge. Even if someday we humans travel to galaxies far, far away, we will still be captive of Earth's natural forces manifest through our physical and mental limitations.

Earthquakes, hurricanes, asteroids, volcanoes, floods, disease, pestilence, and droughts remind us that nature has us on tenterhooks and that no matter how much in control we humans think we are, we're not. From nature's point of view, we humans are cosmic ants. Actually, we're not even that significant to the natural world; we're more like microbes on the back of a cosmic ant. We human beings are only important in our own minds. The natural universe doesn't care one wit about us—zilch, nada, nil. Nature will never change its ways to accommodate us, and we'll only outwit nature on the margins.

All the glorification and self-adulation we humans claim is simply our species thumping its exceptionalist chest. Being human myself, I have to say there are many reasons to be proud of our species; we humans are highly creative and inventive, but we've gone way overboard with our self-consciousness, our appetites, and our feelings of superiority.

Considering the indisputable scale and power of nature, it might behoove us to exhibit more humility toward this world that gives and supports all life. In nature's protracted scheme, humans play a role no more significant than those of other species; nature can rid itself of humans just as it did the dinosaurs and millions of other species. From a natural world point of view, we human beings have only ourselves, other living species, our atmosphere, and our beautiful planet—hard facts that should help guide our survival priorities now and into the future.

At the root, we *Homo sapiens* have created innumerable human-made systems and behaviors that separate us from nature rather than align us to it. Capitalism considers nature little more than a source of raw materials. Rather than emulating nature and working with it, our many depletive and polluting human practices challenge nature in the name of economic gain, political benefit, or individual advantage.

In our quest for life's basics (sustenance, security, comfort), we have developed and sanctioned human-made systems that voraciously take from nature and give nothing back but wastes. **To replace the carbon-based Industrial Age, we now need to openly declare a Sustainability Age, a series of human generations dedicated to realignment with and learning more from nature as to mutually assured survival.** This needs to be the baseline for politics and economic development moving forward. The value of human-made systems to the species must be thoroughly reexamined considering nature's increasingly apparent limits and then refashioned with nature as a guiding template.

What are nature's limits? Here are a few:

- **Global warming/climate change.** Over the past millennia, nature has created numerous climate shifts of its own—ice ages, periods of warming, wet, and drought—almost all of these without any human presence or effect. These changes allowed life to change, as evidenced by faunal succession, and to develop in innumerable new ways, but none of these epochs ended life. It is entirely possible that today's global warming could eventually be categorized as just another climate shift whose effects are no more deleterious than earlier ones—possible but not likely, at least for our species. If even half the negative impacts that scientists predict of a warming climate ring true (rising sea levels, acid oceans, temperature increases, permafrost loss, decline of biodiversity, desertification, coral reef destruction, stronger cyclones/hurricanes), the impacts on the human-made world will be extraordinarily painful and expensive. These impacts will generate massive social, political, and economic issues along with untold human misery. We are already experiencing many of these travails well ahead of scientific predictions. Simply put, we humans will hurt ourselves as much or more than the rest of nature if we continue contributing heat-trapping gases into our shared atmosphere. We need to err on nature's side of this equation by doing what we already know we need to do—reduce/eliminate emissions that exacerbate global warming; produce energy more efficiently; conserve energy and transition quickly to renewable/low-to-no-carbon-footprint energy technology; and reduce, recycle, reuse, and eliminate wastes.

- **Finite natural resources.** Nature will slap us silly if we keep gobbling up resources to satiate our excesses. We humans are so smart. We're so creative. We're so brilliant. We can outfox nature! Right? In your dreams! We know nature has limits, yet we keep pushing them and pushing them to satisfy human-made desires and ethereal fantasies. Our capitalist economic model still depends on compounding growth that, unless regulated, exploits nature without conscience, all in the name of consumption, ever-upward profits/comforts, and capitalist/politician ego validation. Without better stewardship of our air, land, water, and other living species, we will exhaust our natural resources in the name of lesser deities: the balance sheet, social/digital status, and human comfort toys. If there was ever something obvious that we could not see during the Industrial Age, it is that nature, its ways, and its limits should now set the boundaries for economic growth. Anything less constitutes creeping species suicide.

- **Nonrenewable fuels.** While there are considerable reserves of oil, coal, and natural gas left in situ, no natural process is creating more oil, coal, or gas fast enough to offset our insatiable consumption. Unequivocally, human use of carbon-based fuels exacerbates global warming and climate change. Solar, wind, geothermal, tidal, biomass, and other renewable resources will slowly replace exhaustible and problematic fuel supplies as these alternatives become cost competitive at a commercial scale (as some already are) and/or through decentralization and subsidization. Getting to net-zero greenhouse gas emissions is the oft-stated goal, hopefully by 2050; this is a mind-boggling challenge. We humans are just too smart not to take advantage of these clean energy sources and to leverage the huge economic opportunities that come with their development. Successfully emulating nature and optimizing what nature gives us will enhance human survival once the importance of these priorities gets political recognition through a governmental cap-and-trade system, carbon tax, low-carbon-electricity standard, or other legislation in America and elsewhere.

- **Cosmological apathy.** Our puny three dimensions, our beautiful but small planet, our glorious human achievements get nothing but a yawn from the cosmos, if that. Black holes, quasars, quarks, supernovas, unfathomable distances, billions of stars in millions of galaxies—on and on, the universe goes well beyond human influence. The cosmos is cold, endless, and averse to human life. Its primary gift to us is perspective: our orb with a twenty-four-thousand-mile circumference is all we humans have and all we are ever going to have, period. Space travel intrigues us, but it has yet to discover any reachable place as good or better for our species than Earth itself, and if it did make such a discovery, we couldn't afford to go there and colonize it at any useful scale. Preserving and honoring planet Earth are the only realistic choices for our species' survival.

- **Population limits.** Scientists estimate that our planet will struggle to support more than ten billion living human beings, yet we keep having sex and babies and more sex and more babies. Along with economic growth and prosperity come more mouths to feed, all of whom require more economic growth to fulfill their needs and expectations. At some future point, the earth's capabilities to support human population growth will be exceeded. The United Nations predicts we will exceed the ten billion mark by 2030—then what? Arable land, potable water, and breathable air will be at a premium. On the other hand, if humans continue down traditional behavior paths, more wars will help depopulate the planet, and nature's countervailing forces (disease, disaster, pestilence) will probably thin our ranks for us. Fewer children willingly or a Four-Horsemen-like backlash from nature seem to be the main paths before us regarding population control.

Acknowledging nature's limits and living within them is the most realistic option available for continuing life on planet Earth. We now need to ask ourselves why our dualistic human behaviors and differentiated interests have more political importance than sustainable species survival. Why do we, the human species, waste so much time, energy, and resources in endeavors that exhibit our weaknesses and antipathies rather than our intelligence and similarities? Why have dualism and differentiation come to dominate human thinking? Why is nature a lower priority than self-indulgent, short-term, human-made economic and political desires? Why do we citizens let ourselves get seduced by dualistic leaders who have no plan for sustaining life and planet? Why are human politics so bound by differentiating traditions/values and so potentially destructive of the species and nature? Also, some of us have granted to holy forces power over humans and nature that cannot be proved, that dilute resources and energy away from life on Earth, and that divert thinking away from species-level survival and planetary integrity.

While the human-made and ethereal worlds have shaped our personal ideals of happiness and salvation, they have paradoxically led us to confusion, conflict, and despair. We do not appreciate our sameness as human beings because, as already discussed, we have created a world that thrives on dualism and differentiation in multitudinous forms. Fear of and devotion to ethereal forces and worn-out ideals consume time and resources better spent supporting life on Earth. Selfish, individual concerns about the exceptionalism or fanaticism of one political/religious/ethnic pod or another consume energy that could benefit the species and the planet. The truly evil people on this planet are those who claim that humans are more or less than natural beings and that life on this planet isn't important. **Life on this planet is the only thing we humans know for sure and, truly, the only thing we can control. Our political and religious leaders need to focus on this indisputable, common-sense fact.**

Most human knowledge exists because we humans strove for millennia to improve our life's station in the face of intimidating natural forces. Many of these forces still mystify us, but we now understand so very much about the human–nature bond. Another inarguable fact: we *Homo sapiens* are all-natural beings wholly dependent on nature's gifts and devices for survival. Every branch of science and agriculture begins at the trunk of nature, every human economic system depends on nature's resources, and every "thing" we own or want ultimately stems back to nature. Instead of recognizing and living within our natural selves, however, we try to live the paradox. We have created an economic system that encourages endless growth; we have split ourselves into countless cells of political, social, and religious differentiation. Individually, we hedonistically pursue a personal happiness that always seems just out of reach or one that gets constantly redefined with higher expectations. We dualistically rend rather than sew our own species' fabric.

Also, virtually every mental fascination we conjure up bases its claims on outwitting natural forces or overcoming them in some fantastic way. The ethereal world of me/us plays off the basic paradox of all humans being the same but each one being unique. Every mortal would love to have the powers of our supernatural heroes, would love to be godlike, would love to be so exceptional that even the boundaries of nature cannot inhibit us, but we can't quite pull that off in the real world, the natural world, can we? We humans have a hard time accepting our physical/mental limitations because of our ethereal egos, our special blessedness compared to others/them, along with the rightness and purity of our identity pods, especially our political ideologies and religions. To reiterate, we humans currently value individual and pod differentiations *exponentially* more than natural species sameness.

We need to grow up as a species and take responsibility for our collective fate from this point forward. Nothing less will do. We must move away from politics, religion, and tradition that regard nature as something to be conquered, depleted, or ignored. We need to leverage human greed and aggression in new ways, to pull in the reins on unsustainable growth, and to change the view that nature is our garbage can.

We need to empower ourselves as individuals, as nations, and as a species to distinguish between the responsible management of natural resources and the destructive exploitation thereof. Yes, we are smart enough to figure this out, and a lot of sustainable activity is already underway, but there's so much more before us.

It's time to admit that we are part of nature, not something apart from and superior to it; this is humanity's premier challenge with the natural world. We must temper insatiable human appetites for more and more stuff that may make corporate annual reports happy but just ends up in an attic, storage shed, or landfill. We need to moderate our appetites and our behaviors, or some natural force may very well do the moderating for us.

Nature's Rules

Nature can't give more than it's got or move faster than it moves, and we humans seem unwilling to accept these simple truths. Our impatience with nature, our growth/consumer economic model, and our emphasis on the short term over the long term result in pollution, global warming, climate change, resource shortages, huge income disparities, and a lot of other ugly residuals. We humans have a deep and ever-expanding scientific understanding of nature and how we're affecting and infecting its processes, yet we paradoxically live our lives as if this knowledge had no real effect on us as individuals or the species. Oh, how we adore our human comforts! Oh, how human economic prosperity and individual exceptional desires outweigh nature's needs and limits! "We want it all, and we want it now!" That's the undeniable life credo for today's consuming humankind.

Scientific knowledge spells out clearly nature's tendencies and limits as they apply to our species. If we all lived up to our natural potential and took care of our bodies by eating a perfect diet and exercised like we should, then some of us would live to be over 125 years old, but we don't do that because we're having too much fun *not* doing those things. We deem ourselves fulfilled when we are in control of our lives, when there's money in the bank, and when we're busy, busy, busy with human affairs.

As consumers, we have no idea (and often don't care about) what the costs to nature are for our latest purchase. All we care about is whether the product or service meets our expectations to sustain us, make us feel more secure, or improve our comfort. Costs to nature for the things we consumers want to fulfill life's basics are rarely evident in the price tag, and we never express much curiosity about these costs. (Actually, we don't want to know the real costs of our pleasures because that may induce guilt, a disquieting no-no in comfortable lives.)

Nature tends to repeat the same patterns in the short term (the four seasons) and only changes in big ways through eras and epochs we humans can't comprehend. We struggle to envision life beyond our own lifetime or, at most, that of our grandchildren. Individually, we are so focused on leaving a mark on life, making sure that life is as good or better for our kids and grandkids and that we are remembered fondly after death that that becomes the extent of our personal legacy. All the long-term, high-minded ideals about saving the earth get too air-fairy, too big, and too far away from everyday life for most of us to do anything about them. We may have a lot of high-minded thoughts and feelings about nature, yet we take little action compared to our commitments to the human-made and ethereal worlds.

Also, we continue to propagate the old dualistic saw that the earth is here to serve us, not us to serve it, and that is how we live our lives. Today the ultimate truth of emerging planetary limits proves how outdated this premise is. For individuals and nations to have a worthwhile legacy, our species must find workable compromises that include lots of greening and giving back to nature in addition to sustainable economic development that provide life's basics.

Up to this point of human existence, the act of facing climate change, the destruction of eco systems, and biota species extinction has generated sympathetic emotions but little concerted action. Why? Because we humans heavily discount what one individual, one interest pod, or even one nation can do to cure such long-term challenges. We do not value the long term as much as the short term because we are finite beings who won't be around when the long term gets here. We underestimate how much impact an individual can really have on nature; most Americans have no idea what their carbon footprint is, and many don't give a damn. We're selfish. We love being in-charge-of-our-own-life consumers. We've got higher priorities than nature. We're determined to get our share of the economic pie, so that's where our energies go, and as a nation, we Americans don't want to give up the superpower edge we have over other countries because that keeps us aligned with the ideal of America's exceptional/unique self-concept.

Politically, we don't want to jeopardize economic progress or job creation with too much government regulation on the private sector because that might threaten our personal pursuit of sustenance, security, and comfort. We rationalize away overly consumptive behaviors while we struggle to acknowledge that problems with nature exist at all.

To be completely honest, in our heart of hearts, natural concerns aren't all that important to most Americans. We average American citizens have a difficult time elevating nature on our list of priorities because it has been taken for granted for such a long time, and all the dire predictions made by experts have yet to affect our daily lives. It's hard to believe all the doom-and-gloom talk when there's food on the table, clean water to drink, and survivable air to breathe. Nature's long-term changes haven't really smacked us in the face yet. We don't recognize the pernicious effects of excess and neglect; we've quietly agreed, through apathy or intent, to pass that buck to upcoming generations. Après moi le deluge.

Also, our species does not react to long-term natural harbingers whose impacts may be difficult or impossible to reverse once they arrive. We are largely in denial about most natural-world issues, and we resent others trying to scare us into changes that upset our personal priorities and daily lives. Like everything else in our short-term mentality, we will deal seriously with natural changes when they are kicking the door down, when we can smell, taste, and touch them. It will take a lot more persuading and fearmongering by the government, science, and save-the-earth interest pods before most of us give up even a few creature comforts for the sake of natural integrity. It's entirely possible that we will procrastinate too long. **The ultimate danger for our species may come as our exceptional sense about ourselves as unique individuals and identity tribes takes us beyond what nature can abide.**

We human beings have yet to internalize that we all share the same blue-ball planet and that our species represents its major threat. We deny our individual and collective responsibilities regarding nature's debasement. We rationalize away behaviors that we know hurt nature but put money in our pockets, and because of our dualistic conditioning, we see arguments about saving the planet as just one side of an issue, with the other side being economic/business development. We have yet to accept that species survival is a more basic priority than the dynamics of dualistic arguments and human-made world priorities. Yes, as members of the species, we are beginning to think about nature and its problems, but we are terribly slow to understand their primacy and to act in meaningful ways—an ill omen for species survival, if there ever was one.

Adapting to Nature

Human beings became culturally different because nature did not give everyone an Eden. Every tribe had to adapt to the terrain in which it found itself. Natives of the Fertile Crescent apparently started agriculture twelve thousand years ago because there weren't any forests in their locale in which to hunt and gather food. The Arctic Inuit ate meat and blubber and lived in houses made of ice and snow because their white world was the only world they had. Polynesians fished and boated from island to island because the sea ruled and they knew of no other landed places.

Every society adapted as best it could to what nature provided; every culture shared a strong will to live and prosper. If there weren't enough resources to survive, they moved on or died out. **Another paradox: human adaptability to nature's gifts and constraints has led to unique societies that distance our species from recognizing human sameness. Today's highly differentiated cultures ill-serve our species and nature's long-term well-being.** A society's pride of culture as well as self-proclaimed nationalistic, racial, or religious uniqueness can encourage hubris, which often leads others within the species to admire, envy, or hate it. Nature may be a contributing factor in human differentiation, but it is us human beings who sustain and overemphasize our differences.

The exploitation of nature has been the prevailing theme of *Homo sapiens* from our species' earliest days. Because we come from nature and are a part of nature, we can't escape the essence of our being. We must eat food and drink water, we have to move so our bodies don't atrophy, we need shelter from the elements, and on it goes. Contemporary civilization and economic progress give us more time away from these basic mandates. Today we don't have to obsess about food, water, and shelter as much as our ancestors did. We have created cities and modern societies where common citizens demote natural survival to low levels of concern. Modern civilization assures that food, shelter, and other elemental aspects of life can be obtained with much less physical effort than in the past—a reality that frees humans for more abstract thought, intellectual endeavors, and social development.

Human progress mirrors natural processes in that both change relatively slowly. Compared to geologic time, human progress moves at the speed of light, but compared to the span of a single human lifetime, social progress trails a snail. Living conditions have improved during my lifetime: the average age for a white male in America has gone from 63.2 years to 75.2 years.[5] That's great, and kudos to those who made this possible, but progress in politics and the social sciences has progressed much more glacially thanks largely to dualism and differentiation. Discrimination, ignorance, crime, poverty, environmental degradation, and other human-made world maladies that existed before my birth will continue after my death. Sure, there has been progress in these areas, but entire generations of human beings, along with their dated belief systems and prejudices, need to die out before significant change can be achieved for the species—or so it seems.

The generational attitudes of those in power and the support of those who confer power upon them tend to dominate species dynamics by accommodating established modes of productivity and behavior and by rationing change and progress. **Every human generation wants to ensure that its contributions to achieving life's improvement continue until that generation dies out—a legacy that invariably lauds human-made world achievements and politics at the expense of nature.** Of course, for a few in our species, progress isn't a goal at all; some mono-world humans would rather dwell in the imagined perfection of the past or fight for an idealized utopian future, items we will touch more on later.

Through continued population growth, dependence on carbon-based resources, and rising economic expectations, we humans have painted ourselves into an environmental corner. We are flirting with exceeding the natural capacity of our own atmosphere to sustain us. We are overwhelming natural limitations in the name of human-made or ethereal goals. We're in love with reaching further economically and living large because improving financial and social pod status is more important than natural integrity.

In our tendency to delude (and exonerate) ourselves, we humans think that we can exceed nature's limitations and get away with it or that technology will somehow bail us out in the nick of time. We have a hard time believing that nature will cause a backlash during our lifetimes or those of our offspring. Also, because we don't believe in species sameness, our politicians waste precious time bickering about or denying responsibility for solving global environmental problems that America and the rest of the industrialized world created and continue to exacerbate.

Climate change isn't the only negative impact humans have on nature, only the most publicized. In our quest to conquer nature, we humans have reduced the natural resources available to future generations, polluted land, river, and sea with synthetic products and toxic chemicals, generated billions of tons of solid/liquid waste, decimated forests and seas, and eliminated other living species that had roles in natural ecosystems—that is, flora and fauna that may have value for human survival.

Edward O. Wilson's *The Future of Life* spells out clearly how harming the natural world diminishes the human-made world. "Ecosystems services are defined as the flow of materials, energy, and information from the biosphere that support human existence . . . If humanity were to try to replace the free services of the natural economy with substitutes of its own manufacture, the global GNP would have to be raised by $33 trillion,"[6] Wilson says. In other words, the things that nature provides for free (e.g., clean air, clean water, the pollination of crops, the detoxification and recirculation of wastes) would have to be paid out of our pockets.

Jared Diamond hits on the same theme in his book *Collapse*, which examines in part the loss of biodiversity. "But biodiversity losses of small inedible species often provoke the response 'Who cares? Do you really care less for humans than for some lousy useless little fish or weed, like the snail darter or Furbish lousewort?' This response misses the point that the entire natural world is made up of wild species providing us for free with services that can be very expensive and, in many cases, impossible for us to supply ourselves. Elimination of lots of lousy little species regularly causes big harmful consequences for humans, just as does randomly knocking out many of the lousy little rivets holding together an airplane."[7]

LOSS OF SPECIES

A United Nations report predicts the loss of one million species (half animal, half plant) over the next near decades. This is the fastest extinction rate the world has ever seen.

Virtually every argument made by Wilson, Diamond, and other naturalists affirms the need for the human-made world to begin to take more seriously how we humans are squandering our planet's natural equity. We are, right now, amid the largest decline in biodiversity in the history of the planet, yet most of us don't know or care much about this fact. This natural diminishment is no longer a goody-two-shoes, guilt-tripping issue; species survival will depend in large part on how we respond to human-made world impacts on nature day to day over the next near decades.

The depletion of nonrenewable natural resources, the poor management of soil and water resources, the destruction of tropical and old-growth forests, flora and fauna extinction, toxic chemical and nuclear material production/ use/disposal, and the handling and elimination or reuse of massive amounts of solid and liquid wastes all need to replace or, at least, gain political parity with national patriotism, economic development, defense, human rights, and other macro political issues. The more we delay facing and resolving these issues, the more our progeny will suffer, and the more they will rue our shortsightedness.

On an upbeat note, perhaps dealing with climate change will be the first progressive step our species takes together. We got a head start on unified species efforts with the Kyoto Protocol, which seeks to limit carbon dioxide emissions, and the Montreal Protocol, which aims to control ozone-destroying chlorofluorocarbons (CFCs), but not every nation got on board with these initiatives. Even the Copenhagen Accord and Cancun Agreements initiated some fledgling carbon-reducing actions, but all these endeavors fell short of unified, species-focused consensus because of overriding national self-interests. The Paris Accords obligated 196 nations to begin their efforts to keep global warming well below two degrees Celsius (preferably one and a half degrees Celsius) by 2050. The United Nations' November 2021 COP26 conference saw 197 countries sign on to the Glasgow Climate Pact, which made a commitment to lower coal use and to provide more financing for developing countries to deal with climate impacts. Since the threat of climate change affects virtually every life form on the planet, a global commitment will be required to reduce or eliminate carbon dioxide, methane, mercury, nitrous oxide, and other emissions with especially significant commitments needed from the large industrial nations that contributed most to climate change and global warming.

If international consensus is achieved to offset climate change, this will be the first time humankind has politically acknowledged natural limits and heeded them, the first time the species has come together to solve a shared natural problem, and the first time our sameness as human beings has taken priority over narrower human-made and ethereal-world priorities. We are not there yet, but hopefully, we're inching toward concerted, species-focused action on global warming/climate change.

As glorious as this universalistic vision may be, the paradox rule comes into play through emphasis on the second half of the axiom: human beings are all the same, *yet each one is unique*—uniqueness as defined by individuals, by cultures, by religions, by nationalities, and by other differentiated pods that still dominate world thinking today. It is highly unlikely these forces will yield to the idea of species sameness during our lifetime. It is pure idealism to believe that the pillars of civilization (religion, business/commerce, nationalism) will compromise their differentiated status to accommodate species sameness or nature's limits. The question now is can dominating pods find ways to make concessions? How can anyone claim to be an exception to the rule when we are all the same and the natural rule is that there are no exceptions? How much guilt can a "we/us" citizenry tolerate in the face of undeniable climate degradation? How vicious will nature's karma be on the next near generations? We all need a survivable atmosphere, we all need water and food, and we all need to deal with wastes; these are not issues our species can hide from any longer.

As much as humanity may say it wants peace and prosperity for all, species survival will not take root until thinking *individuals* within each culture, religion, and nationality acknowledge the merit of human sameness and the fact that nature has limits. Even with the Internet and other useful tools, this recognition probably will take decades if not longer because it requires so much systemic change of thought and compromise. The haves will struggle mightily against ideas that dilute their have-ness. The powerful will resist rationales that challenge their power base. Influential ethereal idealists will cling to their exceptional beliefs and mono-world self-righteousness. Whether there's enough time for these pods to adjust (or to disappear) without permanently damaging the species and the planet becomes the question.

Whose calendar will prevail? Nature's? The human-made world's? The ideologues'? What, specifically, do humans need to do to reduce negative impacts on nature? Who is going to lead and pay for global systemic change? The challenge will be to change our ways at the individual, national, and other pod levels before nature knocks us to our knees, something it most assuredly can do.

The Human-Caring Value

How would a species-conscious planet work? From a natural-world perspective, we are all made from the same genetic materials, so let's quit kidding ourselves that one race is superior to another, that God favors one religion/race/polity over another, or that rich people are somehow different or inherently more worthy than poor people. That gets us and nature nowhere.

Our basic physical, psychological, and spiritual sameness as a species cannot be denied and must be acknowledged and continually referenced as a primary motivator for a global reorientation. Dualism and differentiation need to be humbled by a species-wide focus on the importance of human sameness, the sustainable achievement of life's basics, peace, and the need to preserve and reestablish natural integrity. **Is sameness recognition not the next step in humanity's social evolution?** Again, what priority rests higher for nature and living human beings than preserving natural integrity and sustainable species survival?

Ideally, at our very core, in the innermost thinking and feeling part of every human being, there needs to be a value that respects the existence of every other human being on the planet. Call this value humanism, tolerance, or common decency. Call it love. Call it a fried-egg sandwich. The label isn't as crucial as individuals having the value itself. What is important is that this value exists in as many human beings as possible and is held as a core belief. This value sees in each person as much sameness as there is apparent difference.

When I, an adult American Caucasian male, look into the eyes of a teenage Chinese girl sitting on a bench opposite me on the Star Ferry crossing the Hong Kong harbor, I see another member of my species who has the same basic wants, needs, and desires as I do. After we make eye contact, we acknowledge this sameness to each other with a polite smile. We have a lot in common. I realize our commonalities, but she probably does not because of her age, her limited life experience, and so on. She may be smiling at me simply out of respect for an older person just as she has been taught (or maybe she thinks I'm cute). Despite the differences, my core value contends that we two human beings have more traits in common than those that make us dissimilar. My core belief, my innermost human sensibility, places more value on human sameness than on language, appearance, age, nationality, politics, or any other variable. I would rather help her than hurt her if given a chance to do so.

Actually, I believe the core value of human caring for others already exists in most of us . . . and dare I say, it's probably stronger in most women than in most men. I believe it is a natural value, and I think that's why our species still persists on this planet today. Perhaps it is an innate part of our primitive past, some remnant of a distant herd mentality, or perhaps something more mystical. I don't know, and it doesn't make any difference. **The point is that the innate human-caring value has been so beaten down, so castigated and sublimated by human-made doctrines, power politics, competitiveness, and ethereal dogma, that it has become a precious commodity that is hardly ever openly talked about.**

By the time human civilization began recording its activities, the core belief in human sameness and human caring had been corralled down to the tribe or family unit and to the individual, where it largely remains today. To feel sameness with strangers has become anathema within our species because of perceived differences and resultant fears; we reserve caring only for those whose sustenance, security, and comfort matter most to us, namely, ourselves and our families. Additionally, interest pods such as nations try to leverage this caring value into a unique identity for their citizenry (patriotism), but by doing so, they dilute species importance.

Not so ironically, those of us who believe in an innate caring value tend to share this sentiment with other living creatures. Nature's rules for most species seem to be consistent with an innate caring value. Love of any kind can be defined as caring for the sustenance, security, and comfort of another form of life.

Very few large-brained species hurt their own kind or kill one another the way humans do. The natural tendency among these animals is to protect and nurture others of the same genetic makeup, not to harm them. Males of a species often fight among one another for the attention of females, but this falls into the classifications of fitness, dominance, and species survival rather than an urge to maim or kill one of their own. Kindness and caring for one's own species—what a concept for humans to consider!

Darwin's *The Origin of Species* and concomitant findings by A. R. Wallace confirm differences from one species to another, but their work supports the essential physical sameness within one species (because that's what makes a species a species). In their view, any given species will change over time, and the strongest among that species will survive and continue to evolve; that's the process of natural selection.

As for humans in particular, Darwin concludes in his *Descent of Man* that "man is descended from some less highly organized form" and "the grounds upon which this conclusion rests will never be shaken, for the close similarity between man and the lower animals in embryonic development, as well as in innumerable points of structure and constitution, both of high and of the most trifling importance . . . are facts which cannot be disputed."[8] Until some more provable and logical theory comes along, Darwin's evolutionary ideas will continue to serve as the scientific baseline for human development on this planet.

Dualistic-obsessed humans with highly differentiated beliefs, not surprisingly, rejected Darwin's conclusions or took his proof about the natural world and created a wide variety of social Darwinist theories. Eugenics, for example, tried to weed out some members of a society because of their physical or mental deformities. Eugenicists believed that purging a society of "inferior" beings would clean up a population and make it more hygienic; their goal was a human-assisted form of natural selection.

The writings of Thomas Malthus and Herbert Spencer, much of which pre-dated Darwin, would later fall under the moniker of social Darwinism. Malthus said that population growth would always surpass the food supply, so the population would only be controlled by war, disease, pestilence, or famine (the Four Horsemen). If the laws about poverty that existed in England during Malthus's time had not existed and, therefore, if the excess population had never existed, "the aggregate mass of happiness among the common people would have been much greater."[9] In other words, according to Malthus, short of strict population control, those with superior intelligence and skills could rationally separate themselves from the common hordes that were doomed to poverty, misery, and early death; these lesser humans were beyond hope and ignorable in his view.

Spencer affirmed the notion that political, economic, and social elites were the strongest and most fit among the populace, so they were the worthiest to survive. He coined the term "survival of the fittest"[10] after reading Darwin's work and helped instill within elite ranks a sense of moral superiority that the strong prosper at the expense of the weak and that that is okay.

In the ethereal religious world, some religionists in the past, in their efforts to differentiate their sect from other faiths and from the natural and human-made worlds, also created attitudes that made followers feel special. They were tapped as the "chosen few," "God's children," or "the blessed ones"—all higher beings and, of course, separate from anything that evolved from Darwin's lesser life forms.

These differentiated stances exemplify how human-interest pods distance themselves from now evident and provable natural species commonalities. Social Darwinism, in its darkest corners, provided rationales for secular and religious elites to dissociate themselves from the common value of human caring described above. Many of these supercilious attitudes persist among today's elites and their interest pods. For the sake of species survival, this type of thinking must now be relegated to the classic dustbins of history; **the ethos of an elite few dominating and exploiting the many needs to be replaced with an elite few nurturing and sustaining the planet in the name of the many.**

In the long run, the argument as to whether man descended from apes or whether elites and "chosen ones" should feel guiltless about their status isn't all that relevant to the moral importance of species sameness. **What matters right now, today, and tomorrow is how successfully we living-and-thinking *Homo sapiens* can sustain life on this planet for our own sake and for that of other flora and fauna.** No national, dualistic, or differentiated philosophy has higher priority from a species survival point of view.

How should we go about this considering that humans must consume resources to obtain life's basics? How can we go about this given the human-made world's diverse and complex priorities that value nature differently? How will species advocates overcome deeply implanted dualistic and highly differentiated political interests and inherited social Darwinist philosophies that are still used to justify pod and individual exceptionalism?

In the broadest sense, our species, through its existing nation-states, needs to identify species-wide problems, to develop understanding and consensus among the populace as to the primacy of these challenges, to facilitate new thinking and behavioral change, and to select leaders committed to species' common ends and then to implement appropriate solutions (economic incentives, moral guidelines, government regulations). This is one of the largest challenges civilization has ever faced, if not the greatest. To fund these species-wide remedies, currently differentiated goals such as dualistic political ideologies, wars, and carbon-based dependencies must be demoted to priorities of lesser concern or eliminated and their government subsidies, funding, and tax breaks shifted to species/planet-targeted ends.

New technologies and new markets that work *with* (that is, net-zero carbon footprint) rather than *against* nature will provide jobs and development opportunities for the private sector; for example, renewable energy and biotechnology are already gaining economic prowess. These emerging markets need government encouragement and consistent support, not marginalization. Aligning life's basics with natural processes and limits will generate new jobs in a greener and smarter information-based economy. Organized religions should have no grounds to object to this shift in governmental and economic focus since their goals include (or should include) saving the planet God created and achieving peaceful coexistence among human beings; to the contrary, religionists should be major expounders of this transition.

The results of such a priority shift will lead to improved homeostasis between humankind and nature and a new status that replaces human destructive habits and technologies that no longer serve the species or the natural planet's best interests. Yes, I know, this is all pure optimism/idealism, and the hardest part will come with the details and nasty politics, but we humans have to set some goals to keep life interesting and challenging for ourselves. These decades-to-centuries-long goals will sustain the species, not destroy it, along with our atmosphere and the natural planet.

Our Carbon Nature

Life knows only life; that's why all living things put so much effort into staying alive. All we really know about death is that it is the absence of life, a prospect that frightens the living and provides a broad landscape for mono- and bi-worlders to exploit. Every living species wants to survive and reproduce; every natural instinct comes from these priorities. When we humans commune with nature, it is the appreciation of life in its varied, unique, and beautiful forms that ties us back to our natural roots—we realize that all life is connected in some mysterious way.

The competition for natural resources does not usually turn brutal until resource depletion forces the issue, a basic truth applicable to all living species. More floods, more droughts, more intense hurricanes, higher crop-wilting temperatures—the list of catastrophic possibilities associated with global warming and climate change is daunting. Also, even if these scientific predictions are only partially accurate, the deleterious effects on millions of people will be life altering. The competition for resources will increase, as will the havoc associated with a more desperate struggle for life's basics. Considering that scientific predictions have so far underestimated the timing of climate change, such as glacial and ice sheet melting well ahead of earlier predicated levels, it's highly likely the impacts of climate change will be greater and more immediate than many Earth scientists anticipated. By following the divisive habits and courses now plotted by today's self-centered cultures and politics, the effects of climate change will probably reverse our species' potential long before we humans do anything to offset them.

The Intergovernmental Panel on Climate Change (IPCC), in its first installment of the Sixth Assessment Report, said in August 2021 that the impacts of global warming will worsen throughout the twenty-first century. It issued a "red alert" for humankind. Irreversible global sea level rise is already in motion. **Without immediate, rapid, and large-scale reductions in greenhouse gas emissions, limiting warming to close to one and a half degrees Celsius (the Paris Agreement target) or even two degrees Celsius will be beyond reach, according to the IPCC.**

Climate change is not just about temperature. Further warming includes changes to wetness and dryness, winds, snow and ice, coastal areas, and oceans. Examples from the IPCC report the following:

- **Intensifying the water cycle**. This brings more intense rainfall and associated flooding as well as more intense drought in many regions.
- **Rainfall patterns**. In high latitudes, precipitation is likely to increase and to decrease over large parts of the subtropics. Changes to monsoon precipitation will vary by region.
- **Sea level rise**. Coastal areas will see continued sea level rise throughout the twenty-first century, contributing to more frequent and severe coastal flooding in low-lying areas and coastal erosion. Extreme sea level events that occurred once in one hundred years could happen every year by the end of this century.
- **Permafrost thawing**. Further warming will amplify permafrost thawing and the loss of annual snow cover, the melting of glaciers and ice sheets, and the loss of summer Arctic Sea ice.
- **Ocean changes**. Changes to the ocean—including warming, more frequent marine heatwaves, ocean acidification, and reduced oxygen levels—have been clearly linked to human influence. These changes affect both ocean ecosystems and the people who rely on them. These changes will continue throughout this century.
- **Urban areas**. For cities, some aspects of climate change may be amplified, including heat, flooding from heavy precipitation events, and sea level rise in coastal cities.

Another fact: global warming cannot be stopped for at least a century because carbon dioxide stays in the atmosphere for an exceptionally long time. Temperatures on the earth will continue to slowly rise because of the CO_2 that's already in the atmosphere plus each day's new contributions. Once CO_2 enters the atmosphere, it stays there for more than a hundred years, so the impacts of yesterday's CO_2 emissions will continue to affect us tomorrow. Obviously, global warming will get worse before it gets better because we have not stopped pumping CO_2 into the atmosphere, and millions of fossil-fired combustion sources keep contributing CO_2 to global warming every minute of every day. Deforestation continues apace as land is cleared for monocrops such as palm oil. This reduces the natural vegetation/trees that absorb CO_2 and release oxygen.

The major problem with climate change is its invisibility. Our species' healthy future hinges on our ability to accept and plan for something that is totally inconspicuous. Scientists have identified steady increases over the past decades in numerous greenhouse gases, carbon dioxide being the most common. Odorless, colorless, and tasteless, CO_2's creeping increase within the atmosphere creates impacts within Earth's natural hierarchy that are slowly working their way up the food chain through global warming.

Individual citizens, even those who don't believe in climate change, have begun to notice subtle changes in their local environment, like crocus and daffodils popping up earlier in the spring, shorter/warmer winters, or longer/hotter/smokier summers. Seeds that could only be planted in temperate zones a few decades ago can now be planted farther north and at higher elevations. Long-time coastal residents notice that high tides are creeping a bit higher on the beach than they used to. Our collective human instinct is affirming scientific statements and predictions about global warming, yet many political tongues still deny this reality.

BP's Deepwater Horizon disaster in the Gulf of Mexico had enough shock value for daily media coverage and quick political action. Slow disasters, like climate change, are usually below the fold and politically procrastinated.

Perhaps the best way to think of global warming is to picture BP's broken pipe at the bottom of the Gulf of Mexico in 2010. Black crude oil flowed into the sea at high rates twenty-four hours a day for eighty-seven days before it was stopped. The same thing is happening worldwide in our shared atmosphere, except these invisible gases come from millions of sources. The volume of gases flowing upward is exponentially higher than the crude oil that invaded Gulf Coast beaches and marshlands, but this pollution is invisible. Politicians from both parties attended to the gulf's problems with fervor and commitment because the public could easily see oil pollution on their TVs. It is much easier to put off remedial action about climate change that citizens cannot see and of which they're not constantly reminded. Without some media frenzy or citizen uprising about climate change, conservative American politicians will continue to stall remedial actions until they are forced to take them or get voted out of office.

Tim Flannery, in his book *The Weather Makers*, relates in understandable scientific detail the deleterious effects greenhouse gases have on our planet. "There is not an ecosystem on earth that will be unaffected by climate change," he writes. Data indicates "that at least one out of every five living things on this planet is committed to extinction by *existing* (emphasis added) levels of greenhouse gases."[11] Tens of thousands more species will vanish unless greenhouse gas emissions are reduced. The obliteration of living species interrupts the dependencies other species have on one another to survive; disruptions within the food chain will become more common. Flora and fauna won't be the only victims. "If humans pursue a business-as-usual course for the first half of this (twenty-first) century, I believe the collapse of civilization due to climate change becomes inevitable," he says.

As we will see in the next chapter, advocates for endless growth and profits in the human-made world pooh-pooh the alarming message of atmospheric scientists. Powerful and rich elites subsidize their stances by leveraging their money, influence, and reliance on human law to create illusions that natural laws can be broken without incurring costs for the species. Ironically, these same people avoid facing big issues pending within their own self-sustaining doctrines. For instance, from the point of view of nature, how are democracy and capitalism going to continue down the growth/profit/individual-freedom path once natural resources reach their tipping point? How can a depleted planet adequately supply rising human populations and expanding markets? How can individual freedoms be guaranteed without sufficient natural resources to give that freedom expression? **Question: when and how will the human-made systems of democracy and capitalism recognize nature's limits?**

Big questions like these are ones most capitalists and politicians haven't given much thought to because it's not their specialty, their responsibility, or a current issue; they're best at marginalizing discussion of such concerns because they interfere with short-term priorities. How ironic that these intelligent, organized, and usually thoughtful leaders will not broach these topics among themselves, much less with the public! They don't want to touch these simmering issues because they have no politically palatable answers—very few to none at all. These macro issues scare them to death. The thought of making changes to the human-made-world organizations that make them and their backers powerful and comfortable must be distressing for them. All the capital invested in plants and equipment, all those sunk costs, all the high level of organization and specialized employees—shareholders expect solid returns on their investments annually if not quarterly. Executives and boards of directors don't want to waste time shillyshallying around with invisible gases that generate no revenue and just increase costs. Prospects of systemic changes or modifications to democratic institutions and capitalistic practices apparently have these leaders mortified or baffled, or they simply don't believe that nature has limits (or they don't care). Still, even within the blinkered human-made world establishment, there are some who recognize species-wide challenges as economic opportunity, something we will talk more about in the next chapter.

So far, our species and American leadership have done little to offset climate change threats. President Biden has shined the light on climate change, but many champions of short-term, status-quo politics have yet to even acknowledge that climate change exists. Interestingly, Americans who claim to be conservative are not interested in conserving the planet because of their bi-world human-made and ethereal priorities. What are they conserving that's more important than the species and planet?

Our Personal Nature

At the individual human scale, we citizens have conflicted thoughts and feelings about other natural life forms. We love some flora (lawns, gardens, house plants) and loath others (weeds, kudzu, spinach). Out of the millions of species of plants on this earth, we humans rely mainly on cultivated vegetables, fruits, and twelve grains for our sustenance. We Americans have reached the pinnacle of flora heights in that we can control their presence or absence in our lives as we please. As for forests, tundra, and jungles, we know only what we are taught at school, see in TV documentaries, or know from our travels. These natural expanses appear so vast, it is sometimes difficult to believe that there aren't enough trees in the world to offset climate change, but alas, there are not.

As for fauna, we simultaneously nurture and exploit the animal world as we eat, fear, and coddle other living creatures. McDonald's has sold billions upon billions of hamburgers, and only the eternal colonel knows how many chickens KFC has served up. Like other animals, humans need protein, and meat products are one way to fill that hunger, but burgers and chicken are just the start. Venison, elk, emu, alligator, turtles, scorpions, chocolate-covered ants—we humans eat it all.

Zoos and television shows expose us to the wilder side of the animal kingdom, and that's simply fine. Few of us—except for adventurers like Steve Irwin, the Crocodile Hunter, rest his soul—want to come face to face with wild animals in their native environments, unless we are armed to the teeth or hovering above in a helicopter. Time spent in the wild proves that animals have their own communities just like we humans do. They also seek sustenance, security, and comfort, and they communicate within their own species and have complex lives just like human beings.

"It is clear that animals form lasting relationships, are frightened of being hunted, have a horror of dismemberment, wish they were back in the safety of their den, despair for their mates, look out for and protect their children whom they love," says Jeffrey M. Masson and Susan McCarthy in their book *When Elephants Weep*. Animals "are individuals and members of groups, with elaborate histories that take place in a concrete world and involve a large number of complex emotional states. They *feel* throughout their lives, just as we do."[12]

Because *Homo sapiens* is the apex species, we encroach upon the domain of wild animals at will. Human beings throughout history have felt virtually no concern whatsoever exploiting animals to serve human ends. Only since the latter years of the nineteenth century have we given wildlife and their natural domains much consideration.

Me/us cultures exist in the animal world as well as human civilization, but only we humans can make corrections at the species level.

Our domestic pets—now that's another matter. There is no doubt in any pet owner's mind that their pet communicates and shares emotions with them. As pets are regarded as members of the family, Americans spend more than $82 billion annually feeding and caring for over 164 million dogs, cats, and other animal friends according to the ASPCA and federal government statistics. Where does this affinity for domesticated animals come from? Why can these animals seemingly control our emotions with simple eye contact, a head tilt, or some other seemingly affectionate behavior? Why do we love them and grieve when they die? Because they seem to care about us, they are alive and made of DNA like us, and they usually repay our affections in kind.

I wrote a magazine article about a wealthy woman in England whose Rhodesian ridgeback had a leaky heart valve. Her dog was dying. She wanted the best surgeon available to perform a valve replacement. Working through British veterinarians, she got in contact with a veterinary teaching hospital in Colorado that agreed to do the surgery for her. However, complications developed when attempting to fly the dog to the United States; the dog would have to stay in quarantine for up to eight weeks after surgery before returning to the UK. That wouldn't work for her, so rather than flying the dog to Colorado, she flew the six-person surgical team from Colorado to London to perform the operation. She also bought a heart-lung machine for the procedure that she subsequently donated to the British veterinary hospital where the surgery took place. No source for this story would identify the woman, at her request, or tell me exactly how much all this cost, also at her request; it had to cost close to $100,000. The operation was a success; the dog was doing well one year after surgery.

Human regard for others in the animal kingdom ranges from the extreme caring of this British pet lover to acts of unspeakable cruelty. While we humans are all over the board emotionally about other species, without question, we humans can choose to control both future domestic and wild animal populations through our economic and political decision making. At the same time, nature will not change its laws because humans do. Nature will continue to press forward with species diversity, adaptability, and mutation as conditions warrant. New species will arise as others disappear, but remember, there are two clocks at work here. Nature's slow pace of evolution and regeneration will always be outpaced by the human-made world's ability to consume/destroy/pollute, especially if we choose to continue to run the human-made world unaligned with nature. **A key element in the Sustainability Age has to be more emulation of natural ways to solve human-made world problems even if they don't prove to be optimum from an economic point of view; if our species chooses to survive, dollars cannot be the ultimate determinant of how humans deal with nature.**

Changes keep happening at the microorganism level as well as with larger animal species, and these changes will continue to affect human health and longevity. Up to this point in scientific development, most microorganism research and medical practice has focused on disease abatement, cure, and prevention. Humans can be rightfully proud of having eradicated or controlled polio, tetanus, measles, plague, and other contagions, but for every disease or pathogen we eradicate, a new one seems to pop up. AIDS, Legionnaires' disease, dengue fever, SARS, methicillin-resistant *Staphylococcus Aureus* (MRSA), Gram-negative bacteria, *Klebsiella*, *Acinetobacter*, *Clostridium Difficile*, *Enterococcus*, COVID-19, and others challenge researchers and health providers. Vector-borne diseases of all sorts will expand their range as global warming pushes up average temperatures in wider climate zones. Mosquitoes and other disease-carrying animals will spread contamination to animals and humans in new ranges as these areas warm up.

Poise, counterpoise—that is the major theme of our species' relationship with nature. Human progress in the Industrial Age was built on the back of nature. Since the dawn of industrialism, manufacturing has depended on extractive industries for raw materials. The transportation sector developed a heroin junkie's dependency on carbon-based fuels, and we consumers demanded more and more standard and custom goods that made life easier, fun, and comfortable.

It's taken more than two hundred years of this behavior for us to see that we can't keep doing this forever. Nature has limits that it would be insane for us to disregard. Our creativity in tipping the scales back to a more balanced position with nature during the Sustainability Age will set the course for humanity for generations to come.

New and innovative ways of accommodating nature will also provide significant economic opportunities for developers (for example, skyscraper urban vegetable/fruit farms, fusion power generation, hydrogen fuel cells, direct-aid capture replacing oil pump jacks, freshwater recovery from under ocean floors, nanotechnology, AI). As specialists develop new technologies, we citizens need to reorder our political priorities and our money away from dualistic/differentiated/high-carbon footprint technologies to more sustainable, species-conscious ones. Leave oil in the ground until we can find ways to use it cleanly.

Sustaining Nature

One thing we need to remember as we move toward a sustainable future is that nature obeys its own laws in its own time and has no interest whatsoever in human affairs. Nature's neither friend nor foe to human beings; it is simply indifferent, uninvolved, uncaring. **We now have to adapt to nature to benefit nature just as fervently as industrialists exploited nature to benefit the human species.**

The image of man conquering nature began with René Descartes' seventeenth-century view that gained widespread acceptance throughout the Industrial Age. Descartes, the creator of his own form of dualistic philosophy, determined that "I think, therefore I am" and that everything outside of the human mind was mechanical; ergo, things mechanical can be understood and possibly controlled by the human mind. "Descartes offered an antidote to idealism—the conception of an objective world completely mechanical," said Will and Aerial Durant in their *Story of Civilization*.[13]

Descartes' way of thinking is something we're all familiar with even if we don't know it. It includes understanding complexity by breaking elements of a problem into separate parts. By understanding the parts, we can understand the whole; we gain assurances about the whole by understanding its components. The scientific method (observation, hypothesis, experimentation, conclusion) stems in part from Descartes. This mind-over-matter way of thinking has become second nature to modern human beings; it is the skeleton upon which capitalist economics muscles up its growth activities and in which scientific organs fulfill their research functions. It is the basis of today's normative economic, scientific, and engineering thinking.

However, there's a problem. Modern scientists have unraveled a new model to replace the Cartesian mechanistic view—a view of the mysterious way humanity is tied to nature. "Twentieth-century physics has shown us very forcefully that there is no absolute truth in science, that all our concepts and theories are limited and approximate," says Fritjof Capra in his book *The Turning Point*.[14] "Descartes' method is analytic," Capra continues. "Overemphasis on the Cartesian method has led to the fragmentation that is characteristic of both our general thinking . . . and to the widespread reductionism in science—the idea that all aspects of complex phenomena can be understood by reducing them to their constituent parts . . ."[15]

"The classical worldview was materialistic and individualistic," writes Ervin Laszlo in his book *The Systems View of the World*. "It viewed objects as separate from each other and from their surroundings. The 'systems' view of life perceives connections and communications between people and between people and nature and emphasizes community and integrity in both the natural and human world."[16]

Capra, Laszlo, and other systems proponents present in their writings a different, holistic view of nature. "The universe is no longer seen as a machine, made up of a multitude of objects, but has to be pictured as one indivisible, dynamic whole whose parts are essentially interrelated and can be understood only as patterns of a cosmic process,"[17] writes Capra. At the subatomic level, it is relationships that matter most, not matter itself, according to this view.

"In atomic physics, the sharp Cartesian division between mind and matter, between the observer and the observed, can no longer be maintained. We can never speak about nature without, at the same time, speaking about ourselves,"[18] says Capra. Every physical thing on the planet, including humans, is tied to every other thing on the planet through subatomic interrelationships. In fact, in modern physics, there really aren't any "things" at all; what we call things (solids, liquids, gas) are just bundles of energy, waves, and particles and the interconnections among them.

What's important for our species to recognize now is not so much any constituent element itself but the system in which it exists. "The systems method always treats systems as integrated wholes of their subsidiary components and never as a mechanistic aggregate of parts in isolable causal relationships,"[19] writes Laszlo. Systems methodology has identified our mystical tie with nature; every thing, every creature, and every person on the planet is part of one big system comprising millions of other smaller systems located within it. **A sustainable future for our species will be based on our ability to understand natural/ecological *systems*, so human activity aligns with them as we eliminate or vastly reduce our impact on them.** We are just as connected to nature as we are to our families, our jobs, our daily routines, and our visions of heavenly peace according to the systems view.

Humans will not allow regression back to simpler times. "Man's mind, once stretched by a new idea, never regains its original dimensions,"[20] said Oliver Wendell Holmes. We call this trait growth or progress, and it is what the human-made, Cartesian-addicted world uses to justify its existence and priorities. Most humans will ignore, deny, or demand intractable proof before a new systems or holistic paradigm of nature replaces the more comfortable and adapted-to Cartesian model.

Considerable time will be needed before a systems view becomes understood and accepted by most citizens because it is as yet new, widely unknown, and discomfiting to the human-made world status quo. Not many citizens understand complex theories like those elaborated by modern physicists; most citizens revere the simple and the practical, those things that help advance life's basics. Systems/holistic thinking may yet be a lesson learned by our species, but it will be widely accepted only through its proof of utility, simplified comprehensibility, moral relevance to day-to-day living, and inclusion into species' focused goals.

Instead of cathartic transitions, the most likely way forward for our species and nature for the rest of the twenty-first century includes the following:

- A slower drawdown of natural resources through the increased unit productivity of available resources
- Eliminating/reducing/recycling wastes
- Developing innovative ways for humans to achieve sustenance, security, and comfort without denuding, polluting, and exhausting the planet

- Developing clean, renewable energy and higher efficiency and cleaner energy from nonrenewable resources
- Preserving ecosystems for the benefit of native species along with their potential benefit to humankind
- Getting to net-zero carbon emissions as quickly as possible
- Leveling off population growth
- Migration away from Cartesian habits to systems-holistic thought
- An acceptance that our powerful species, *Homo sapiens*, exists along with millions of other species that come and go as nature determines in its harsh and dispassionate wisdom

All this, of course, is the optimistic scenario for the Sustainability Age based on the continuance of more realistic democracy and capitalism as root drivers. These outcomes will proceed more smoothly and expeditiously if human sameness is recognized as a global norm and the human paradox becomes second nature.

You can conjure up bleaker scenarios on your own, but don't forget to include privation, power perversions, greed, hate, war, early death, huge income disparities, apathy, discrimination, and all the other time-worn, unnatural injustices we've done to our species throughout history—virtually all of which occurred because we valued our differentiated pods and ideologies more than our species sameness and planetary integrity.

Natural Human Traits

Survival ranks number one in the long list of instinctive traits all humans share; everyone wants sustenance, security, and comfort in their lives. Beyond these basics, most of us also evidence attributes that seem to be universal and natural within our species, namely, adaptability, dignity, beholdenness, recognition/love, and persistence. Of course, there's jealousy, hate, and other emotions and behaviors that don't need a lot of discussion because we're all familiar with them. The five traits discussed here are ones we will need more of during the Sustainability Age to reinforce our core value of human caring and to enhance our understanding of the human paradox.

Adaptability

We human beings have an extraordinary ability to adapt to our surroundings, be they natural or human-made. We are good at this because we want to survive, to feel safe, and to find some physical and mental comfort.

Comfort for human beings has always been and always will be relative and conditional to circumstances. Soldiers can make themselves comfortable in a hole in the ground if it keeps them out of the enemy's line of fire and the wind. A Hollywood celebrity can feel comfortable in the back seat of an old VW bug if she is getting a ride home after her limousine breaks down. Grandma willingly feigns comfort sitting in a tiny straight-back chair if it gives her time to drink pretend tea with a granddaughter. We tolerate physical discomforts if there's a payoff for us. Adapting to longer-term uncomfortable surroundings, well, we're not as formidable here; we Americans tend to bitch and moan when expectations aren't as fulfilling as we anticipated them to be.

Because every human being has his or her own take on reality, there is an individual tick mark on life's adaptability meter for every one of us. This is one area where our uniqueness as individual human beings kicks in. Life requires that we adapt our individual selves to the circumstances of the worlds in which we find ourselves at any point in time. We drink Mother's milk, we grow, we learn, we work, we socialize, we have fun, we suffer, we die. How we adapt our exceptional sensibilities to realities outside our control helps shape our personality and ambitions and helps define our attitudes, fears, and politics.

Ultimately, the adaptive choices we make and how we manage them determine our character and personal dignity or lack thereof. Prevailing dualistic and differentiated thinking now channel lives into mono- and bi-world outlooks that usually shortchange one or more of the other worlds. Such lives defy the Socratic maxim of "know thyself" because of their shortsightedness. Those of us who become complacent about life usually adapt to skewed versions of reality because we get tired of considering other options that seemingly don't work for us, or these options make us feel uneasy, or we fervently believe that our current beliefs are best and right and others should live by them as well.

Many of us stop learning as we age. The mono- and bi-world attitudes within us close doors to other ways of thinking because "things are finally going our way," "I finally made it!" or some other expression of self-sufficiency. **Because we currently don't know about or accept the human paradox, the three worlds of reality, human sameness, or systems thinking, we tend to be maladapted to species-focused ends.** We think adapting to local/personal wants and needs are all we need to do to attain and retain life's basics. The "big fish, little pond" scenario beats other options for most of us.

Also, as individuals, we sometimes like to play the allure game, some parts of us not known or knowable to others. Being aloof or coy keeps us interesting to ourselves and temptingly curious to others. As we employ these techniques of captivation, we bask in our individual uniqueness while we deny that we are just as much a part of the universe as the other forces and objects that compose it. At the species level, most of us have not accepted any responsibility for our common fate yet; we're so fixated on "me," "ours," and "mine," we never think in species terms because there never seems to be much reason to think that way.

Still, despite the strong pull of our personal exceptionalism, we human beings on occasion do sense a greater whole, a bigger system beyond our personal and local one, something universal that is hard to define and explain. We don't understand systemic/holistic notions that say we're all connected to one another and to every other place and object on the planet because we don't allot much thought for such grand ideas. Thinking in species terms ranks extremely low on most human priority lists, especially in America.

Rather, if we humans could live out our fantasies and have every human comfort imaginable, then life would be perfect, wouldn't it? Oooh, to be rich and famous, to have all the gadgets and gizmos, to live atop the pyramid—"I could really adapt to that!" Right? Actually, having everything you want and being ultra-spoiled can place you on a fast track to boredom and disappointment. Call that sour grapes, if you like, but answer this: what's left after you have everything? What's left to do after you've done "everything"? How do you cope with affluent boredom? Sex? Drugs? Rock 'n' roll? It all runs thin fairly quickly.

Learning about reality as you grow, adapting yourself to reality, and customizing reality to your own desires pretty much sums up what any person's life is about. Without new curiosities, new physical and mental challenges, and new explorations into other perspectives, life can be a real drag, the ultimate snoozer, suicide city. Discovery and adapting to new findings in your life comprise a sizable portion of life's enrichment and energy for every thinking human being; without physical, spiritual, and intellectual curiosity, enthusiasm for life dwindles. Alternatively, accepting narrow rote living and fear tends to castrate life's wonders and can leave you burdened with constricted routines along with a severe case of exceptionalist myopia, frustration, and pent-up rage. In today's dualistic world, adapting to life's changes enriches a life; non-adaptation to change leads to boredom, frustration, and anomie.

There is absolutely nothing new about human adaptability; it's natural and timeless. All living things either adapt to their environment or perish. Peoples defeated by Rome adapted to their new lives as slaves. Political prisoners in the Soviet Union adapted to gulag privations. Nelson Mandela adapted to eighteen years of prison life on Robben Island. At the other end of the spectrum, nouveau riche Americans adapt to their McMansions in gated communities, owners of new cars adapt to all the buttons and screens in their new ride, and season ticket holders adapt to better seats on the fifty-yard line after moving up from the goal line. For the former, these adaptations come involuntarily, reluctantly, and with smoldering rage; for the latter, their improved circumstances come with a smile and a sense of deservedness. The effects of one set of adaptations last much longer than the effects of the other; challenge and adversity provide more teaching moments than add-on enhancements to already comfortable lives. Having everything you want tends to reinforce ethereal illusions over reality and generates anti-species–driven behaviors to achieve more illusory, selfish, and often vacuous ends.

Nelson Mandela's cell on Robbin Island, South Africa. For eighteen years, Prisoner 466/64 spent his time breaking rocks with a hammer.

Today we *Homo sapiens* live mostly off the momentum established by our forbearers. The truth is they did most of the hard work of invention, production, and distribution. They suffered most of the pain, heartache, and discomfort. We have simply improved upon their accomplishments and have thrown in a few modern advances of our own.

Human beings have excelled at mastering the provision of sustenance, security, and comfort for more and more people planet wide. **We now need to acknowledge our need to adapt to what the planet can no longer do for us, specifically support endless population growth and materialism, accept our wastes without aftereffects, and provide endless raw materials and carbon-based fuels to subsidize carbon-based economies.** Denying and deferring these challenges to future generations attest only to a maladaptive attitude that simply wants to coast into the future, riding on the coattails of past accomplishment and political intransigence—that is, lazy, stubborn, and self-righteous conservatism.

America has so much comfort now, we have become complacent and rather smug; as a nation, we have yet to acknowledge this fact. We are fat and change resistant as a people because we believed our own propaganda about the benefits of hard work, pursuit of the American Dream, and moving up the hierarchical pyramid. We are really suckers for the fantasy of having it made. Once you hold in your hands that pot of gold at the end of the rainbow, you wallow in it, you acquire all the toys you want, and you live the high life of affluence, self-indulgence, and physical/mental comfort. Hmmm, hmmm . . . delicious. But, as noted above, adaptation to this dreamed-of lifestyle often disappoints because the natural world does not support "fat and happy" for long.

Our species was not physically or mentally designed to wallow in ultra-comfortable ends. We were designed to strive, think, and adapt. We were designed to stay busy and involved with life and the planet of which we are only one part. Not attending to the macro questions that now face the species means we are not acting naturally. We are dallying; we are not changing and adapting our abilities to serve the species and the planet's best interests. We are lethargically attending to inherited adaptations rather than aggressively attacking those of a needful future, and we continue to seek more comfort, believing it has a panacea-ic, ultimate, end-reward value. Once we reach comfortable ends, we're often disappointed, so we dream up new goals that we're sure, this time, will make us genuinely happy. Oh, how we adore our ethereal aspirations and perfectionist ideals!

As for the other elements in life's basics before comfort, once an individual starts a business or begins to climb the career ladder, the issues of sustenance and security get addressed first because they are more primary. Adaptable human beings will put up with discomforts to achieve their goals, but as time passes and success/profits become more standard and as strivers age, increased comfort becomes a higher priority. There are worries and fears along the way, of course, but the goal always seems to be creating a more highly desired level of comfort.

Comfort manifests itself in financial security and materialism in America. An individual's apparent comfort with his or her own material circumstances reflects on that person's self-esteem and social status. The Beverly Hillbillies in the TV comedy never reached a balance between their circumstances and their mental comfort level. They never attained a dignified, high status in their wealthy community; they adapted their circumstances and community to their hillbilly values, not the other way around, hence the humor.

Every nation credits its citizens with amazing adaptability and lauds them for enduring hardships or for working to achieve life-enhancing and national goals. America honors its soldiers with Memorial Day and Veterans Day, both ways of saying thank you for adapting to selfless service for a national good. Russians provide similar recognition for their veterans, as do England, France, Germany, and virtually every other nation with a history of armed conflict. These acknowledgments are appreciated, but all these honoraria parse the fact that adaptability to challenging circumstances remains a species attribute, not one exclusive to any nation, ethnicity, or culture. As long as we humans have air, food, water, shelter, clothing, and a way to dispose of wastes, we can adapt to and survive virtually any place under any circumstance. **The challenge now is to adapt human brilliance and energy to a natural world with increasingly limited resources for a shared future and to act responsibly about that reality.**

Dignity

What constitutes human dignity?

Here are three *Oxford English Dictionary* definitions:

1. The quality of being worthy or honorable; worthiness, work, nobleness, excellence.
2. Honorable or high estate, position, or estimation; honor; degree of estimation, rank.
3. Nobility or befitting elevation of aspect, manner, or style; becoming or fit stateliness, gravity.[21]

Because we don't have royalty in America, we ramp down the grandiose wording and tie our definition of dignity more to self-esteem, honesty, and respect for and from others. Rather than being noble or stately, our dignity tends more toward being responsible, accountable, straightforward, and hardworking. If we are sincere in these attributes, then we have internal dignity. If our family, employees, peers, and coworkers respect us and listen to what we have to say, then our dignity has a foothold with others. How we consistently behave with, speak to, and share with those around us evidences how we think and feel about them and ourselves.

A lack of self-consciousness deepens dignity along with a degree of humility. Telling the truth and avoiding deceit and gossip also affirm a dignified stature. Accepting responsibility, not avoiding it, evidences dignity. Being dignified doesn't mean being snooty or humorless. On today's interconnected and interdependent planet, individuals who work hard to balance the three worlds, who evince an acceptance and understanding of the human paradox, species sameness, and life's basics, who serve the long term as much or more than the short term, and who treat all other human beings with respect will achieve the trifecta of honor, style, and gravity that connote dignity anywhere.

Of course, there are people in America who think themselves dignified because of a corporate or political title or social rank or for their mono- and bi-world accomplishments. Some leaders, celebrities, and elites truly are held in high esteem by the citizenry; many are not. The latter have differentiated themselves into realms of separateness and exceptionalism that seem to affect all their senses. They can't see, hear, or touch anything that counters their own self-importance and ambitions. If they do sense any counterarguments or piercing truths, they dismiss them out of hand because their pseudo dignity is a house of cards that they know could topple quickly. Their status depends on a few key relationships, a few high-risk investments, a few legal documents, some good press; there is nothing truly honest or substantial within these egotists because dualism, self-created differentiation, and commercial competitiveness have been their life's focus.

McKenzie Scott, Jeff Bezos's ex-wife, got $38 billion in her divorce settlement with the founder of Amazon. She's given away nearly $7 billion so far to three hundred or so charities. Scott told CBS News that she and her charitable team are "attempting to give away a fortune that was enabled by systems in need of change." Pete Peterson, former secretary of commerce under President Nixon, became a billionaire in one hour when the Blackstone Group went public. He could have opted for pseudo dignity and surrounded himself with adulating sycophants, but instead, he set up a foundation to propose workable solutions for the long-term challenges that face the United States. "These challenges all require sacrifice," Peterson told *Newsweek*. "That means everyone. We fat cats will have to pay more taxes. The government will have to spend less. Everyone will have to save more."[22]

Munib al-Masri, a Palestinian billionaire, could have easily moved to Switzerland and hunkered down in luxury, but he chose another path. He put his money where his mouth was by establishing an International Peace Center to expedite establishment of an independent Palestinian state and by putting Palestinians to work. He employs over fifty thousand Palestinians in his various companies, and he may yet become prime minister of a unity government to replace the Palestinian Authority's Hamas-led regime. He wants to achieve a two-state solution to the Israeli/Palestinian problem during his lifetime.[23]

Most leaders give off "vibes" that we who follow them sense. Dignity may or may not be one of these sensory-radar blips. The appearance of dignity may be part of a first impression because of title, style, or some other surface attribute, but to assign dignity to someone else, especially politicians, you really need to know much more about them. I have tremendous respect for the Office of President of the United States, but I don't respect the "dignity" of some individuals who held that office. Lyndon Johnson and Richard Nixon made giant strides in civil rights and foreign relations, respectively, and I admire their achievements, but their botched handling of the Vietnam War, among other sins, diluted their hope for a dignified legacy in my mind. George W. Bush will remain infamous for his decisions regarding the invasion of Iraq and the incompetence in Iraq's subsequent multi-year occupation, along with torture policies and other non-accomplishments. These political leaders willed their country significant indignities in the form of costly and disastrous conflicts along with their lingering aftereffects. Donald J. Trump is probably the most undignified leader America has ever had because he has no comprehension of selflessness and service to others. His attempted coup d'état after the 2020 election brought America to a new low. These presidents' legacies will forever be tainted because they were unwilling or unable to think and act beyond the bounds of political dualism and differentiation; they had no apparent awareness of the human paradox or species sameness, or if they did, they assigned these realities no regard.

Tagging well-dressed politicians or handsome/pretty celebrities as dignified in your mind can also fade quickly when their behavior does not reinforce an expectation. We usually love our illusory mental models much more than the actual human beings who reside therein. **Not knowing more about a person sometimes keeps them more dignified in our ethereal-world minds, where media/mental impressions and blind admiration count more than reality.** Within your own local world, don't be surprised to discover dignity where you least expect it. Some of your coworkers, employees, or members of the janitorial staff may be a lot more dignified than those you exalt.

The act of bestowing dignity upon someone else or retracting it can be a complicated endeavor because every individual's ethereal world includes a pantheon of perfect traits/looks/values. Every human being wants to find that ultimate companion or role model for their personal life, another person who can help fulfill deep-seated hopes and dreams. Whether that expectation is for a spouse, friend, or mentor, the reality will fall short of expectation because no human being is perfect or ever will be. Also, if you are the person being admired, you will probably blow your cover once there's intimacy. Dignity founders on the shallow reefs of human vanity and base instincts.

Undoubtedly, the only person's dignity you can control is your own. Social life offers three points of view: what you think of yourself, what you think of others, and what others think of you. If you have self-dignity, then you have principles and live up to them; if you are a real and sincere person, there is nothing fake within you for others to see. Few people get to this point early in life, while some never get there at all. However, maturity and a more balanced outlook on life may help you get to a place where you consider yourself dignified or at least striving to be.

Everyone who works for a living believes their individual contribution is vital to more than their own life's basics; work can yield personal dignity. There is intrinsic and fulfilling value in the work individuals do, and there is also pride of accomplishment in personal achievement, teamwork, innovation, and goal fulfillment. Everyone wants to experience these good feelings that extend beyond their personal sustenance, security, and comfort. At the same time, no one wants their life interrupted to the point where they no longer have employment or they have to retrain themselves for a completely different set of specialized skills. Life interrupted has little appeal for the vast majority of American citizenry (yet most who are forced to adapt to new circumstances do so with resolve, even alacrity).

America's paradox for the future boils down to the supposed timelessness of its basic values. Reality begs to differ and asks these questions. Can every individual be guaranteed unfettered freedoms in a world with limited resources and known natural/ecological limits? Can capitalism be granted wide latitudes for growth and profits on a planet that does not have sufficient resources to support unlimited growth? Can representative government effectively serve its citizenry when it puts off making decisions about species-wide and planetary survival issues? In the future, America's dignity will be determined by how it answers these and related questions.

Getting to a species-focused agenda is where personal values of thinking *individuals* come into play. Self-esteem, respect for self and others, integrity, honesty, courage, duty, patience, reason, reverence, wisdom, and all the other intangible virtues humans hold so highly need to be a part of the dignity that tri-worlds realists exude. But these values must be understood and actionable before they can affect the political sphere. That is the hard part, the time-consuming part, and the part where education, commitment, and personal dignity come into play. Breaking away from established thinking never comes easily or fast; there are way too many confused retrograde thinkers with power who own today's political equity along with the hearts and minds of go-along, get-along followers.

The definition of dignity needs to include considerations of the natural world and our species. Who can be more dignified on this planet than someone who recognizes nature's limits and does something about them? Who can be more dignified than one who advocates acceptance of human sameness? Who can be more dignified than a leader who helps his or her citizens achieve life's basics in a sustainable fashion? Who can be more dignified than someone who has the bravery to lead humanity away from self-destruction to self-preservation?

Slow, incremental progress will dominate the tri-worlds political agenda during the Sustainability Age because such efforts always move ahead through dense existing interests, not a vacuum. Expect relatively fast political progress in some areas (probably renewable energy) and glacial political progress in others (modifications to democracy and capitalism) within upcoming years. The only things that matter, ultimately, remain understanding of the human paradox, recognition of human sameness, elevation of life's basics on political leadership agendas, sustainable development, peace, and a commitment to the integrity of the planet upon which all life depends. Attending to these goals will lead to a more dignified future for us all.

Beholdenness

Beholdenness stems from feelings of deference and obligation—and maybe some guilt. **Within a family, we love and respect aging parents and grandparents who have sacrificed for us because we feel duty bound to them; we feel we owe them payback for all they have done for us.** Deep down, we may like or dislike them as people, but as they grow visibly older and needy, we feel a duty to share more time with them. We bite our tongues when they say things we don't agree with; we smile and nod when they mumble non sequiturs or retell stories just told. We see in them the truth of aging and its merciless rents, obligations we will soon have to pay ourselves. We love them either sincerely or from a sense of duty. We do our best to accommodate their needs and wants because they have already done the same for us and, selfishly, because we want to avoid future guilt feelings for not attending to them. People of conscience all want to say in the end, "I was there for them. I did the best I could."

Beholden feelings are deeply rooted in the subconscious mind. We usually struggle to relate our feelings of indebtedness to any particular acts of love our parentage extended, to any special recognition or discipline they imparted, or to any specific event, time, or place. Rather, the nebulous but overwhelming obligation of beholdenness within us exists as an emotional counterweight to all the nurturing, love, and discipline that was so one-sided when we were suckling infants, innocent youths, or defiant teens. How did we ever make it to adulthood if not for them? How much are we like them? We can't remember the details of childhood; we're just left with a lasting sense of regard and connection that really doesn't need to be and usually cannot be explained.

Feelings of obligation/love/caring for siblings and other relatives and friends can also be of the beholden type. Proximity plays the biggest role here, as it does in most love relationships. Being around brothers and sisters all the time, growing up with their fears and dreams, playing with and picking on them year after year—these are essential elements in familial socialization. Cousins, aunts, and uncles who live nearby can be endeared almost as much as siblings, parents, and grandparents depending on how active they are in one's life. Relatives far away become more of a curiosity than members of the inner family circle, people we may be able to have fun with and get to know better when given the chance. Good friends may also be part of a welcoming clan that acknowledges our senses.

Even in households where familial love is not well expressed or even in homes where there has been abuse, a sense of obligation and deference to family may still exist. Honoring thy father and thy mother can be the easiest commandment to obey when parents act in loving and caring ways or the toughest to obey when they do not accept their roles and how to play them. How many people were born of parents who should never have been parents at all? How many wounded children have become parents and passed their psychological infirmities on to their children? How many of the world's troubles stem from familial dysfunctions and their resultant wounds? Despite all these woes, most children usually find ways to forgive their parents' and siblings' faults over time, to honor them despite past painful mistakes—this endearment coming from a sense of beholdenness.

In a more destructive way, feeling beholden to those above you in a family, organizational pyramid, or religious hierarchy can subvert your ability to think and act independently. Being loyal for loyalty's sake requires a non-thinking mindset, a devotion that lacks reason and balanced sensibilities. Doing doubtful favors for someone cooler or more "in" than you or any act that makes you feel like you're selling part of your soul—these can be the self-deceptive and corruptive forms of beholdenness. Powerful and influential people (and psychopaths) often depend upon their ability to generate such feelings among acolytes. Dualism thrives on beholden feelings like gang loyalty, political bias, intimidation, and hate.

Beyond human relations, we may also feel beholden to Mother Earth or God. These feelings may manifest themselves through activism for natural causes or financial support, or perhaps they are more subtle, like picking up a piece of trash off the sidewalk and putting it in a litter barrel when no one else is looking or simply communing silently with nature/God as you walk through a park. **On the one hand, feeling beholden hangs as a repressive emotion—an obligation, a familial burden. On the other hand, it generates a sense of good will, of fulfilling an obligation to something larger than your exceptional self.** While God gets his share of reverence through religious faith, nature could benefit from more beholdenness of a conscientious and active sort. Evidencing an affinity for nature in word and deed keeps you aligned with your natural sense and extends the possibility of a sustainable future for the species.

Recognition

Everyone wants to be loved, to feel special, and to be recognized; few can deny this fact. Even the toughest, nastiest criminal on death row wants someone to care about him. We humans are social in nature, yet we each want individual recognition for worldly achievements and love returned for love given. A first holding of a child or grandchild, an exotic vacation, winning a blue ribbon, getting married, presents under the Christmas tree, the retirement gold watch—these, along with countless other gives and takes, compose moments of special recognition in our lives.

Come on, admit it! You love it when someone does or says something to make you feel special! Everybody does, and it's a great feeling when you make someone else feel special! Feeling recognized and appreciated bridges all worlds—it's natural, human-made, and ethereal. Few things make your day better than acknowledgment of your importance, affirmation of your worth, or giving other people positive feelings of acceptance and warmth. Friendships and deeper affections grow in this special ground.

Families survive because individuals within them give and get recognition from others they hold dear. Dogs and other pets get special treatment from their owners, who feel deep ties of intimacy and commitment to their attentive companions. Trophies, medals, diplomas all make recipients feel exceptional for their accomplishments. **A look, a**

smile, a caress can feel really special when they're needed, especially when unspoken anticipations get fulfilled. Everyone wants inclusion, acceptance, and love in their lives.

Not all recognition is nice, however. Some special treatment only gets recognized after a desired result takes effect. Some teachers I had growing up recognized me in special ways that I didn't appreciate at the time but did later. Discipline, order, knowledge, and a host of other attributes only make sense and have lasting value once they are instilled. Understanding and accepting social parameters along with all the other underpinnings of civilized behavior come only with physical, mental, and emotional maturity.

Some recognition goes too far. By its very nature, treating someone special differentiates that person from others who are less so at one point in time. Dictators and others with dualistic bents recognize and adulate followers because of their race, nationality, devotion, or other traits, and of course, they expect their followers to adore and obey them in return. Political parties differentiate themselves based on their platforms/leaders and provide special identity for those who follow. Religions make believers feel unique and blessed because of their devotion to certain creeds and tenets. Special recognition can deceive and corrupt followers of politics and faiths into valuing their differentiated selves more than the species, peace, or a higher universal purpose like preserving natural integrity. For dualists, the concept of evil often gets just as much attention as that of good, enemies get as much attention as friends, and the wealthy get way more attention than the poor.

People who receive too much recognition get spoiled and start to think special treatment is normal and due. People who get too little recognition become mad/hurt/criminal. In a dualistic sense, "special" can be both good and bad. Acknowledgment of intelligence, effort, ambition, acceptance, forgiveness, love, dedication, devotion—these are good types of "special." Deviousness, lying, stealing, and murder—these acts may make the perpetrator feel special for a while, but they are really bad types of "special." In the human-made and ethereal worlds, "special" depends on the details of who conveys the feeling, who receives it, and the circumstances therein.

Humans consider parts of nature special, like the Grand Canyon, the Great Barrier Reef, or a favorite fishing hole. However, nature doesn't play favorites; it obeys its own laws in its own time, and no place or no species gets a better deal than any other. Balance and slow change within the biosphere/atmosphere/cryosphere are what count. God makes people feel special through feelings of love, inclusion, and salvation expressed by clerics, fellow believers, and holy books, and God makes people feel bad when they break the rules of their faith by sinning and letting others down. Ethereal storytellers make people feel special by transcending them out of daily routines into fantastic alternative worlds where heroes survive deadly challenges, time flies, and all usually comes out right in the end.

Emotions constitute the essential element of recognition for human beings. I'm sure neuro- and other types of scientists are working in university labs somewhere trying to uncover the chemistry and physics of love, caring, affection, and every other emotion that make up special feelings. These researchers' findings will give us revelations of discovery and extend our knowledge and understanding about ourselves, but the deeper, subtler aspects of recognition and special feelings, their variables as to impact, transience, and permanence on the human mind, will remain hidden and personal within each of us. Science can only dig so deep.

The antitheses to recognition, love, and specialness in a dualistic world are feelings of being un-special: rejection, discrimination, hate, and so forth. Many of these feelings originate in our human-made world hierarchy. There is just so much room at the top of a social or economic pyramid. The few who occupy the heights have to cull down the many who want to infiltrate their ranks; they only have so many options to do this, all of which involve un-special tactics no matter how tactfully they are applied. Objective and subjective criteria populate the minds of decision makers who allow some people to ascend higher while keeping others out or down. Flawed, self-serving, and sometimes cruel hierarchies are inherently divisive of the species as they seek to achieve their own human-made and ethereal world goals.

Unlike old hierarchies where position, class, and ethnicity dominated national histories and stratified societies, America's large middle class short-circuits a lot of un-special feelings. That is a primary value of a large bulge in the middle of the human bell curve. The domain of the middle class in America extends so wide and so deep that individuals can find a home pod that recognizes them and makes them feel special just about anywhere in the country—if for no other reason than that the middle class has value to American society. A large middle class also goes a long way in satisfying life's basics for more people, which moves them toward their subjective ideals of happiness.

American society thrives on recognition and special events. Every day of the year is special to someone or some pod: a birthday, an anniversary, a holiday, Arbor Day, ride-your-bicycle-to-work day, employee-appreciation day—there is always something special going on. We populate our calendars with anticipated events that may ring true to expectation or fall short when they occur, but that doesn't really matter. What's important is that there are more recognition events upcoming, each with the potential for fun, business opportunity, or entertainment. Americans are healthfully addicted to anticipating special events because of the potential for social interaction, some laughs, and receiving or giving recognition.

What the planet needs more of is recognition—the giving and receiving of emotional and psychological support in the here and now. Too many societies limit special recognition to holidays or exceptional circumstances. Here's a simple idea: recognize someone as special every day, and the benefits of the activity will make you feel better, will exhibit your humanity, and will make the recipient feel appreciated, cared for, loved. Surprise is the gift of life, said C. S. Lewis. Surprise someone. Extending these tendencies to other living species won't hurt either. It's easy, and what you give, you will get in return. Kindness, generosity, and love strengthen your dignity and self-esteem.

Persistence

The image of loving and caring individuals trying to sustain the species and the planet seems rather puny when compared to nature's awesome power, the heartlessness of many human-made systems, and the long reach of a loving yet vengeful God. How could such idealistic attitudes ever take root and gain ground on a harsh planet? Isn't such imagery just appealing to the good side of people conditioned to dualism? What about the bad side, the evil side of humanity that also resides within us? Won't this side win out, as it has so often in the past?

I contend that our species is blessed with millions of thinking *individuals* whose basic decency and caring for humanity and the planet quietly outnumber the more vocal pods of mono- and bi-worlders who want everyone to live by their limited life scripts. This is the upside of individualism (and the beauty of democracy). People who acknowledge tri-worlds reality know that every individual has to provide some form of specialized labor to obtain life's basics, yet at the same time, every individual is a system within a system within a system. We are all individuals, and we are all members of families, peerages, teams, committees, and congregations. We are all workers, managers, or owners of proprietorships, partnerships, and corporations. We are all residents of unincorporated areas, towns, and cities. We are all citizens of states and a nation, and ultimately, we are all members of the same species. Who can deny these identities, each a system unto itself?

Reality guarantees that when you die, virtually all of these human-made world systems will continue to exist. New individuals will take your place as consumer, worker, believer, and so on. Unlike less immutable natural and ethereal world systems, these human systems will survive as is or in some form as they are modified to more adequately serve the needs of living human beings. Every human-made world system continually seeks its own improvement. Without continuous adaptation to the needs and wants of the living, every system will be replaced with something better/more relevant, it will end up as a paragraph or two in a history book, or it will disintegrate into dusty obscurity.

Because every human being lives in three worlds all the time, the question of species survival depends on how humans define what can be changed, what cannot be changed, and how the seemingly immutable can be better understood. For thousands of years, humans yearned to fly, but that happened only a little more than 115 years ago. Scientific evidence proves that humans had no significant effect on the atmosphere until the Industrial Revolution, when carbon dioxide measurements began their upward climb. Perhaps in the future, time travel will be a reality, but as of the early twenty-first century, we have no idea how to make that happen.

What we know now about our species and planet is that human beings will continue to pursue life's basics because we have no choice in the matter. We will continue to generate wastes. We will continue to affect natural systems for good or ill. We will continue to maintain differentiated national, political, legal, economic, and social identities among ourselves. We will continue to study, innovate, and explore, and many among us will continue to believe that differentiated and dualistic values and faiths make some people morally superior to others who do not share those beliefs.

Greed, animosities, hate, wars, superciliousness, ignorance, and a host of other countervailing forces will continue to infect species behavior. Humans will continue to dualistically struggle between values incarnate in modern/scientific thought and the thinking and faiths of more traditional beliefs. Clashing human-made systems will always generate sparks of animosity; the prevention and control of resultant fires concerns advocates of the human paradox and tri-worlds realists.

Ultimately, persistence in the pursuit of three-worlds goals (understanding the human paradox, fulfilling life's basics sustainably, human sameness acceptance, natural integrity, peace) can have a significant impact on the species and the planet if practiced now and taught to those who succeed us. Establishing tri-worlds systems, accepting their potential for species-planetary survival, and then applying them are the issues upon which our energies must now coalesce.

Imagine the impact of dignified individuals advocating human-paradox understanding, of tri-worlders extending a sense of beholdenness to our species and the earth, of recognition of actions and systems that enrich/extend/elevate life of all sorts, and of thinkers and doers who dare to go beyond black and white, right and wrong, us versus them. Acknowledgment of commonly shared instincts, values, and faiths and the overriding importance of these commonalities will persist in the future because they are so totally human and omnipresent within all decent and thinking individuals.

CHAPTER 4

Human-Made World

Chains of habit are too light to be felt until
they are too heavy to be broken.[24]
— Warren Buffett

Picture this. You're walking in the countryside. Rows of crops on rolling hills extend as far as your eye can see. An azure sky hosts patchy white clouds. A cool, gentle breeze caresses your face. Ahead, you see a farmhouse with a barn and some animal pens. Kids play in the yard. Mom hangs laundry on a clothesline. Dad plows a field. Stands of tall cottonwoods shade the house, while cattle graze in a nearby pasture. A red-winged blackbird dives and swirls at a hawk to keep it away from its nest.

As you talk with the folks who live in this picturesque setting, it is clear they know every nook and cranny of their work and living space. They know that hard work, smarts, and a little luck provide life's basics. They rely on common sense and time-proven practices to accomplish their tasks, and they use as much laborsaving technology as they can get their hands on. Their economic wells—their fields, their crops, their irrigation system, their livestock, their machines, their know-how and energy—are all they have to provide life's basics. They seem content and happy, yet they admit it's a struggle to eke out a living on a farm because a hailstorm can wipe out a season's plantings, bovine spongiform encephalopathy can make their cows mad, or they can lose a finger or an arm in a chain drive if they're not careful. They are sure that if they invest their energy conscientiously and use proven techniques, they will get the results intended.

You continue your walk. As you crest a hill, you notice more human presence before you—more human-made infrastructure along with houses and buildings grouped into a town. As you visit with the locals, they tell you there are more options for work here than in the countryside but not much more. Serving those on the farms and ranches is their focus. There are just a few local employers of note, along with a few franchise restaurants and discount stores out by the Interstate. Township residents hang on to their jobs with both hands because that's what puts food on the table. Only when work options fade do they develop new skills and chase a career rainbow in the city. A few large corporations may have a presence at a local plant, pipeline, or discount outlet. Citizens in these communities usually don't aspire to lofty goals; they just want to make enough money to raise a family and to control their lives. The axis around which their priorities spin includes family ties, work, friendly surroundings, and familiar faces—all related to the pursuit of sustenance, security, and comfort.

You walk over another hill, and there before you stands a mammoth city, sunshine glistening off mirrored office towers. When you ask a man on the street about his economic wells, he responds, "There are no wells in the city. What kind of bumpkin are you?" However, standing right before you are skyscrapers emblazoned with corporate logos, each business dependent on natural resources, human labor, and capital for its assets. Every economic well in the city has its own experts who claim knowledge and experience with every conceivable aspect of each well's existence, each asset's purpose, its components and performance. Data, details, and complication rule here.

The simplicity and straightforward thinking of rural and township life yield to roll-up abstractions in the city, to arcane lexicons, and to executive-suite decision making. The apparent honesty and friendliness found in rural America give way to the mandates of well-defined titles and departmental functions defined by an organizational pyramid and specialized work assignments that are more mental than physical. Highly differentiated brands come to life behind these business walls as commodities take on new identities; there are no earthy smells and green-cropped fields tended by accessible folks like you met earlier. This business arena of the human-made world primarily serves the interests of its executives, employees, stockholders/bondholders, and customers; this environment has a completely different feel and sense of purpose about it than rural or township life.

Undoubtedly, where you live and how you earn a living shape your social, political, and cultural points of view. Few can deny this fact. Your job molds your individual destiny as much as or more than genetics or any other physical or social factor. Also, how you personally adapt to your locale—country, town, city—helps configure your human-made world identities and shapes who you become as an individual. These identities become what others in the human-made world think and feel about you and how you, in turn, regard them.

For many Americans, human-made world identities sculpt an individual life into a mono-world that minimizes the natural and ethereal worlds to near-total obscurity while it subverts the concept of human sameness in the process. Socially, we link up with others who share "our" goals and interests, who think like "we" do, who can do "us" the most good. Everyday routine, pursuing the almighty buck, and trying to make it financially often become life itself in today's competitive, human-made world.

Ironically, the human-made world can be extremely inhumane. **America and other Western cultures offer opportunities, not guarantees.** Workers learn quickly that even level playing fields in the human-made world are full of trip holes, razor wire, and mines. The dreams of a cap-and-gown student living a life of prosperity run smack into this world's harsh and merciless setting once that tassel gets flipped.

The human-made world lays bare the virtual nonexistence of common species identity within its boundaries. "Us/we" has a parochial meaning here. Everyone and everything must react to a company's vision, the business plan, government rules, and market forces. There is no sense of species sameness here because virtually all players in this world believe money, power, and status ultimately rule, so that's where their energy flows. An individual's hopes, dreams, and expectations vastly exceed this world's ability to fulfill them, except for a willful and sometimes unscrupulous few.

It is axiomatic in the human-made world that anyone who depends directly on nature to obtain life's basics will concentrate on that relationship more intensely than distant human affairs. Rural and small-town citizens know what they need to know to attain life's basics, and that is where their energy goes. They aspire to improve their lives within the geographical and economic context in which they find themselves. Their waking hours are consumed with the endless tending demands of their farm, ranch, or small business. They know first-hand nature's challenges, along with its occasional bullwhip ferocity, over which they have no control whatsoever. Nature's destructive flare-ups along with inherited human traditions, prejudices, and fears often lead them to religious ways of thinking and a sense of fatalism.

At the other extreme, in the cities, millions of jobs exist to service existing economic wells and to drill new ones. Most Americans, about four out of five, now live in or near urban areas because that's where the jobs are. To the common-citizen job holder or careerist, her work, her expertise, and her niche within her organization are what really matter. Winning a new contract, meeting sales goals, getting a promotion, depositing a year-end bonus check—these are about as big as her career concerns ever get. Her specialized on-the-job connections are dedicated to coworkers, customers, and bosses, while off-the-job community connections likely run more shallow than deep because job and family consume practically all of her energy. Because there is so much to know and do within her own career framework, this urban worker focuses on who and what she needs to know and leaves the rest to higher-ups in the organizational hierarchy.

All economic wells, no matter where they are, generate common outputs of products, services, money, and information for use in the human-made world. **Unlike the natural world, the human-made world cannot exist on its own. It has no autonomic, genetic, regenerative forces to sustain it. It depends totally on human energy, knowledge, natural resources, and money for its existence.** It relies on tradition-bound business practice and politics for its structure and human interest and ambition for its momentum.

Human-made wells in capitalist societies create wealth that creates growth, which, theoretically, creates more wealth and more growth.

Private-enterprise capitalists assume risks, make investments, and then set about producing a product or service. Nature provides the resources for economic progress, while human workers provide the skills and drive to spur and sustain growth. The ethereal world contributes inspiration to make growth and profits happen through leadership and worker ambition, determination, and motivation. Without economic growth in modern capitalism, the belt around life's basics tightens for just about everyone.

As described earlier, what the human-made world has created beyond all its glorious economic growth, arts, and sciences is a planet divided by human-made nations, languages, cultures, and diverse ethereal beliefs. Currently, these differences carry more weight in citizens' minds than human physical sameness, nature's limits, and the commonality of needs and wants shared by all *Homo sapiens*. Reinforcing apparent differences in the human-made world are the behavioral aspects of competitiveness, advantage/position, and exploitation/intimidation that one individual or pod may hold or seek to hold over another, a.k.a. the stressful workaday existence described as the "real" world by everyday citizens.

Work for most Americans means applying a learned set of skills and knowledge that becomes more specialized over time through its application in specific ways for specific purposes. **We all become both enabled and entrapped by our specialized job skills because these talents only have value when and where there's demand for them. When demand for them surges, so do life's comforts; when demand fades, so do life's basics.**

Capitalism's Pull and Push

The human-made world has tipped the scales of humanity away from the best interests of the species to those of various pods of interests within the species. Large and powerful corporations, for instance, are elements within the whole that operate strictly by the laws of their own self-interests—that is, the rules of capitalist economics, along with and secondarily the laws of the nations in which they work. Species-wide issues are usually not within a corporation's purview of concern unless they hold a profit potential.

Transnational corporations have become large, powerful, and influential because they create jobs and provide usable products/services at low or reasonable costs and because they are willing and able to take on more risk in specific areas than government. To give credit where it is due, major corporations have achieved giant status because they focused on and excelled at their portion of providing life's basics to the masses; they're masters of specialization, and economically, they shine at what they do.

A major goal of capitalistic private enterprise includes the growth of residual/discretionary income for owners—that is, create wealth that enriches owners. More capital accumulation and control thereof is every owner's goal. Anyone who does not understand this point does not understand capitalism. The achievement of this goal usually does not recognize or value human beings any more than other business assets. Capitalism requires arms-length objectivity, knowledge, resources, and decision making that extends no consideration to the human species per se; any such commitment, by definition, is dualistically labeled as antithetical to capitalist practice.

Corporations have no soul; advertising and branding campaigns seem to give them one, but that's facade. It is pure self-deception to believe that business enterprises exist for any purpose other than making money; that is the *only* reason for their existence. Jobs, brand integrity, good will, community relations, public image—every facet of a business is ancillary to its assets, cash flow, and profits. No assets, no cash flow; no profits, no business.

Species and natural considerations beyond a corporation's business focus have no place in its operational affairs unless imposed by a higher power, namely, the law. Environmental laws are a primary example. These laws exist because no business would impose such restraints upon itself willingly; to do so would place it at a competitive disadvantage and negatively impact cash flow and profits. Whenever possible, private-sector businesses will externalize expenses like pollution and other social costs rather than include them in their product or service prices. Current modes of corporate operation privatize gains and externalize costs as much as possible, thus providing prima facie evidence that capitalism does not have an inherent, long-term species and planetary focus. Taxes, regulations, permits, fees, and other governmental requirements also impose themselves on pure capitalistic endeavors.

The dualistic nature of capitalism reveals itself in its name. Those with capital are the owners/elites; those who do not have capital work for those who do. Owners work to attain *financial* security; common-citizen workers seek to attain *job* security. Owners and elites have mastered the systems that represent capital (money, contracts, stocks, bonds, patents, and so on). Working citizens know about these representations but know little about how they work or how to use them. Owners grow their residual income, which generates interest and other sources of income that usually do not require a lot of physical effort or time on their part. Interest, dividends, and rent are examples of residual income. Workers who want additional income have to work overtime, get a promotion or a second job, or move to a better job to improve their financial status.

Owners invest their capital in transactions that generate profits that they consume, save, or re-invest to generate more income/profits. Workers swap time and skills for money and benefits that they expend on sustenance, security, and comfort for themselves and their families. Owners and elites tend to make investments that *ap*preciate in value (securities, real estate, art); workers tend to invest in basic assets that *de*preciate in value (appliances, cars). Most workers aspire to be owners of, at least, a home and a car.

In a capitalist society, the rich get richer because they know the rules of making money and they are willing to take risks or appear to take risks. Workers fulfill their job requirements, build seniority, and try to grow middle-class status. The poor stay poor or get poorer because they do not know about, understand, or choose to follow these rules, and they tend to be risk averse and have no money to invest.

Because all human beings share the same needs and wants, there are multitudes of competing self-interests that service life's basics. Corn flakes are corn flakes, but some people like the crunch of Kellogg's more than the texture of Post. Burgers are burgers, but some people like McDonald's over Wendy's or Burger King (or maybe it's the fries). Gasoline is gasoline, yet some people purchase Shell, Exxon, or Valero to the exclusion of other brands because of a perceived, differentiated benefit. We consumers love having all these companies cater to us; we love accepting or rejecting an offer, of being in control of our buying decisions. Having money in a consumer economy generates feelings of individual empowerment that can be aphrodisiacal to our exceptional sense about ourselves.

Within a highly differentiated consumer society like America's, there is not much profit potential in emphasizing human sameness. There's no commercial reason to justify a species-wide consciousness about species survival or natural integrity. There's no reason to bring human commonalities and natural priorities into the realm of discussion, except possibly for public relations purposes. **The thrust of progress within today's capitalist society favors a bias toward differentiation, dualism, and competitiveness that paradoxically threatens the long-term interests of our species and planet.**

Ironically, while corporations make differentiated claims about their mostly generic goods and services, the business practices that produce them are essentially the same. Every corporation keeps a set of books (or two), has productive operations, personnel, and inventory to manage, and has sales and service goals to meet its basic objectives of income, profits, and growth. Every business uses double-entry cash or accrual accounting practices, markets its products/services, and pays taxes (maybe).

Generally accepted accounting and business practices are time proven and widely used because they are sensible and reliable. Just like individual human beings, businesses are unique yet the same. Each is held accountable to owners, stakeholders, regulators, and the IRS, and of course, there are exceptions. A few risk-loving business leaders will try to manipulate operations/accounts to meet personal ends or to satisfy some dualistic or differentiated personal/political goal.

Overall, to believe that private-enterprise capitalism operates within a broad, humanistic ethic is to believe that cows lay eggs. Capitalism simply is not set up to work humanely; it is too detached from the species and nature for that. Humans have developed and advanced a capitalist economic system that eliminates human caring in its concepts and operations (except for we/us insiders) and adulates little other than numeric progressions (profits, positive cash flow). Capitalism: a heartless, soulless, cold (but supposedly level) playing field. **Only *individual* executives and employees**

have the potential for advancing the human caring value within today's impersonal capitalist parameters.

Economics

Economics, the study of human productivity, carries the moniker of a dismal science because of its sangfroid. Its self-assurance comes from its neutrality in a human-made world rife with slash-and-burn, win-or-die capitalists. The integrity of economics rests upon its objectivity, which is the source of its widespread rational appeal. Economic principles and methodologies seem ultimate, fair, and sensible to most players within industry, commerce, and government.

Capitalist economics holds such powerful sway in the human-made world because it embodies the means to attain sustenance, security, and comfort for more and more self-interest pods and individuals. However flawed, capitalism works. It is the primary tool available to fulfill life's basics, along with some political promises that keep the middle-class and poor sated. Economic forces set the tone for domestic and global trade and underwrite peaceful alternatives to bellicosity.

Economic activity plays to humans' common sense in that those with specialized skills and tools can produce goods that others with different skills and tools will purchase to sustain and enrich their lives. All working people benefit themselves and others from their endeavors; these are the productive activities economics observes and measures. Our species accepts and trusts capitalist economics because of its potential to generate some degree of widespread prosperity. As for capitalism's complex inner workings, most average citizens don't have a clue and don't care.

Capitalistic economic activity plays to humans' exceptional sense in that it provides the means to achieve fame and fortune for some business leaders, innovators, and risk takers. Economics does not provide much guidance or wisdom regarding humans' natural sense—that is, our recognition of Earth's limitations and our dependence on it. The index to my 1970s-edition 780-page economics textbook, for instance, cites no references within it for the word "nature" or "natural."[25] A second economics text of similar size and date only uses the word "natural" to refer to natural gas, natural monopoly, and two short references to natural resources as they involve economic growth in developing countries.[26] (Note: Checking indexes in more up-to-date economic texts generates the same minimal information regarding the words "nature" and "natural.") Bottom line: economic activity assumes at its foundational level that nature will give and humans will take; nature apparently has no accounts receivable, only accounts payable.

Economics' major weakness is that its theories, principles, and rules have to be applied by human beings. We will never get economic theory/balance exactly right because we're not that smart or that considerate of others in our species. Greed, for instance, another word not listed in an economics textbook's index, remains a human behavioral constant from one generation to the next, but economics makes no moral judgments about it; that's a subjective human problem that's well beyond economics' objective purview. Economics can measure greed's effects and provide the corrective actions needed to return to more economic equilibrium when greed takes its toll (as in the 2008 financial meltdown), but human beings cannot rely on economics to wax ethical or to correct human immoralities; we've relegated those responsibilities to the individual conscience, politics, pundits, the law, and religion rather than to a social science focused on human productivity.

Also, economics paradoxically liberates and imprisons our species. The beauty and symmetry of economic activity that provide life's basics also inhibit the decision making required to deal with global natural challenges. **Mono-world capitalists and dualistic politicians pose natural issues as competing with economic interests rather than as immutable forces that, at some point, will demand compromise from the human-made world.** The human-made world has a deep bias for the soundness of economic principles and gives them more political weight than natural laws. However, reality, from a three-worlds point of view, shows that the planet cannot accommodate an endless procession of sanctioned self-interests, each one seeking to become a leader in its field, with its owners sitting atop bales of cash. There are limits in the natural world that the human-made world patronizes rather than accepts, natural limits that business and economic interests ignore or work around to meet their own mono-world goals, and wasteful private sector endeavors that politicians abide to the detriment of the overall common good.

By setting the parameters for normal day-to-day productive activity within the human-made world, economics reaches no conclusions about the natural world in which we live, about the changing needs of the natural world, or about how everyday economic activity may need to change to accommodate a limited planet. Also, individual business leaders almost always make decisions that lead to some short-term economic benefit for their interests rather than for the longer-term or the common good, and no one should expect them to decide otherwise according to the current rules of capitalist economics and the politics that support it.

Ironically, it is capitalist excesses like those of the business-gone-wild years of the 1990s–2007 that generate outcomes that require the imposition of common-good/government-imposed "socialist" reforms. More government regulation and resultant changes appear inevitable after such hedonistic periods because human-made world capitalism will always resist putting earthly and species realities on a par with its sacred goals of growth and profits.

The dualistic conflict between the common good and private interests serves as key evidence that modern civilization has not given the human paradox, human sameness, and the need for pervasive sustainability much thought. All human-made world incentives and proof must work within the rules of economics in its role as the final arbiter of worth. Economics has evolved into the ultimate determiner of value for the species within capitalist/consumer societies. Without much doubt, capitalist economics sits atop the list of human-made world systems so far in the twenty-first century; it is the heavyweight of human-made world ideations despite its inherently limited vision.

Numerous recessions and depressions have plagued capitalism since the beginning of the nineteenth century, some nearly threatening capitalism's very existence. The Great Depression and the 2007–2011 Great Recession and the economic gut punch during the COVID-19 epidemic resulted from human excesses, inadequate government policies/oversight, and pandemic denial that created huge economic imbalances and human pain.

American free-market capitalists in the twentieth and twenty-first centuries stretched the limits of economic activity through bubbles that ultimately popped and threatened capitalism's future. No matter. Free-market advocates believe capitalism contains the bandages and medications that business/governmental systems need for self-healing over time, and they can count on humans having a short memory, a condition that allows speculators to create new, more creative bubbles.

Highflyers who love their risky speculative extremes, especially those in the overcrowded financial sector, look for and find ways to outmaneuver existing laws and economic constraints. We taxpayers pick up the tab for their ambitious overindulgences, and we have to suffer hard times because their gains are privatized, while taxpayer relief socializes their gambles. Wall Street gamblers hardly ever go to jail. Economics interpreted by one political faction or another provides either the inspiration to create bubble greed or the reins to moderate and reform bubble excesses, all actions that contribute momentum to the left or right swing of the political pendulum.

Paradox: economics emphasizes ideals of normalcy and balance and cause and effect that, compared with human behavior, present a template of moderation that proves anathema to capitalist risk takers. Fast-tracked, greed-inspired capitalists regard economic norms and government constraints as mere speed bumps on their exploitation highways. Immoderation plagues capitalism like fleas on a mangy stray.

Within today's human-made world of private enterprise lies an obsession with measurability. Determining the numbers and what they mean is inescapable in modern business practice no matter how big or small an enterprise may be. Business leaders regard the balance sheet, income statement, and other financial reports as their report card because these documents measure achievement compared to the business plan, to last year's performance, and to the competition.

What executives decide, how well employees perform, how the markets accept or reject an enterprise's products/services/performance all show up in business statements. Love and kisses greet good financial reports; questions and second-guessing greet bad ones. This paperwork, these impersonal figures, set the tone for policies that ripple their way down to the lowliest individual within the business ranks.

The dualistic demands of financial imperatives make each business a strict mono-world dedicated to its own growth and profits through performance, timing, and differentiation. BP's affinity for profits at the expense of drilling safety in the Gulf of Mexico in 2010 exemplifies how important the numbers are to top corporate executives along with their potential to err on the side of extreme risk—and how expensive and damaging such a choice can be. Legal action against BP, Exxon, Shell, Chevron, and ConocoPhillips goes well beyond one spill. Cities, states, and other jurisdictions are suing industry giants for knowingly deceiving customers about global warming. These corporations knew their products were causing the problem, the suits contend, yet they continued to promote and profit from those products. Fossil fuel companies are responsible for the consequences of that strategy, which resulted in increased wildfires, drought, and numerous other climate crisis outcomes.[27]

For growth and profit goals to be achieved, the current year's financial statements of any business need to reflect more favorable numbers over last year's financial statements. This is a main pumping chamber in the heart of capitalism, especially large corporations. Did we make more profit than last year? Is the value of our stock higher than last year? Can we keep paying dividends? Is our leadership taking us in the right direction for more income, profits, and growth?

For these questions to be answered affirmatively, many in the private sector now need to think globally. **Every private enterprise, in its wildest dreams, would like (1) every potential customer on Earth to purchase and repurchase its products or services, (2) to establish and maintain the lowest costs of production and distribution, and (3) to profit by each customer transaction.** These goals constitute the inspirational growth hormones in every organ of the capitalist corpus. Also, in today's image-conscious consumer world, there's more than operational performance at play; there's commercial identity and brand loyalty. Appealing to consumers' exceptional sense has become big business.

The success of Apple's iPods, iPhones, and iPads attests to the human-made world's ultimate commercial push for individual consumption, for information customization, and to reinforce individual differentiation. Apple's devices allow each buyer to create their own personal commercial-free radio station or MTV, to input their own telephone directory, to read electronic books/newspapers/magazines, and to watch movies, among many other customizable features. This high degree of personalization appeals to the specific desires of individual consumers because each buyer can create an electronic space that is completely their own, their own private galaxy of human-world contacts, information resources, and recreational diversions. Every*one* can be a master of their own mix of worlds, a customization that will, they believe, enhance personal happiness and fulfillment. It's no coincidence that most Apple product names start with an "i."

Apple's promise of control and selectivity is the ultimate in personal differentiation and unique identity that is all available through a sleek electronic box. For Apple Inc., this strategy of building brand loyalty will, it hopes, keep customers coming back to buy the next iteration of the i-whatever so next year's financial statements will improve over this year's. Every corporation strives for an enamoring relationship with its customers like Apple's successful one, a customer intimacy that affirms trust in the products and services provided—all traits affirmed by increasing revenues and profits from a dedicated and growing product line and customer base. That's heaven for one of America's largest corporations!

The markets in which Apple operates did not exist until the 1970s. Part of capitalism's claim to fame is its ability to create new markets and to match a market's seller and buyer efficiently. eBay is a marketplace, just as is the Mercantile Exchange in Chicago and the New York Stock Exchange. Your grocery store or the local flower shop, the cattle auction company out on the highway—they are all players in specialized markets. In every market, people with money trade that money for goods, services, labor, debt, or ownership in a company at what they consider to be an acceptable price. The process of creating goods and services and then exchanging them for money or other goods and services has been the economic backbone of civilization for thousands of years. The ultimate inspiration for economic progress has always been obtaining and improving life's basics for owners, working individuals, and their families.

One of the human-made world's greatest achievements has been the development and improvement of markets into the world of business and commerce we enjoy today. Humans have a tremendous amount of equity built into business and trade systems; millions of people have spent thousands of years improving markets, products, and services from one generation to the next. Whether you view economic progress with awe or disdain, there is no doubt that economic prosperity allows billions of individuals to achieve physical sustenance, security, and comfort in their lives. For those less fortunate, it is the potential for economic prosperity that gives them hope that their own and their children's lives can improve. **As long as humans exist on this planet, we will strive to attain and improve life's basics for ourselves, our families, and our pods of self-interest. This remains the essence of human-made world activity for now and the foreseeable future. This is the essence of species survival, one of this book's major themes.**

Democracy and Capitalism

Ultimately, despite their many faults and challenges, the most functional systems the human-made world has devised to govern itself are democracy, which hovers somewhere between the extremes of total government control and ultimate social chaos, and, to feed and house itself, capitalism, which, in some form, has gained acceptance in the world as the predominant economic system to attain life's basics. **Both democracy and capitalism provide a way for more and more individuals to pursue and achieve individual dignity, self-esteem, and physical prosperity.** That is why they're still around. But the limitation with these systems comes with their relevance in a shrinking natural world.

Democracy gives individuals freedom to pursue happiness as each individual defines it, and capitalism provides the mechanisms for achieving this happiness—yet both systems assume that nature will silently and continuously provide the necessary resources for individuals to realize their dreams. That may be true in the near term, but in a world of finite resources and increasing population demands, how long can this dream scenario go on? Where will more resources come from on a planet facing increased physical depletion and natural systemic exhaustion? How can our small planet support capitalism's vision of 3 percent compounded annual growth ad infinitum? When should human-made world systems start adapting to nature's limits, and how will that work?

If democracy and capitalism are to retain their worth and dominance, political and economic models established by Enlightenment philosophers, America's founding fathers, Adam Smith, David Ricardo, and others will have to be tempered to accommodate nature's limits, and we will need to get vastly more productivity/efficiency out of the natural resources (and recycled resources) still available. This is where human intelligence, creativity, peace, and species sameness recognition can play big roles—by shifting emphasis from compounded growth to sustainability. This is where a new, saner economics resides.

Formal control documents that assure individuals of their right to pursue their dreams based on their talent, intelligence, and capital will probably continue in some form as ideological underpinnings in future societies, yet paradoxically, these ends will be less achievable because of natural constraints. **The recognition of natural limits will, at some point, have to become a part of democratic and capitalist guiding principles.** The natural world simply cannot provide enough resources (air, soil, water, minerals) for every human being on the planet to pursue a dreamed-of lifestyle, yet that is exactly where capitalism and democracy will try to take us on their presently charted paths. That outcome would be great if global warming, pollution, and limited natural resource issues can be addressed and solved along the way, but such an outcome defies current scientific prediction and prevailing economic/political realities. Some root changes are inevitable simply because we are finite beings living on a finite planet.

Economics/politics that does not construct a Sustainability Age will invariably trudge along the same income-disparity, belligerent, partisan-laden trails they currently plod. Without a reversal in natural resource consumption (decreased demand), higher productivity per unit of natural resource (new technology), and a more ubiquitous effort to reduce pollution and global warming (higher costs), human-made capitalism and democracy will face increased natural pressures antithetical to their basic tenets; their numbers won't add up. What about planned obsolescence? How deeply enculturated is this practice in corporate business planning?

We cannot have unlimited economic growth, ever-higher profits, and unimpeded individual freedoms in a physical world unable to support these ideas. That simply won't work. Something has to give, especially on a planet where ethereal forces (God/gods) don't favor our species with their reputed powers of intervention, caring, and generosity. Ethereal powers that remain aloof and inactive in human affairs make no practical contribution to species survival and cannot be counted on to do so. We humans are the only thing we can depend on.

Affirmation of our human-made world dilemma (that is, more economic growth from declining resources) comes from the fact that most of the planet's low-hanging fruit has already been picked. There simply aren't enough untapped oil fields left in the world to cheaply supply long-term carbon growth, and the crude oil that is available will be more difficult to find and more expensive to extract and transport. Oil prices will rise and fall with supply and demand in the short term, but without a more rapid change to alternative energy sources, petroleum costs will undoubtedly track higher. There's plenty of coal and wood around, but their combustion contributes carbon dioxide and other pollutants to the already overtaxed atmosphere, and we need trees to stay in the ground to store carbon. China's extraordinary economic growth has turned it into the world's largest consumer of cement, aluminum, and steel, resulting in a push to higher prices globally while its economic growth has massively polluted its own and the planet's living and breathing space. Prices of food stocks will increase as world demand for corn, rice, and wheat exceed supply. Potable water has already become an explosive political issue in countries where corporations have tried to privatize it and even more so in countries where supply is dwindling or deficient. Farmers are deeply concerned about the condition and erosion of topsoil or the lack thereof, along with shrinking aquifers and the overuse of insecticides and herbicides.

All this activity plus much more confirms the conclusion that our species has a deep and sincere interest in improving life's basics for more people and that governments and the private sector are more than willing to facilitate these ends, but the snag comes with the one-way sign inherent in unbridled consumerism. Nature cannot supply resources for consumers endlessly and accept our wastes without hurting itself (and us) in the process. The planet is only so big and not getting any bigger. We are burning through nature's resources at an ever-increasing pace, and we're in deep denial as to the costs and consequences involved in this behavior. Après moi le deluge, Act II.

Every benefit has a cost that modern consumers do not want to know or think about, especially Americans. Private enterprise and the politics that support it do virtually nothing to bring these costs to mind because that may adversely affect sales and profitability (and image). We American consumers want to enjoy our treasures and pleasures guilt free. We don't want to have to consider the costs of our lifestyles on the species and the planet. That's very unpalatable and disruptive to our exceptional self-concepts and our comfortable lives.

We live in hedonistic denial sustained by denial politics. In our dualistic and highly differentiated human-made world, we citizens just want to focus on the linkages that generate life's basics and that affirm our differentiated beliefs. We don't want to delve too deeply into the whys and wherefores associated with achieving improved status in the human-made or ethereal worlds. We don't like change that dilutes our sustenance, security or comfort; we don't want to give up our ethereal, aspirational dreams. Political conservatives especially thrive on these "don'ts."

Democracy and capitalism, in their essence, have yet to acknowledge natural limits within their basic precepts, and proponents of these systems find it politically difficult to emphasize costs as well as benefits. **It will probably be growing *individual* citizen awareness of costs, innate human caring, and conventional wisdom working up from the citizenry through the governance structure that set the parameters within which capitalism and democracy will function on a resource-limited planet.** If this doesn't work, then there are autocratic/totalitarian alternatives to help citizens realize when enough is enough—the least attractive alternative and one that can be purposefully avoided.

As a species, we are just beginning to manifest understanding and support for a more realistic state of mind about our appetites, our resources, and our planet, and we have an exceedingly long way to go before actualizing an enlightened consciousness. Our denial tendencies will not transition easily or quietly into one of sustainable species and planetary survival. Deniers will cling to their priorities of materialism and status and the inviolability of local values. The transition ahead will be a long, nasty political slog or, through enlightened leadership, perhaps a transition to realistic acceptance of our shared humanity.

A Hopeful Future

What may seem hopeless really isn't for either democracy or capitalism. Democracy keeps trying to extend its common sensibilities of individual freedom/rights, pursuit of life's basics, and governance by the people to more and more countries because all humans have the same basic needs and wants. The same human inspiration, creativity, and genius that developed capitalism can and should now be applied to modify traditional business practices to fit today's species and earthly realities. The business community's obsession with profits now needs to find ways for private enterprise to operate on a planet with limited resources, something that is already beginning to happen, at least in the productive economy. The wasteful, nonproductive, and unsustainable greed games of the status-quo financial establishment and its casino economy need to be exposed for their unproductive nature and their destructiveness to the nation, the species, and the planet. Assets need to be productive, not purely speculative; reform of financial gamesmanship is where a sustainable capitalism can begin. Also, the one-way sign in consumerism needs to be turned into a loop by eliminating wastes and curbing irresponsible appetites. No one stands in the way of these transitions except "we the people"—our attitudes and our unthinking habits.

An alternate idea already exists for capitalism's compounding growth economic model. Steady-state advocates say "enough is best" rather than "more is better." Rather than the ideal of constant, never-ending economic growth, a steady-state economy envisions a constant level of population with the things people need to attain life's basics produced at the most efficient rates and with the least amount of waste and pollution.

"If we use 'growth' to mean quantitative change and 'development' to refer to qualitative change, then we may say that a steady-state economy develops but does not grow, just as the planet Earth, of which the human economy is a subsystem, develops but does not grow," says Herman E. Daly in *Steady-State Economics*.[28] Daly notes that such an economic model has dominated 99 percent of all the time humans have inhabited the earth. Only for the past two hundred years, during the Industrial Age, has economic growth become the obsession it is today. "In the long run, stability is the norm and growth the aberration . . . it could not be otherwise," he states.[29]

Elaborating on the steady-state idea in his book *Prosperity Without Growth*, Tim Jackson describes the economic problem succinctly: "In pursuit of the good life today, we are systematically eroding the basis for well-being tomorrow." Economics needs to be redefined away from consumerism/materialism and ecologic ignorance into "a robust, ecologically literate macro-economics" that replaces growth with new conditions for a sustainable economy.

"The fundamental macro-economic variables will still pertain," Jackson states. "People will still spend . . . and save; enterprise will still produce goods and services . . . government will still raise revenues and spend them in the public interest. But new macro-economic variables will need to be brought explicitly into play. These will almost certainly include variables to reflect energy and resource dependency of the economy and the limits on carbon. They may also include variables to reflect the value of ecosystem service or stocks of natural capital." Also, ecological investment "must play an absolutely vital role. This will mean revisiting the concepts of profitability and productivity and putting them to better service in pursuit of long-term social goals."[30]

Creative entrepreneurs and planners in the productive economy have already identified renewable energy, waste reduction/elimination, more efficient industrial productivity, climate-specific agriculture, and other strategies and technologies as ways to offset pressures on natural resources and to reduce pollution while providing new profit and employment opportunities. These are the startup endeavors of the Sustainability Age, and there are thousands of them. Brilliant minds are already at work trying to meld capitalism with new ways of meeting human-made world needs.

"We can, in short, use the power of the market system to climb out of the hole created by flawed markets," say Fred Krupp and Miriam Horn in *Earth: The Sequel* as they elaborate on the implementation of a cap-and-trade strategy. "We can offer a pot of gold to those who develop new ways to generate carbon-free energy and new technologies to remove carbon from our smokestacks and atmosphere. **We can channel the full range of human impulses—ingenuity, idealism, ambition—into undoing the damage and healing our planet. America's greatest strength has always been its boundless capacity for invention.**"[31]

At the end of the nineteenth century and in the early decades of the twentieth century, American economic growth reached its highest peaks. Indoor plumbing, electrification, telephones, automobiles—all the devices and services we now take for granted were finding their ways into American daily life. Paved roads, water and wastewater systems, skyscrapers, subways—these were heady days for conventional infrastructure. These "one-time" growth spurts, as economist Robert Gordon calls them, will not happen again.[32] True, but components of the Sustainability Age will rebuild rusty infrastructure and add new job-generating scientific and engineering elements. For instance, Bill Gates is a leader in private capital investment/grants that fund technological breakthroughs. His concept of Green Premiums emphasizes the difference between what's being replaced and what that product/system is being replaced with. Example: "The average price for a gallon of jet fuel over the past few years is $2.22. Advanced biofuels for jets . . . cost on average $5.35 per gallon. The Green Premium for zero-carbon fuel . . . is $3.13 . . . a premium of 140 percent." Green Premiums can be established for virtually all alternatives to carbon-based products/systems. The technology/political/business challenge comes with closing the gap between the two.[33] This high-risk arena is one he's committed a substantial portion of his fortune to addressing.

Klaus Schwab, founder and executive chair of the World Economic Forum, emphasizes in his book *Stakeholder Capitalism* the need for a holistic response to the issues facing economics, planet, and humankind. He acknowledges that "economic growth of less than 3 percent per year seems to be the new normal."[34] He believes that business, civil society, governments, and international organizations should "shift to a long-term perspective, looking beyond the next quarter or fiscal year, to the next decade and the next generation, and they take the concerns of others into account."[35] The World Economic Forum meets annually in Davos, Switzerland.

While there are alternative ideas about modifying capitalist practice, there has not been much talk about modifying democracy. Most proponents think democracy is pretty perfect as is. The U.S. Constitution serves as a strong basis for this pride. Interestingly, this founding document does not include the word "nature" in it or the word "natural" except in Article II, Section 1, about who's qualified to run for president (a "natural" born citizen). Understandably, the natural world was not something America's founders could conceive of as limited or exhaustible; they had millions and millions of acres yet to explore.

For modern nations, the next steps in the evolution of democracy and capitalism are at hand. How will we handle them? What will these steps look like? Aren't these issues our leaders should be addressing now? Are democracy/capitalism the right answers for every country? What ideas do you have? What are you, as an individual citizen, willing to do to accommodate the long-term needs of the planet for the sake of your children, their children, other living species, and the planet itself? Do you feel any responsibility for these issues? If not, why not? If so, what are you going to do?

In modern societies, human-made laws support individual liberties and the endeavors of capitalists, while politicians who make the laws benefit from the wealth accumulated by those in the private sector. Anyone outside inner power circles gets mostly lip service and short shrift no matter what party occupies the White House—or so it seems to us average citizens. Hoi polloi blue- and white-collar workers only get more of the economic pie when they become owners or when they rely on strikes or other production-threatening options to increase their power. **Capitalism's differentiation techniques and dualistic mental programming do not allow for concepts such as "humanistic capitalism" or "profitable socialism" or "sustainable capitalism," although some ideations like these are probably where most modern societies will end up because of planetary limitations.**

Americans, especially, seem light years away from comprehending that traditional capitalism and democracy will not work on an overpopulated, limited-resources planet; both systems have to be modified to accommodate natural-world realities. To think that America can go it alone in an interconnected, interdependent world is downright idiotic and self-damaging, as the George W. Bush and Trump administrations so clearly demonstrated.

From a species survival point of view, it's obvious that capitalistic economics and American democracy will have to make concessions to the species and the planet, or they will fade away, and a burned-out

America will crumble because it could not adapt. Morph intentionally by accepting earthly and species realities or get morphed—that seems to be the ultimate choice for today's dualistic, differentiated, democratic, and capitalist America.

Human Paradox Asks

Underlying all economic theory rests the supreme driving force within every capitalist endeavor: profits. That is the pot of gold at the end of the rainbow, the pathway to growth and success, the new Lexus in the driveway. Every successful product or service vendor in the world, from a modest trade stall in Baghdad to the corporate towers in Manhattan, understands the concept of profitability, but not everyone understands the complexities associated with cost recovery, accounting, personnel, productivity, competitiveness, distribution, branding, and efficiency that lead to profits in today's complex human-made world. Also, every capitalist understands the price to be paid by not running a profitable operation (unless you are a Wall Street too-big-to-fail bank).

Attending to one's own self-interests can provide life's basics within the human-made world, yet continued personal success only comes from directed mental and physical energy, knowledge, experience, and risk taking, functions that many average citizens cede to leaders and bosses. Not having well-defined goals and/or not attending to these goals can bring struggles and hardships that dilute sustenance, security, and comfort for any individual or pod seeking profits and growth.

Here are the basic rules of survival in today's human-made world of business: know your specialty inside and out, plan for the short to long terms, pay attention, mingle and endear yourself with others who can benefit you, meet/exceed your plan, avoid debt if at all possible, turn a profit, anticipate the unforeseeable (like the COVID pandemic) with some savings, reinvest to achieve growth, and then repeat—so easy to say, so exceedingly difficult to achieve.

Once a business finds a way to reach its goals profitably, it locks into that specialization and then seeks to grow through marketing, expansion, innovation, and diversification. As stated in the vernacular, "grow that cash cow [and] then milk the hell out of it."

Industry, finance, and commerce function to gain advantage over competitors by landing exclusive and profitable contracts, by applying new technologies that lower production/transit costs, and by employing as few human beings as possible. Here's a general rule of thumb in business: hire only as many employees as you absolutely need and weed out the unproductive ones; utilize cost-efficient technological alternatives to humans whenever possible; consider employees as units of production and evaluate their performance accordingly; get the most productivity you can out of your human capital at the lowest possible cost; and develop a small coterie of trustworthy insider employees. Also, when a downturn hits, eliminate jobs first along with all their associated costs; this seems to be the preferred way to alleviate financial pressures and to match output with reduced demand.

Perhaps the ultimate irony for a capitalist economy comes from its self-interested nature—that is, to provide life's basics for principals and employees (and profits and dividends for stockholders) while concurrently resisting all temptations to pay attention to other humans outside its own interests. Beneath its feel-good/do-good public relations mask, private enterprise must remain steadfast to its legally binding and self-protective nature. Common citizens digging for a warm geothermal layer within capitalist private enterprise will find only a thick layer of permafrost instead. **Private-sector capitalism exists to serve the interests of *some* human beings, not the species, nature, or God;** these realms go way beyond the scope of any business or industry's vision statement.

In the dualistic and highly differentiated human-made world of business and commerce, economic laws outweigh natural laws. Nature's limits are little more than challenges for humans to overcome. Looking at the planet through the lens of human-made private enterprise yields an extraordinary array of options to supply and enhance life's basics at a profit. All of the earth's resources are fair game to capitalists who hold a strong economic and political hand via their abilities to create jobs and to fulfill life's basics for employees and stakeholders. Economic growth also includes within itself the concept of accountability, which may, ultimately, bring natural limits into play within economic growth theory and practice—either inculcated voluntarily or through government imposition.

The government assumes the role of tending to common interests that private enterprise will not assume; it takes (or should take) action for the common good. Members of the common good include those outside the purview of a private enterprise. The government does what the private sector cannot or will not do because it lacks the scale, interest, or resources to take on such challenges. The government taxes citizens and businesses and then redistributes this money into various programs and services that, purportedly, it can provide more efficiently than individual citizens or private interests. Also, the government's role includes mollifying the compulsions and greed of the private sector when these behaviors threaten the public interest. Even the government applies economic principles and business logic to its operations because these practices enhance productivity, efficiency, and fairness; these practices are judged inescapably basic to responsible human interaction.

Hypocrisy shows its ugly face in the high end of capitalism as mega corporations and banks that fall on hard times get rescue funds from the government, like the $700+ billion bailout for the financial services industry in 2008 and the multi-billion-dollar assistance package for the automobile industry in the same and the following years. Business-sector leaders justify passing the buck to taxpayers to save the global financial system from total collapse or to prevent another depression. Admitting publicly that the private-sector masters of malfeasance made a trove of bad decisions and went overboard in their speculative and highly leveraged bets comes sparingly, if at all.

Add to this the Ponzi schemes of Bernie Madoff types that cost numerous investors and charities their wealth, and it becomes apparent how dysfunctional the financial sector can be, and all of this occurred under the auspices of a conservative Republican administration that espoused lax regulation for free-market capitalists. Also, the Trump administration brought the federal government to its knees through unqualified leadership, institutional trashing, lies, and poisonous partisanship. The Trump tax law of 2017 just put more money in rich folks' pockets; it came nowhere near paying for itself, as promised.

OPM: "other people's money." This cliché within the business/finance community was a big factor in triggering the 2008 economic recession and Trump's ever-wandering mindset. Aggressive, gaming capitalists inspired by a free-market, hands-off government concocted elaborate products and deals to make profits in the casino economy using dollars provided by investors who didn't really understand what they were getting into or who naively trusted their banker/broker. Not even the Federal Reserve Bank, through its own admissions, had a grasp of how much risk these banks were taking on. For every dollar of a dealmaker's capital, another $30+ in OPM would back many fanciful schemes. (The key to selling these schemes was the carrot of increased residual income; investors could make good money without having to do any calorie-burning labor to get it. Everyone with capital to invest loves easy-riding residual income.) The Trump world thrived on OPM; "I love debt," he famously boasted.

The profit margins for the financial institutions involved in the misplaced trust of the Clinton–George W. Bush-era rip-offs rested in the mysteries of the deal, the incomprehensible complications of unregulated investments, and the reams of paper supplied by financial specialists all trying to make a pass-through profit with no to little risk for themselves. They trashed the economy through arcane verbiage, through financial products that let them slough off responsibility to some other party, and through flawed basic assumptions (for example, "real estate values will always keep climbing").

The pity in all this was that Wall Street bankers weren't content with simply making profits; they had to develop new and riskier ways to make mega profits through leveraging straightforward financial instruments like mortgages into complex, out-of-this-world financial contrivances. As the housing market crumbled, the banks' unregulated products started to vaporize. Everyone with private capital sat on their cash, causing the credit markets to dry up; no one trusted anyone else, so borrowing shrank, and the economic growth clock started ticking backward. In the fall of 2008, the stock market tanked, and the Bush 43 administration clamored around, looking for a solution to stanch the panic. Their solution included huge outlays of public money to buy toxic assets in struggling banks, an outcome that Naomi Klein characterized as "George W. Bush's final pillage" of the U.S. Treasury.[36] Zealots of unimpeded free-market capitalism had to rely on government solutions/funds to resolve financial problems their own free-market, unregulated greed created. None of the famous capitalist captains went to prison. Socialism for über-capitalists—how's that for irony?

During the go-go years of the 1990s and early twenty-first century, including the Trump presidency, greed, arrogance, and ethereal fantasy replaced sensible economic parameters and responsible management within the financial sector of the American economy. Too few people had too much surplus capital and too little interest in putting it into the productive economy; instead, they invested in bets that many of them didn't really understand, all in hopes of making a significant and quick profit. The ultimate victim in this farce was human trust; when it died, everyone pulled back into their shells to protect their remaining capital.

Recessions provide the opportunity for the government to take the lead in transitioning away from a traditional boom–bust mentality toward a more realistically based economy that launches the Sustainability Age. President Obama indicated such tendencies in his first-term stimulus package and financial reform policies and in his proposed budgets, which contained some encouraging tri-worlds aspects to them. President Biden's Build Back Better program includes $500 billion for climate change.

It remains to be seen if the transition to longer-term goals for the American economy can be enacted by the government or whether the shorter-term bubble-building practices of free-marketers will start to gain momentum again. Congressional Republican intransigence to Biden's policies indicates how difficult and time-consuming changing to a more sustainable future will be. High rollers are still playing a lot of yesterday's risky games, and there is a lot of surplus capital around looking for places to bet.

What tri-worlds reality seeks to obtain from both public- and private-sector power brokers are some realistic concessions so humanity can survive. A tri-worlds goal: to reshape capitalism and democracy so they fit more clearly into a planet with limited resources and a burgeoning population. This will be accomplished with the good will, support, and leadership of capitalist elites or, perhaps, more aggressively in the face of their narrower interests.

The sharp edges of capitalist excesses and greed must be rounded off in the name of species survival. The inspiration behind democracy must be reconstituted to include earthly realities. Everyone must realize that God will not give humankind a golden parachute; we must take care of ourselves, which means giving as well as receiving. Capitalists need to acknowledge that there really is a commonwealth that is just as important as private wealth.

All this is bitter medicine for a dualistic and differentiated human-made world obsessed with its own appetites, comforts, and social status. Ironically, business leaders who understand these new realities and then nest their enterprise's future within them will have the greatest potential for long-term prosperity because they will have anticipated needed transitions. They will have adapted their enterprises accordingly, and they will have gained the confidence and trust of employees, customers, and the citizenry. Their decisions will evidence dignity.

Tri-worlds politics wants to harness leadership energy and capitalist values into a re-focus of private enterprise toward species survival, economic sustainability, and more emulation of natural processes in productive technologies (green steel, green cement, green energy). Any company that achieves these ends will achieve profitability and success because common citizens will support them. Veterans of the Industrial and Information Ages need to take the lead in the transition to the Sustainability Age and natural capitalism, not fight these ideas.

Company vision and mission statements need to align more clearly with the reality of life's basics, limited natural resources, and the sameness of species needs and desires. Holding on to highly differentiated status, denying human sameness, and obsessing over ever-growing personal wealth degrade a leader's life and legacy; these priorities deny new market opportunities and are also a fast track to vociferous resistance, obsolescence, and failure. To believe that profits cannot be attained within a greener and more sustainable economy is delusional and simply pig-headed, old-style capitalism.

Also, for business leaders not to see or to deny the sea change going on within the minds and hearts of individual American citizens regarding species survival and natural integrity is to bury one's head in the sand. "Groundswell," "catharsis," "metamorphosis"—words like these barely scratch the surface of how deeply many citizens feel the need for more consideration of planetary limits and sustainable economics. Our collective common sense yells out for new directions, new leadership, and new politics. Why? Because carbon-based fuels and a service-driven, consumer economy can no longer sustain the United States as a nation or retain the Unites States as the role model for realistic progress and hope for the world.

Both business and governmental leaders lag the thinking and concerns of common citizens regarding these issues because transitioning to a less carbon-dependent economy interferes with ongoing, vested mono- or bi-world interests—interests that keep traditional leaders in power and established elites ultra-comfortable. The productive, thinking majority of American citizens see clearly what many public- and private-sector leaders do not. We accept the need for self-interests to modify traditional drives in favor of alignment with practices that stop denaturing the planet, and we see the value of a sustainable and healthful common good.

Accepting the human paradox and tri-worlds thinking has a long-term conscience that private mono- and bi-world thinkers lack. Special interest arguments that run contrary to species survival will peter out at some point because these arguments will no longer make sense. The current mindset of enriching the already rich will run its course as a species/planetary consciousness gains hold. How many more Cuban cigars can oligarchs smoke? How much more twenty-year-old Scotch can they sip? How many Patek Philippe or Jaeger-LeCoultre watches can they collect? Excuses made by oligarchs as to why they deserve their billions will run dry. Increased momentum within the mass of humanity to attend to natural issues and species survival will make demands on the human-made world that downplay exceptional sensibilities about elites in favor of ones more balanced with our natural and common senses.

Through all its machinations and guises, the human-made world and its precedence-based tendencies have created a bind for our species. Capitalism, excessive materialism, and representative government are heading for the un-scalable wall of nature's limits. Our status-quo economic and political systems do not acknowledge the problems these limits bode.

As innumerable reputable scientists have proven, humanity will face significant challenges within this century just in the areas of climate change, adequate foodstuffs, overpopulation, and declining natural resources (irrigation water, potable water, soil erosion, carbon-based fuels), among others. Short-term, profit-driven establishment capitalists respond to these macro concerns with denials, pseudo-science, and deferrals, while like-minded politicians shape the law to support those who support them. To reiterate a major point, capitalists and politicians almost always squander the long term in favor of the short term. They want paybacks now so they can enjoy the kudos and admiration (and reelection) that come with attending to the present and near future. Why keep playing this game?

Political and capitalist leaders need to commit to longer planning horizons that acknowledge known inevitabilities along with financial commitments and incentives to assure the actualization of new, longer-term policies (renewable energy, net-zero carbon emissions, sustainable development practices). With regard to nature, we humans have spent our cash, and now we're approaching our credit limit; nature can't support our appetites for more of everything for more people forever. Economic progress needs new, more sustainable directions and leadership with the chutzpah and persistence to take us there.

Proven leadership already exists within the private and public sectors. These leaders need to recognize the importance of human sameness, life's basics, sustainable development, and natural integrity and then acculturate these values into their own areas of influence and control. The reform of institutions and processes needs to dominate their political instincts, not just quarterly performance and compounded-growth obsessions.

Elites

Capitalism and democracy play large to the possibility that individuals can become rich and powerful—the much-admired rags-to-riches story. Implicit in this potential rests a separation of the elite individual from average citizens and their lesser ways, and capitalism and democracy have delivered.

Most of the world's elites achieved their status through industry, commerce, finance, technology, or political/military power. Some elites rose through intelligence and hard work, while others had wealth given to them through bloodline (or crime), facts that may not matter much in the end. **Status is what counts for elites, however vague and mercurial that concept may be.** Sitting on the yacht, enjoying the sea breeze; enjoying the company of A-list celebs at an exclusive soiree; limos, tailored suits, designer originals, vintage wines, private jets, smiley pics in the newspaper's society section or even in *Vanity Fair*—all pleasures of elitedom.

Earned status, inherited status, stolen status—these are the goals of subspecies *Homo elitus*, especially within their domain of the human-made world. Of course, elected leaders of governments get included in elite circles while they are in power; at least they are tolerated (and potentially useful). Some politicians even get full-time elite status by dent of accomplishment or recognition like a Nobel Peace Prize.

The underlying premise of a planet essentially run by *Homo elitus* types stems from the centuries-old precedent of the few leading the many and the belief that "might makes right." Kings, emperors, and presidents have brought forth both glamorous and disastrous results for followers during the span of human history. Captains of industry and financiers have generated tremendous economic wealth along with greed-spawned recessions and depressions. Elite clergy have dangled salvation carrots in front of the masses and given them eternal hope on a planet dominated by cold and unforgiving natural forces.

Elites of all sorts feign having a conscience and caring about humanity, but their actions often belie their words. **The gods of status, wealth, and power give elites three trump suits in a four-suit deck. Middle-class citizens and the poor will always feel the pressure of elite thumbs upon them as long as humanity regales the elitist myth of "wealth + power + status = happiness."**

Just like a teenager infatuated with a rock star, humanity will continue to live a manqué existence as long as it idolizes its exceptions at the expense of human sameness. The mindless adoration of elites costs the species much more than such adulation benefits it; in fact, it is corrupting. Celebrity status, mind-boggling riches, and hero worship—how can such accolades not warp a human mind (like Donald Trump's)?

The survival mechanism upon which elites depend most is the desire of the masses to be like them. Elites with power and high profile believe they will survive in style as long as they never shut this ajar door—that is, the possibility that everyday citizens can rise to elite ranks, at least in America. Also, so as not to betray their status ideals, elites will hardly ever reveal their innermost secret: personal fulfillment and happiness remain elusive no matter how much wealth, celebrity, or power one has.

The paradox with *Homo elitus* status is magnetic. The crème de la crème, their world of haute couture and luxury, their wealth/power/celebrity all play to the exceptionalist fantasies of most citizens. That is the attraction. The repulsion comes with their betrayal of their privilege, their hauteur and greed, their childish manifestations of tabloid brattiness and ingratitude. Many of the beautiful people have an ugly underbelly. They often do not live up to the fantasy expectations admirers have of them; they disappoint us when they turn out to be just flawed human beings like the rest of us. The most admirable elites tend to be the dead ones—the saints, the heroes, the personifications of mostly differentiated values that populate historical volumes and holy books.

Elites work hardest at staying elite. Whole industries exist to service this endeavor. Fashion, prime real estate, decor, art, jewelry, vintage automobiles, yachts—all play to the whims and wiles of the rich and famous. **What elites have that the rest of us do not is a surfeit of comfort; they love this fact and always want more. Sustenance isn't something elites worry about much, but security plays to their neurotic and/or paranoid fears.**

A key element of being elite is being known but inaccessible, being distant from the everydayness of common people. Elites want lots of privacy—mansions behind gates, private islands, exclusive elevators for penthouse use only. *Homo elitus* love projecting the allure of separateness from the crowd, of svelte persona and appearance, and of complete uniqueness and deservedness. Reinforcement for their vanity depends on affirmation from their family, their peers, and the admirers who revere and stroke them.

Elites think they have outwitted paradox, contradiction, and irony by being rich, clever, and separate from the rest of us. Being exceptional lifts them above the woes and stresses of workaday life and provides a chrysalis of spun gold in which they can enjoy their *vie blessé*. Being a part of elitedom and being surrounded by others in their class creates a somehow cleaner existence for them, a life actualized from their happy-ever-after childhood dreams, a higher existence where elegance and only the well-qualified few mingle. Actually, all elites have done is to change the setting in which paradox, contradiction, and irony occur. In truth, elites face the potential for more deception and treachery than do we average citizens because the games they play involve higher stakes.

All elites depend on formal power of one kind or another for achieving, maintaining, and elevating their status. Constitutions, laws, bylaws, corporate charters, wills, trusts, portfolios, contracts—some legal paperwork somewhere gives elites the power to own and control their private interests. All the rigors of planning, bargaining, negotiating, and commanding resources justify their reward; they are convinced of that. They are the masters of deal making. Ooooeeee, to be such a genius— and to be lucky too! Every elite wants to stay on the right side of income inequality—the 1 percent side.

Elites do not see any moral dilemmas with capital hoarding. The top eighty-five wealthiest people in the world, according to the Oxfam committee, have more wealth than half of the world's seven-plus billion population combined. Also, more likely than not, those eighty-five individuals believe they deserve every penny they have. Elites suffer from the incurable affliction of deservedness, a plague that is rampant throughout the upper tiers of capitalist cultures. Dedication, smarts, hard work, determination, killer instinct, right-time/right-place thinking, kissing the right ass—these are the symptoms; beautiful arm-candy wife, mansions on both coasts, crushing the competition, taking no prisoners, being the ass kissed— these are the just rewards. The species and planet have no squares on the Deservedness board game.

Billionaires seem common these days. Perspective: Spending $1,000 a day, it would take 2,738 years to spend $1 billion.

No matter how much wealth elites accumulate, it never seems to be enough. Elitism generates huge appetites. Democracy, through its laws, and capitalism, in its essence, support elitist tendencies by encouraging and accommodating massive accumulations of private wealth. Even criminals and their gangs have their own governance structures and ways of concentrating power and rewards, to a select few. At the other end of the scale, the global poor, with their extralegal property agreements, also evidence elitist tendencies because everyone wants to feel and be exceptional.[37] The species has never been without elites of one kind or another and probably never will be. Get used to it because this innate separation tendency within our species will not go away.

Elites, no matter how despicable or admirable they are, don't constitute a major concern for the species; however, **it is what elites do with their status, power, and money that concerns human-paradox realists and tri-worlds advocates.** Decisions made by *Homo elitus* types need to be evaluated on three factors: (1) wealth management and disposition; (2) recognition of the human paradox and tri-worlds reality; and (3) humility/empathy (or at least the appearance thereof).

Most rich people amassed their fortunes through repetition and deal making rather than innovation or giant technology strides. They got rich by making the same corn flakes and the same burgers and the same gasoline they made yesterday and will make tomorrow. Success in one area allows elites to consider investing some of their capital in other interests to diversify their holdings, but most of their profits come from producing the same widgets the same way, day in and day out—the cash cow we referred to earlier. Sure, there will be some failures for elites along the way, but prudent management of their assets will keep cranking out profits and wealth at least until these assets are fully depreciated and, the elites hope, a lot longer than that.

The privileged few *do* have responsibilities to others no matter how they became wealthy—some version of noblesse oblige. Everyone in a society knows that wealth comes from the efforts of workers and other assets, not solely from the efforts of a decision maker, owner, or wealth holder. Old wealth recognizes this more readily than new wealth. Elites can be found on every disk of the establishment backbone because their own best interests and those of the economic, social, and political structure that supports them oblige them to help the less fortunate. No smart elite wants to alienate the source of his/her power and comfort, and it is simply good business practice and public relations for elites to give back something to the communities that provide the wealth that makes them exceptional. The richest and most comfortable *Homo elitus* cannot reside exclusively in their champagne bubbles forever, although some try. With age, some wisdom, and inured feelings toward luxury, elites eventually arrive at the Peggy Lee moment: "Is that all there is?"

Guilt may drive elites to share their wealth; perhaps they may even have sincere interest and caring for others behind their philanthropy. It's sometimes hard to tell. Vanity, tax advantage, or old school ties may also move them to share, but what's most important to philanthropists is control of their donations; *they* have to decide where their money goes, not any vestige of government. Large endowments to universities, for instance, usually contain constraints on how the gift can be used. Being elite connotes superior taste and discernment when it comes to dispensing private wealth. Elites do not consider the government a peer within their ranks; after all, it's "my money, and I can do whatever I want with it." The government is more like the competition, the opposition, the resource of last resort. Yes, elites tend to think dualistically (surprise!).

Elites, especially those in the business community, also tend to be politically conservative because they helped create the status quo and profited from it. Progressive politics that encourage change threaten processes that supply their wealth and high comfort. While elites may have admirable eleemosynary tendencies, they will fight tooth and nail to gain and retain power in their corporate and political worlds. Many will bring to the political process the same level of commitment, audacity, and exploitation they used to gain power in the private sector.

Actions become relative to the wealth in hand or the need to add more wealth to an elitist's strongbox. Considerations of the natural world that do not serve elite interests will be opposed and denigrated at all costs by *Homo elitus* because these are interferences with their human-made world objectives. Ethereal concerns can also be argued down, elites believe, as secondary to the economic and social benefits gained by achievement of their human-made world goals, or these concerns can simply be patronized. Private interests provide public benefits in the form of jobs, taxes, and increased security—or so elite arguments go; yes, it is the old trickle-down theory that the richer they become, the better off those beneath them become. (Contradiction: despite the growth of the middle class, history proves the trickle-down theory to be a lie—the richer the richest have become, the poorer the poorest have become.)

Most elites attained their wealth through some development or production endeavor using natural and human resources. **Strident advocacy by private interests to continue enhancing the security and comfort of a privileged few who are already secure and comfortable confronts today's realities. The basic problem for elites is knowing when to say enough is enough.** How much more comfortable do elites need to be? How much money does it take for them to feel secure? Why is *more* always the right answer?

Through unthinking habit or simple greed, elites continue their obsession with more and more wealth accumulation along with pursuit of the "wealth + power + status = happiness" myth. Also, in a capitalist economy, usually, the more wealth you have, the easier it becomes to acquire even more wealth because you become a well-connected insider. Elite cliques support themselves, not nature or humanity.

In the not-so-distant future, elites of this traditional ilk will have to realize that the planet can no longer support their extravagance, endless consumption, and exclusivity. Their trickle-down wisdom will be severely challenged by nature's limits; there will have to be compromise or chaos. Again, this may take decades, but it will happen because the earth can no longer sustain unlimited upward mobility for more and more *Homo elitus* along with all the aspiring wannabes.

At some point, elites will have to face their own values, fight to support them, or compromise for the good of the species and planet. Elites will have choices: (1) deny challenges the world now faces and continue me-first/conservative/rising-tide-lifts-all-boats arguments; (2) provide their own solutions as to how global warming, overpopulation, and other species-wide issues can be addressed and solved by the business sector or through philanthropy; or (3) join the transition to a political posture that abrogates private interests to some degree in favor of the common good, species-wide interests, and natural integrity. Humankind should expect variations on all three of these themes throughout the twenty-first century.

Humility will benefit elites in the long run and may help them retain a high yet somewhat diminished financial status. Sincere empathy would help too. Admitting species sameness, advocating stances that benefit the common good, decrying greed for greed's sake—these and other actions that evidence more give than take will generate respect and common identity with the rest of humankind. Images of a newfound generosity for elites should not be hard to present since elites own the communications media. Common citizens tolerate elites, even admire and envy them, but our planet will not be sacrificed just so elites can prance, dance, and romance in ultra-comfort style. That behavior has gone on long enough. Elites who ignored macro issues in the past got the American, French, and Russian Revolutions, among other takedowns. Few want to go down that path today, but it always remains an option.

For their own personal edification, it might also be a good idea for *Homo elitus* types to don a pair of jeans and a work shirt now and then. Silver-spoon/trust-funded/polo-pony elites do not get much respect outside their own social circles, which is why most don't venture outside these circles very often. Elite women who only wear design originals as well as alexandrite, tourmaline, and conch-pearl jewelry, who shop for a living, who bitch-manage the help—how do they benefit the species, nature, or God? Elite men who never question their lives, who feign honesty/patriotism/conservative values yet mercilessly exploit others and keep a young lover or two on the side—what values do they exude beyond status strutting, cutthroat capitalism, and moral hypocrisy? Also, rich children—how many are spoiled, valueless, and confused? How many are druggies and psychologically wounded, the ultimate victims of their parents' status-driven mythologies?

Rich and pampered folks could greatly expand their horizons through acceptance of the human sameness and human-caring concepts and then doing something about them. Set up a foundation dedicated to relieving some slice of human misery. Donate money to the poor. Help build a house for a needy family. Be a big brother or big sister to a one-parent kid. "Adopt" an immigrant family. Put a hair net on and serve turkey at the homeless shelter on Thanksgiving Day. Do something, anything, to admit and internalize your humanity, your sameness with the rest of the species—and get your kids and rich friends involved too. You will be amazed how good sharing with others makes you feel, how de-stressing and possibly life changing such experiences can be.

Elites rooted in the ethereal world also need to reevaluate their importance. The basis for everything they advocate, sell, or preach is mostly emotional tissue paper in the rough-and-tumble human-made and natural worlds. Some elite entertainers gain follower thrall via their magnificent imaginations that they exhibit in a book, theater, movie, video game, or television production. However, unlike entertainers, clerics cannot step out of their professional roles and admit their work is just escapist fantasy. Religious leaders are committed to consistently living their teachings and preachings—the pope is the pope every day, a rabbi is a rabbi is a rabbi, an ayatollah is a Muslim elite 24/7. The farther the promises of a religionist are from the other two worlds, the more dedication and fervor their doctrine requires. Conversely, inclusion of the other two worlds in religious thought and teaching helps subdue radical tendencies and increases the ability of humans to understand one another.

Well-heeled elites of all modes have modeled their modus operandi on royalty and aristocrats of old, most of whom, in the end, valued their legacies more than the fellow human beings who made them wealthy and powerful in the first place. Somehow rich folks, famed rulers, and religious leaders throughout history became better and higher in their own minds and in their local settings; somehow they became made of different protoplasm than the rest of us. As science proves and death affirms, these differentiations simply are not true.

Elites have difficulty admitting their basic humanity and the ultimate low worth of their status to the species because they have created such a huge chest of rationalizations as to why their status is merited. Perhaps greedy and ego-driven elites need to be ridiculed and put down more often. Maybe they need to be laughed at; maybe then, they will see that we everyday citizens have figured out their games and how selfish their status priorities are. Now's the time to call them out, to help them find a better path to happiness by sameness recognition and planet caring.

As just discussed, nature has not made *Homo elitus* exceptional via their physical composition. Elites are made of bone, blood, and muscle, just like the rest of us, and these all wither and expire no matter what a person's station in life. Elite status has value primarily in the human-made world, where it is highly regarded in some quarters but largely ignored by most of humankind. "So you're rich/powerful/a celebrity. That's nice—but what else have you got?" Elites who have internalized ethereal fantasies about themselves are just as wacky as common folks with similar delusions. Political and business egos that seek "their place in history" do so within a pod-centric environment, not a species-wide one. Also, if the Bible is correct, then life after death won't be too comfortable for the rich because they simply won't fit through that needle's eye any more than a camel will.

Introspection, new ideas, and healthier attitudes about the exceptionalism of elites might as well occur sooner rather than later. Most elites attained their status because of their willingness to be the high priests of conformity to the economic, political, and social demands of their time. Even on a global tri-worlds–balanced planet, there will be elites for the same reason. Some citizens have to take risks and provide leadership; we average citizens will still elevate the few leaders among us based on their potential, promises, and performance. **Perhaps a new model for elites will emerge during the Sustainability Age, one that evinces intelligence, eloquence, and caring for others rather than McMansions, condescension, and shady backroom dealings.**

Another paradox for elites gets down to their endless quest for differentiation that, in the end, makes them all the same. Rich folks all have big houses, fancy cars, and lots of stuff. Religious elites all claim knowledge/faith/ credibility for an exclusive path to God. Political elites come and go, rise and fall, yet only rarely do they leave behind results that prove beneficial for their portion of the species. Elite themes on this dualistic and differentiated planet repeat themselves, just like average citizens' themes do.

The earth we live on now moves in directions that threaten traditional human-made and elite precedents. Musty, crusty, rich conservatives who attack the government but fail to manage it well when they have the reins are being shoved aside by voters fed up with their dualistic and hateful self-absorption. Not only in America but also throughout the world, regressive and bellicose rhetoric is starting to give way to rationales that recognize nature and its limits, that modify human-made systems to sustainably meet human needs, and that decry ethereal systems that do not live up to their teachings of love, tolerance, and humility.

What elites probably have to fear most are their own children and grandchildren as well as future generations who will want answers as to why their progenitors didn't advance humankind and the planet when they had a chance: "What happened, Grandpa?" Many a shamed youngster might yet piss on Grandpa's grave.

Elites need to start thinking beyond dualisms, gated communities, and their abundance of comfort toys. Humankind will welcome their input. Business elites who value their status will find opportunities in this transition just as they always have—building green efficiencies into their products and services, supporting eco-tech through new industry and biomimicry, making voluntary industry-wide commitments to reduce social costs and working within nature's limits. There's profit and sustainable development potential in so many areas, not to mention resultant good will among customers and employees. Political elites will follow voters' consciences (and their dollars) by structuring governments that attend to the sustenance, security, and comfort of citizens in sustainable and healthful ways. Religious elites, hopefully, can join together to find common ground that washes away old hatreds and affirms the importance of human interactions here on Earth. Elites have a lot of homework, behavior modification, and soul searching to do.

Middle Class

Earlier references in this book claim the perspective of the common, average, and everyday citizen. All these claims come with authority since I am so completely middle class. I claim to be an average person because I am. I'm not famous, rich, or a genius. I'm a typical American in most statistical ways. I've worked all of my life. My IQ is not off the charts, and I don't have an Ivy League pedigree. I don't think I'm anything special except to my family and friends (sometimes, at least). I enjoy being a husband, father, and grandfather, and I've played by the rules pretty much all of my life. I'm liberal about some political issues, conservative about others, which makes me a self-proclaimed moderate. I vote, I'm a veteran, and I'm a stage four cancer survivor. I've been a single parent and am now a caregiver for my wife (stroke survivor). I value my health by exercising and by eating and drinking responsibly. I enjoy my privacy. I've done things I'm proud of and things I regret.

Having spent my life in Vanillaville, I can offer an experiential view of the American Dream. I'm not alone. I have millions of compatriots right behind me who have baby-boomed their way into a comfortable existence and who are retiring, thinking about retiring, or realizing that they'll never be able to kick back in style. This aging mass of humanity exhibits all the good, bad, and indifferent morality that resides in the *real* America, where the vanilla beans grow and where they are picked and processed into social norms/values, economic trends, and political priorities.

Europe, Asia, and Australia have also created substantial middle classes, but America still has the widest bulge in the bell curve of any nation or continent on the planet. Also, to interject a contemporary irony, one-party China has the fastest growing middle class in history thanks to its authoritarian version of capitalism, another testament as to how varying "vanilla" can be.

A democracy's middle class works well for the human species because it is the great tamer. Not being poor, not having to grovel for daily bread, and not having to be subservient to some intimidating/criminal/militaristic element helps keep fear and belligerent human instincts in check. Having a decent place to live, owning a piece of property, having the opportunity to climb a career ladder, having a few bucks saved or invested keeps common citizens interested and focused on life's basics. Creating or being part of a family, being productive, and contributing to both an economy and a community keeps citizens busy and interested in what is going on around them. Having the resources available to gather more knowledge, to have fun, to love family/friends, and to plan for the future directs energies to fruitful outcomes for individual citizens and the overall economy.

The breadth of America's middle class includes so many different interest pods that there is something out there for everyone's vocational and avocational interests. A growing middle class serves as the species' workshop in which ideas and plans can flourish and out of which extend the tendrils of economic growth, innovation, and prosperity.

We American common citizens do not aspire to live in Hearst Castle because we've got our own little delights going on (but a sleepover would be nice). Art, music, sports, and other cultural/recreational opportunities abound in our lives, along with access to national preserves that showcase nature's beauty. America's middle class provides the means by which education, creativity, and hard work can actualize aspirations by anyone willing to expend the mental and physical effort required. The middle class provides adequate sustenance, security, and comfort for tens of millions of people and, at the same time, provides the opportunity for gifted and ambitious individuals to claw their way up to elitedom. Key to all this activity is the freedom to believe, decide, and act in one's own self-interest—the basic key to America's success as a nation, as guaranteed by our constitution.

Those of us who live in modern societies are a product of where we live and what we do every day. We are the subspecies *Homo localus*. Our daily boundaries are family, career, and finances. We work for a living, carry a mortgage, and love our kids. Our lifestyle is the envy of the world because we have a culture, an economy, and a system of government that allows us to sustain ourselves within a relatively secure and comfortable environment. When the president talks about America, he is talking mostly about us. When economists cite consumers or white-collar/blue-collar workers, that's us. We are the voters who decide political directions and candidates' fates and the patriots who supply the taxes, technology, and personnel to fight America's wars. What we common citizens think and how we act collectively determines the destiny of the world's only superpower, however ephemeral that status may be.

We *Homo localus* citizens have just a few areas in our lives where we enjoy personal power or influence over others, but for the most part, our obligations control our lives. We accept that middle-class reality. Our time and energy go into paying bills, making the boss happy or tending a small business, getting the kids into college, and building a nest egg for retirement. We are straight, we're gay, we're confused and bemused. We are proud of our achievements, humble as they may be, but we realize there is always more to do. We are conservative about keeping what we already have because we worked hard to get it. On the one hand, we're captives of daily routine and rather boring; on the other hand, we have fun and are pretty happy with our lives.

Our main goals are to attain life's basics for our families and ourselves and to establish a sense of community with others around us who share our instincts, values, and faiths. Such a local community allows us to provide the sense of security that sustains our family unit, a community that provides some level of physical, social, and spiritual comfort. Our day-to-day endeavors give our lives purpose and varying degrees of fulfillment and frustration. We want to feel special about ourselves and about those we love so we can enjoy our achievements along with a sense of accomplishment and inner peace. We like to believe that we make a difference in our own and others' lives. We want to have fun. In the best of all worlds, our chosen community provides a sense of solidarity among its members, along with human dignity and happiness for the individuals within it. Also, our community network often provides a local identity that helps achieve success in the human-made world.

Because we are mostly a trusting lot, we middle-class citizens can be easily influenced by our own socioeconomic groups and by media that provide information and insights. Without news, entertainment, and social media, we would not know about things that often move us emotionally and intellectually, and because we don't want to feel left out, we tend to hug our TV screens, smartphones, and computers a lot. We would rather be in the know than not about issues that might affect us. Through our consumer spending, we determine what's popular and what's not. We are addicted to being entertained, and we really like to laugh as much as possible. At the same time, we can be extremely cynical and angry when we are lied to or betrayed.

Except for our job specialties, our tendency is to know a little about a lot rather than a lot about a little; we are information skimmers. We sometimes get emotional about the little we do know. When we see news of a tsunami or earthquake that kills thousands on the other side of the world, we pause and sympathize. We feel sad about the victims' pain and suffering; we are awed by nature's might, and we're glad that we're not the ones suffering. A few of us send money or donate blood, but by the next day, our sympathy is waning because it's back to the daily grind. We have to move on to near-at-hand issues that sustain our middle-class status. We simply don't have the time or temperament to keep a firm grasp on events and problems far away.

We common citizens like to consume; that's part of our role in today's capitalist economy. We are programmed to want a house, to have a nice car(s), and to acquire lots of stuff. Status for common citizens comes with having material possessions and being a stable and contributing member of the local community.

We *Homo localus* have a deep understanding of how to play the middle-class survival game. Every one of us has to provide some level of specialized labor, skills, or knowledge to be of value to others who need and can reward our talents. The key word here is "specialized." There are not too many classified ads seeking well-read generalists with a sense of balance about life who can make $100,000 a year. **We middle-class citizens know that the key to survival is being good at what we do especially well, maintaining interest/enthusiasm about our specialized knowledge and skills, and demonstrating both competence and vigor to our bosses, peers, and customers.**

What we haven't realized yet is how dependent upon specialization our minds have become. Only people recognized as experts in their fields have credibility and influence upon our political and economic decisions—or so it seems. Professional, social, and commercial differentiation has splintered us into thousands of special interests, minutiae-focused pods. We hardly ever think in species terms because of all the fractions that compose our lives, along with the credibility we give these micro units. We have yet to internalize the connectivity of systems thinking.

We also know the basic rules of the deeply seated dualism of formal versus informal organization found outside the home. These two operational orbits overlap and daily affect the lives of *Homo localus* citizens. Virtually all the organizations we belong to (business, professional, social, and religious) have laws and bylaws, policies and procedures that provide formal organizational structure. Administrative hierarchies are established by these governance codes that also include defined job duties and responsibilities. We respect formal rules and those charged with enforcing them because management decision-making power and direction stem from them. We common citizens like structure; it makes us feel secure.

On the other hand, we also know that most of the work/creativity gets done in the informal organization—the workforce, teams, committees, and other groupings. Because formal guidelines are usually general in nature, the specifics get covered by us, the human beings doing the work. What we know, who we know, how many times we have performed certain tasks before—these more informal relationships and functions often make the difference between getting a job done or not. Formal documents and bylaws don't make the honey; we worker bees do that.

Doing a good job and keeping our noses clean (or brown) keeps working citizens in good stead with the formal organization. Friendly relations with peers, being honest and trustworthy, and working hard keeps us in good graces with others in the informal organization. Day in and day out, we prefer life in the informal orbit, but we keep an eye on the formal orbit to see if any space debris from higher-ups may be headed our way. The formal organization provides the rules and regulations; the informal organization provides the talent and wherewithal to get work done. These functions are mutually dependent, and that's not going to change anytime soon because this human-made world system works well.

The price common citizens pay for abiding by formal laws, rules, and regulations is conformity and obedience. By agreeing to abide by formal conditions, we common citizens allow others who control these writs to have power over us in the human-made world. Theoretically, these higher-up bosses are the best and brightest among us. Sometimes that rings true, sometimes not. Business and civic leaders who acknowledge the existence and importance of the informal organization are generally held in higher regard by common citizens than those who do not, so unit performance improves. Leaders who distance themselves from those who get the work done harm the best interests of both formal and informal groups, so unit performance does not improve, or it declines. Common citizens will extend respect to those who manage us as owners/executives extend respect and honesty to those getting the job done. Individual dignity means a lot to *Homo localus* citizens. Mono-world or bi-world decision makers who set unrealistic goals, who set my-way-or-the-highway standards, and who disrespect employees will usually lose in the end; we common citizens will see to that. Karma, karma, karma.

Middle-class citizens get first exposure to the human-made world concepts of conformity, power, and obedience from parents, teachers, and the playground bully. Parents and teachers have power by virtue of their proximity and size; kids know that these big people are the source of love, food, shelter, and knowledge, so they obey and feel secure. The bully intimidates, threatens, and ostracizes; kids feel fear, anger, and isolation. Strength in numbers becomes an early learned concept thanks to bullies who also help children internalize the dualistic concepts of bravery and cowardice. Kids befriend others who will accept them and play with them; they develop their own friendship pods that make them feel secure and comfortable. In addition to the innumerable good things resulting from a child's formative experiences come gangs, cliques, and social stratifications that carry into adolescence and adulthood.

We common citizens will spend billions of dollars taking care of our pets or our lawns but comparatively little to help poor people in Africa and Central and South America; we're mostly tight fisted and local with our charity. Proximity benefits from our largesse; distance brings suspicion and reluctance to ante up. "What are the governments in Africa and Central/South America doing?" we ask. "Why can't they help their own citizens? Don't we send them foreign aid?" TV commercials with doe-eyed children living in filthy barrios may tug at our heartstrings, but there are too many questions and suspicions for most common citizens to donate long distance, especially when there's United Way and other charities helping local needs.

We are also leery about charitable sympathies because we're usually uncomfortable with our personal finances. Either on a spreadsheet, in our checkbooks, or in our heads, we keep tabs of monthly income and expenses and know what depressingly little is left over after the bills are paid. We spend this surplus, save it, or invest it depending on our overall financial health and family needs. Some months, we have discretionary dollars to spend; some months, we don't because we have to buy a new set of tires, the water heater goes out, or the mortgage/rent goes up.

The Great Depression taught our grannies to live within their means and to be grateful for a regular paycheck. We middle-class citizens love these old-timers, but we don't give their advice much heed. We are constantly coming up with new desires, new needs, and broader wants; we want some hot fudge and sprinkles in our vanilla lives.

To get the fun stuff, we often stick our toes in the chilly waters of the credit pool. We know that some people are fighting sharks in the deep end of this pool, so we pay off our credit cards every month or at least try to pay more than the minimum due. We know the importance of a decent credit rating because we live in an economy that encourages debt and is awash in it. Maintaining a cool social demeanor for family and friends in the face of the never-ending challenges of cash flow management, debt repayment, and minimal/no savings just adds more stress to the already tightly wired lives of many *Homo localus*. We are more slaves to finances than masters of them.

Once we middle-class citizens have achieved a desired level of financial comfort, we appreciate what we've got, but we don't linger in that mental state for long; instead, we simply get used to our new comforts, and that becomes normal. As soon as we are comfortable in our new house, car, or school, we begin to think about additional things to own, new vistas to explore, more relationships to build. While most of us will financially stall out on the climb up the consumption and job ladders, the desire to climb higher hardly ever goes away until middle or old age sets in, and even then, it lingers as ethereal thoughts of what might have been.

Security and comfort can be corrupting forms of differentiation among common citizenry in that there is always someone who seems better situated than we are. Working citizens expend a tremendous amount of time and energy trying to match physical realities with self-concepts of values, status, and style. Exactly how comfortable/secure someone is must manifest itself through the home, furnishings, clothes, automobiles, and so on, which others in the same peerage feel an obligation to match, or we feel a need to match them. This keeping-up-with-the-Joneses trap can inspire acquisitiveness, destroy marriages, lead to bankruptcy, and divert a tremendous amount of time and energy away from nurturing family relationships. We *Homo localus* can be blind fools to upward mobility at times.

Comfort also appeals to a behavioral trait that comes with age: coasting. As common citizens enter middle age, the goal becomes retention of the status quo, not career or social climbing. The sought-for end becomes making it to retirement, where one can wallow in one's own superfluousness, where there is no compunction to set the world on fire, where accumulating untold wealth or outmaneuvering business or political opponents generates little enthusiasm. Responsible disengagement from the rat race takes years to achieve, and—don't kid yourself—everyone with some gray hair is thinking about it.

Squeezing by constitutes one aspect of common citizens' darker side. While we middle-class Americans are generally good natured and well-intended, we've been known to present a false front, to cheat now and then, to deceive our family and friends a bit, and to lie if we can get away with it. These are usually little sins and misdemeanors, nothing too hurtful or something we do often.

By hooking our morals/values car to the middle-class train, we commit ourselves to the mores of working for a living, participating in local life, and replenishing the middle class with children who appreciate these values. Hypocrites, we are when we dump used oil down the storm sewer, dent someone else's car in a parking lot and then drive away, or submit a not-wholly-accurate Form 1040. We all speed on the highway, we all gossip, and we all have unspoken lusts. But we know that by not rattling the foundations of the middle class too much and by not shaking the tree of centrist values too hard, we can go along and get along like everybody else. We exonerate ourselves for our secret misdeeds while we hypocritically "tsk, tsk" the sins of others. If there is an edge we can gain for our family and ourselves and we think we can get away with it, we just might take it. We value our good name and status, but we are not beneath a minor transgression now and then if it helps us squeeze by financially.

Relationships are another area where common citizens get flaky. We've got real family, friends, and acquaintances with whom we maintain loving and caring relationships. We also have family we'd be happy never to see again, coworkers we don't consider friends, and acquaintances/neighbors we avoid because we don't want them to become family or friends. Our human-made world is awash in forced civilities, commercial relationships, and purchased friendships that we don't value beyond a potential career or social gain. Many relationships are maintained simply for their usefulness; we really don't like some of these people.

We middle-class citizens carry an invisible case of masks with us to work or school, to family reunions, to religious and social gatherings. We change these masks instantly at the sight or sound of a coworker, neighbor, or pest. Sincerity? Pseudo-affection? Bare tolerance? Sure, we've got a mask for that. However, unlike the easy-to-read masks of youngsters, adult masks are more placid and more prone to an initial, welcoming smile and some pro forma felicitations. These masks are more homogeneous, more apparently welcoming, yet sometimes, they are barely able to contain insincerity or discomfort. It's as if we *Homo localus* adults all went to the same sales training and learned the same manipulation techniques, the same paste-on/corporate smile, and the same social connivances, and during this training, we learned that the ultimate goal of our presence is to seem not to be wearing a mask at all. We can be real masters of faux interest and insincere sincerity when we want to.

Only as we evaluate and categorize others based on our own biases and differentiated priorities do our family, business, business-social, or purely social relations have a chance to spark beyond trivialities into sincere interest in one another. Because we average citizens must maintain so many forced relationships with bosses, coworkers, and customers to serve our interests, the opportunities to go beyond chit-chat civilities may be rare and go unexplored. Status consciousness and maintenance of obligatory relationships often militate against opportunities to better understand family members, to become closer to friends, or to grow acquaintances into truly friendlier relations. Also, our closely held reserve of dualities and differentiations keep us apart from those who may broaden and enrich our lives. We bypass such opportunities in favor of the known and the comfortable—behavior that is the essence of social conservatism and anti-species attitudes. **We common citizens oftentimes struggle to get beyond our own inhibitions to develop deep-feeling and stimulating relationships with others outside our local sphere, and we rationalize away the opportunities.** We let a lot of potential closeness with other human beings slip away, and we often end up lonelier than we need to be, largely as a result of our dualistic, highly differentiated society and our adherence to its demands.

On the other hand, we get payback from involvement and commitments made to local professional/civic/religious/social/sports groups. These pods provide ways for individuals to express interest and caring with others who have similar inclinations. Acquaintances and friendships develop among members of these groups, along with business contacts and varying degrees of respect. We individual *Homo localus* citizens enhance feelings of self-esteem, enjoy the company of others, and feel pride and recognition in our associations within these groups. These interests often play the socialization role schools used to play. Beyond family and religious ties, commitments to these associations can generate feelings of loyalty, obligation, and fulfillment. Concurrently, effective solutions to local problems can also generate hostility and defensiveness when questioned or challenged by outsiders. All politics is local because outsiders cannot possibly know "our world" as well as "we" do.

Perhaps the darkest side to America's middle class comes with our lack of understanding and appreciation for others within the species. We live inside a cocoon located in a cloister deep within the bowels of our individual minds and select communities. We have biases, fears, and prejudices about people who are not like us, and we don't really know why we give these doubts credence. This bothers our consciences sometimes. We oftentimes can't explain what it is that inhibits us. Is it their race? How they dress? Their accent?

We common citizens value the ideals our parents, teachers, and others taught us, yet we know these values may have outlived their worth. We know that having hostile/standoffish/doubtful feelings about others may be morally obsolete. We hold on to these divisive rationales anyway because they seem to protect the securities and comforts we already have; it is better to err on the side of caution to conserve things most dear to us. We value our differences more than the seeming abstractness of human sameness because the familiar is more secure and comfortable than something new and not locally accepted. We trust our cautious intuitions and irrational prejudices long before we open them up to insightful evaluation. Some of us never question our attitudes and prejudices because they are "just part of who we are."

We venture outside our swaddled lives occasionally to investigate new economic, political, and social possibilities, but our primary goal is the preservation of domestic principal—that is, keeping what we already have and growing it when we can. This parochialism makes us feel secure yet distances us from the world's problems, all the woes we see on TV. We become inured to protecting our lifestyle, our routines, and our feelings of security; we are masters at rationalizing away or minimizing our role as contributors to worldwide problems (climate change, pollution, poverty). We are very slow to involve ourselves in issues that fall outside our normal sphere and don't affect us directly. We often default to our ethereal world conceptions rather than to the realities of the human-made and natural worlds. **Our middle-class paradox boils down to the concurrency of centripetal forces that pull us inward toward maintaining and improving our local status and to the centrifugal forces that pull us outward toward more universal activities, ideas, and understandings.**

Managing the struggles of daily work and family life always take priority over issues beyond our immediate influence and control. This inward focus is what we in the middle class call being responsible to ourselves, our families, and our culture. This is the socially conservative frame of mind that comes from successfully achieving self-interests, and it pervades the American middle class. Yet, this is the very sentiment that hinders our ability and willingness to think and act as members of a species. We do not realize that achieving middle-class security is also self-incarcerating, isolating, distancing "us" from "others."

Despite our internal tugs-of-war, a desire for personal freedom lives at the heart of American common citizens' motivations. We can't imagine life without it. The need to control (or appear to control) one's own life, one's time and resources, to make plans and then to carry them out—these are the common denominators of freedom that stoke up yet fracture *Homo localus* lives into so many different motivations and masks.

Promises inherent within the American Dream also have costs that, eventually, we learn we must pay. Socially, for example, it's worth the time and effort to become involved, to befriend others, to become interested in others because these relationships support and sanction personal privacy. But once private time becomes available, its sacred value often expires too soon as the needs of work, relationship maintenance, and other commitments impose themselves. Still, we regard the need for some privacy and introspection as an essential factor of personal life, especially as we age.

To protect our achievements and comforts, we average citizens often dampen our true thoughts and opinions and defer to those of leaders, bosses, or stronger personalities in our midst, those who are more interested, aggressive, or adept at relationship building than we are. Because most of the activities of political leaders and elites occur outside the domain of *Homo localus* lives and do not threaten our personal privacy, we tend more to complacency than to aggressive activist fervor about them. The role of citizen—one empowered by a constitution that guarantees individual rights, a vote—suits us just fine, even if that's as far as we're willing to go.

In the long run, we middle-class Americans don't really believe that one individual can make a big difference in today's world, especially when confronted with the scale, power, and wealth of complex societies. The bosses, the rich, and other elites are under the thin right arm of the human bell curve, and that's okay. We don't value obsessive ambition, greed, and the killer instinct as much as our bosses and political leaders do. We common citizens don't enjoy playing the power game; we'd rather get rich hitting the lottery.

We also know that virtually everyone who gets his or her fifteen minutes of fame fades from the scene fairly quickly. We do respect any individual who can be a hero when standing up for what is "right." (That classic photo of the man standing in front of a tank near Tiananmen Square comes to mind.) We feel for the police and fire crews who risk their lives protecting us and for our airmen, soldiers, sailors, and marines who fight and die in conflicts they often don't understand/support, but they do their jobs anyway.

It takes something titanic to wrest the attention of *Homo localus* away from the strictures of daily local life. The September 11, 2001, attack on the

World Trade Center turned our heads, made us mad, and made us sad. Strong emotions lingered, but most of us didn't have time to dwell on them. While we will never forget or forgive this atrocity, we had to get back to work to bring in a paycheck, take the kids to school, mow the lawn—life's daily routines. Speaking of routines, that's essentially what we common citizens are—people who mostly do what we did yesterday and what we'll do tomorrow.

The harshness of survival, the difficulty of extending and improving life given nature's challenges, the personal challenges we all face trying to make a living and raising a family in the human-made world, living a wholesome life, and being a good person—these are the things on which most common citizens dwell. There's little energy left after attending to these things.

We *Homo localus* citizens do not have the time, understanding, or patience for mega issues like war and peace, macroeconomics, string theory, or dark energy; distant issues like these don't affect us day in and day out, so we really don't worry about them. Leaders, elites, and geniuses need to deal with these macro issues, not us. While many of us would like to be better informed about big issues, we simply don't have the energy or time to devote to them. Our middle-class tendency is to be active and committed to the demands of daily local life, less sure and reactive to issues distant or abstract.

Perhaps the grandest irony we *Homo localus* Americans face is entrusting our children to a future we have affected so little. Because we work in highly specialized jobs, because we commit ourselves to insular American middle-class values, and because we are more passive than active about life outside the home, the only real input we have that affects the public commons is our vote. Often we even squander that power through feelings of inconsequence: "Why should I vote? It won't make any difference. I don't have the time."

Citizenship needs rejuvenation in America today. As of the early twenty-first century, we *Homo localus* Americans have largely forgotten what citizenship entails. Citizenship doesn't mean that someone else will take care of you; it means just the opposite: citizens are responsible for their own well-being, and without conscientious management of your own fate, you will drift around in other people's priorities. However, at the same time, no citizen can deny their own commonalities with other human beings or that the planet has limits, that humans have exceeded natural tolerances, or that you are unique but like the rest of us at the same time. You are local you, but you are also a member of the species; these undeniable truths involve rights, duties, and responsibilities.

During the Clinton, Bush 43, Obama, and Trump eras, we Americans squandered our rights and responsibilities away to leaders and elites who sometimes subverted democratic ideals, who profited from our fears/ignorance, and who exploited our credulity and apathy. We diluted the common good down to a thin gruel that had no nutritional civic value; we spent more time at one another's political throats than guiding the ship of state in a species-wise direction. We acted like adolescents who skipped civics class and couldn't even define the term. We created the red and blue propaganda machines and then let them run over us with hyperbole and lies.

The Sustainability Age can't abide this type of citizenship. We *individual* citizens have to grow beyond hedonism and subservience to antiquated ideals, habits, and attitudes. Old systems and carbon-based mindsets cannot be sustained on a limited planet. We all know this in our minds and hearts. We all know that we have to transition away from our overindulgences, our mindless loyalties, and our denials of provable realities. We middle-class citizens need to acknowledge and advocate Sustainability Age priorities: understanding of the human paradox, species sameness recognition, sustainable achievement of life's basics, peace, democracy and capitalism that recognize nature's limits, and natural integrity/replenishment. The more we hang on to aging and obsolete political ideals, the more obsolete and irrelevant America and the middle class will become.

Unfortunates

Years ago, Seattle's Space Needle Park had a big kinetic box sculpture full of pegs. I don't know if it's still there or not. Shiny steel balls dropped down onto the pegs and then bounced around, distributing themselves into a normal distribution. The end product always came out the same, the bell curve, yet the dropping balls always found their unique way to a final resting place.

Unlike the steel balls, we human beings influence where we end up in the distribution. We think, we make decisions, and we choose to believe or follow one peg over another. Of course, like the balls, we also experience randomness in our lives, events we cannot control, yet we all end up in the bell curve somewhere through intent, chance, or circumstance. At one end of this curve are the poor/homeless, the mentally ill, and criminals; at the other end are wealthy elites, celebrities, and powerful political/religious/ civic leaders. Common citizens of all make and model reside in the bulging middle. The Homo smarmus subspecies will be defined soon.

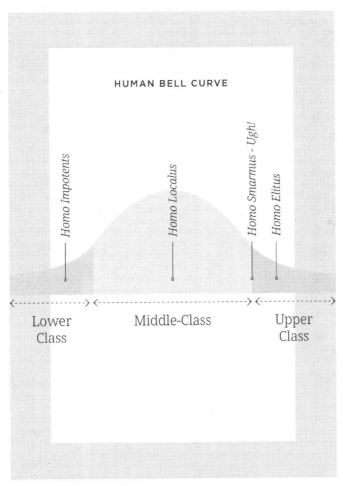

HUMAN BELL CURVE

Homo Impotents

Homo Localus

Homo Smarmus - Ugh!

Homo Elitus

Lower Class   Middle-Class   Upper Class

This tried but true normal distribution still applies to everyone in the human-made world. With a united focus our species can broaden the middle class and keep nature whole.

Nature plays a part in this distribution through pegs of physical largesse, innate intelligence, illness, or deformity. The human-made world plays a big role in an individual's fate by using pegs to qualify, advance, or redirect a ball's progress through human-made job requirements, level/quality of education, and so on. Ethereal religionists provide moral pegs they say will lead to a heavenly or hellish end, and they often claim they can pull a ball out of the curve altogether into some fantastic other dimension.

Unlike gravity, which naturally distributes the steel balls into a bell-curve shape, **human history shows that the bell curve can modify itself. It has over the centuries. We have proof that we can change.** There was no wide bulge of educated, well-fed common citizens, no middle class for most of civilization. That's a fairly recent phenomenon for which we average citizens are grateful. However, historically, there have always been extremes, those under the arms of the curve at the ends. The distance between these extremes generated the concepts of good and evil, virtue and vice, godly and ungodly, rich and poor, smart and stupid—the bases that established dualistic thinking. While most common folks in past times just wanted to live simple sustenance- and security-driven lives with a bit of comfort, warriors/kings/popes/tyrants kept moving the bar of civilization higher or lower with their beliefs and actions, thus reshaping the curve in their wake. It was not until the concepts of individualism and the middle class developed that leaders and elites began to feel pushback from others on the curve.

Humanity expends significant resources attending to the bell curve's extremes—poverty, ignorance, criminality, and other related ills at one end, power, wealth, and celebrity at the other. The lesser end gets attention through charity, movements seeking social justice, legal due process, or incarceration/rehabilitation/treatment. These people are the *Homo impotents*. Interests at the other fortunate end continue their activities largely unchallenged and unchecked because these are the heights to which humans aspire. The *Homo elitus* enjoy the human-made world's imprimatur to pursue self-identified ends; they expend their political capital trying to remove obstacles that stand in the way of their goals. They dispose of excess wealth through philanthropy—sometimes. They enjoy the yacht-y life. Those of us in the middle class work for those at the high end of the curve, and by so doing, we attain an ample enough degree of life's basics to keep us civil. Those at the low end of the curve struggle against poverty, ignorance, illness, discrimination, and crime to achieve some minimal degree of sustenance, security, and comfort. Such is life under today's human bell curve in America.

What is not apparent when looking at the bell curve are two things: the background upon which the curve exists and the threads that tie the extreme ends of the curve together.

Of course, the natural world provides the framework in which this human bell curve rests, just as human sameness provides the template upon which the hierarchical power pyramid sits. As mentioned earlier, without respect for the natural world and deference to its limits, we human beings are headed for avoidably hard times. Continued population growth, more and more inefficient natural resource drawdown, the pursuit of endless growth and profits, greed, and arrogance, all behaviors now extant in the carbon-based economy, undermine the natural platform upon which all human affairs depend. Human-made tracts inspired by ethereal models of individual freedom, high comfort, and universal happiness for all cannot be sustained in the long term because nature can't provide enough resources to meet insatiable human appetites. As much as our ethereal mind-brains would like to believe it, we cannot outgrow the planet's limits. The human bell curve will revert to former less-desired shapes without new thinking, actions, and respect regarding the natural world.

Threads that tie the rich to the poor, the religious to the heathen, and the law abiding to the criminal run thick and thin and span all three worlds. These threads can be fraught with emotions of various kinds. Rich folks pity the poor yet depend on them to buy the cigarettes, booze, and junk food they manufacture. Religious organizations extend a helping hand to those in physical need out of a spirit of generosity, yet they concomitantly hope to convert/save/reform some unfortunates and thereby expand their flocks. Lawyers, judges, and the police work hard to be objective and tolerant when dealing with crimes generated by ignorance, insanity, and recidivism, yet they would have no profession and no income if there were no criminals and mentally ill people. Many of those at the high end of the bell curve depend on the unfortunates at the low end for their well-being.

Self-indulgence, ignorance, bad luck, or mental defects make the *Homo impotens* among us a drag on society; they have low status and little economic worth and are considered society's dregs. These citizens often lead loveless and harsh lives. They escape from the human-made world and nature through alcohol or drugs. They have little money, status, or influence. Their life planning often goes day to day, meal to meal. Their everyday jurisprudence is jungle/street law. They have little security or comfort. Their minds may host ethereal fantasies that can be acted out in self-destructive or criminal ways.

From an economic point of view, occupants of the low end of the bell curve constitute labor markets with small potential for returns on investment, so the private sector avoids investment therein. Elites will sell to unfortunates but usually will not hire them because it's too risky, they're too undependable or unqualified, and there are, usually, plenty of job candidates available who don't require training or rehab. *Homo impotents* are fellow human beings, however, so society makes concessions to them. Improving the lot of the low end of the bell curve is almost wholly a responsibility of the individuals themselves, their families, governments, and private/religious charities.

At the high end of the curve, the wealthy and powerful control the direction of private sector funds so returns on investment (they hope) can be maximized and their own business interests can grow and be profitable. Public funds also flow into private coffers when governments let contracts for defense, infrastructure, and the privatization of government functions. From this private and public sector activity come jobs, innovation, and development that benefit middle-class citizens as well as those on the human curve's more fortunate side. From a socio-political point of view, the business/financial/legal processes inherent in democracy and capitalism have improved the sustenance, security, and comfort of more and more people by broadening the American middle class and thereby assuring these systems' survival for the foreseeable future. Bravo to democracy and capitalism for these achievements!

One of my sisters lives in upscale Walnut Creek, California. When we drive into San Francisco along the elevated portion of Interstate 580, we can see Oakland neighborhoods below. Aging houses crowded together, some boarded-up windows, an occasional tree here and there—all the typical signs of low-income communities can be seen adjacent to the viaduct. No doubt community leaders in Oakland are working hard to improve the lives and safety of those who live near the highway. No doubt there are good people, honest citizens, and hardworking homeowners down there trying to become part of Oakland's resurgence. Probably, there are some gangbangers, ex-cons, and future cons down there too—a thought one seldom has when driving through Walnut Creek's lush, architecturally controlled environs. What a difference a few miles make!

Every urban area in the United States has its own blend of rich, middle-income, and poor neighborhoods. Folks who live in the trash dumps of Nigeria and India would think Oakland's houses are palaces. People considered rich in some countries live in houses that would only qualify as middle class in America. Even in the United States, the sale of a clapboard two-bedroom house on LA's Venice Beach would buy a mansion in Arkansas. Disparities of wealth, varying feelings of neighborhood security, and standards of community comfort differ in every direction and to every degree throughout the United States. It's amazing how much time and energy we citizens expend on one of life's obsessions: trying to find (and afford) *just* the right house in *just* the right neighborhood.

My father was a jazz piano player who made his living as an optometrist. I was born in New Orleans because of his affinity for jazz. He loved his music and simply abided his profession. He was a terrible money manager and went bankrupt at least once; he and my mother argued almost exclusively about money. We never owned a house. We always rented. We moved six times in twelve years, once because we got evicted. I recently returned to New Orleans post Hurricane Katrina to visit my old neighborhoods, including the Ninth Ward, where I went to first grade. Katrina had inundated all my old haunts; only one of our six houses had been refurbished, while the others stood as empty hulks. Even in their most pristine pre-Katrina condition, none of the houses we lived in would have fit into Walnut Creek; all would have easily fit under that stretch of Oakland interstate.

As a kid, I had no idea my family was poor. I had a roof over my head, clothes, a hand-me-down bike, friends, and my imagination. What else does a kid need? I had loving siblings and parents, fun bike expeditions with my friends, and new trousers, shirts, and shoes at the beginning of each school year. Not until junior high did I start to recognize income disparities and assign value to other people's possessions—"Gee, you have a really nice house! You must be rich!" This feeling of having less than others only got worse when my father died and my mother and I moved to Shreveport, Louisiana, when I was thirteen. Being male dependent, my mother chose to move into a house next door to her elder brother in Shreveport, a shingled duplex that looked a lot better at night than in the daytime.

Recognition of one's poor economic condition hurts a young person. It confuses and intimidates them. Adolescents begin to compare their personal worth and potential to others who may have better homes and nicer things, people who always seem better off and more self-assured. With my elder siblings off on their own and just my mother and me living next door to my uncle, only then did the dynamics of family life become important. You never know how valuable your siblings are until they are gone. Friends and their families became extensions of my own family; these folks didn't really care if I was rich or not, which was a blessing. Growing up worked out for me, fortunately; I managed to survive adolescence and poverty and work my way up to the middle class.

One of the most dizzying realities about life in America is how casual we are about family. This most basic institution, this foundation for an individual's long-term emotional health, this cornerstone of self-esteem gets the Rodney Dangerfield treatment from a lot of folks—no respect. In today's human-made world, moms and dads both work over eight hours each day. Sleep supposedly takes another eight hours. The remaining daily third gets divided into all the activities and diversions of daily living. Making money, buying stuff, and maintaining social status all seem to have equal priority to raising kids for many modern American families. Spontaneous time together as a family, honest talk about one another's lives, planning for life's transitions—these can be rare occurrences. Kids spend time alone in their rooms with their computers and iPods or on a smartphone. They retreat to their own customized digital and social domains and ethereal fantasies; they outwardly value friends exponentially more than family. What's a parent to do? We common citizens do the best we can with family life, and we try to have as much fun as possible, but we wish we had more time together. We sometimes wish things could be different day in and day out.

Americans tend to be casual about family life because of our deeply embedded belief in individual freedom. Our freedom guarantees that we can come or go as we please, believe whatever we want, and do whatever we want if we don't step on too many toes in the process. We have no restrictions on travel or work preferences in the United States. We are free to succeed/fail/change our careers as we wish. We can support, oppose, or be apathetic about any political issue at any time. We can date whoever we want, have sex with whoever will have sex with us, and have a child or not depending on participants' inclinations, whim, or condom integrity. Without strict restrictions to guide us or rules of stringent behavior to confine us, America's freedom lets us do whatever we like whenever we like as long as it's legal. If we screw up our personal or professional lives, we can move on and start anew; we can always find a pod of like-minded folks out there somewhere who feel and think the same way we do or to whom we can adapt, or we can be hermits and live in a tent in the woods. Ultimate liberty, ultimate choice, and ultimate room to maneuver—that is what America is all about, right?

Sure, for single adults. When wanting to start a family pops up on the screen of possibilities, a lot of these freedoms get minimized. Getting married, bringing new life into the world, buying a home, and settling down are some of the biggest decisions an individual human being ever makes. These are huge steps, life-changing decisions, and deep commitments that have lifelong psychological and emotional impacts for everyone involved. Many young adults do not see these complications clearly at the outset, however. Entering family-making commitments lightly or without serious evaluation of their implications leads to a potential life as shallow as that of any mono-worlder. You diminish yourself and everyone around you when you make these commitments lightly; the demands of marriage and family life will surely beat you up if you don't understand their boundaries and rules ahead of time. Leaping's easy; looking's hard.

Maturity and responsibility form the basis for a "happy" marriage and family life. Men whose little heads say yes at the marriage ceremony will have big-head issues almost immediately after the honeymoon. To women who think they've got it made because their new husband-prince will take care of everything and all they have to do is shop, be good in the sack, and have a baby or two—*Whammo! Kapow! Bam!* There isn't enough onomatopoeia in the world to express how certainly those dream bubbles will pop. Love may be the reason the affianced come together at the altar, but these emotions will certainly cool. As hot sex becomes a memory and partners scrape baby poop from under their fingernails, their commitment to each other grows, transfigures, or dissolves. Marital love gets tested repeatedly as the daily demands of family life make themselves felt. Making a family work requires reasonableness in numerous forms from both partners: self-sacrifice for the family good, the setting of achievable goals, fiscal responsibility, commitments to emotional and physical health, caring/loving/sharing, and endless patience—it's really a second job. Anyone unwilling to make these commitments should not make the move toward marriage and family; just *don't* do it! Not surprisingly, reasonableness and commitment also apply to family unions joined outside the legalities of marriage.

Who among us can approach family challenges best? Someone whose outlook on life has a mono-world or bi-world bias or someone who acknowledges the human paradox and all three worlds of reality and then tries to balance them? Mono- and bi-world enthusiasts will try hard to raise mono- and bi-world kids who just repeat Mom and Dad's aspirations/ limitations/fantasies. Some parents will succeed in this biasing exercise, but most American kids today lean toward human paradox understanding and tri-world curiosities because there's so much information available to them and it's so easily accessible. Kids are learning sponges. They are constantly soaking up new information from every source available and wiring their brains accordingly. What kid isn't interested in nature? What kid doesn't have ethereal fantasies? What kid isn't interested in the human-made world? Why things are the way they are, what's real and what's make-believe, how things work – it's all mental fiber for every kid's growing mind-brain.

What doesn't matter much to prepubescent kids is whether they are rich or poor. They can't make such distinctions easily. They just want to learn, grow, play, and be loved. Put young kids from Walnut Creek in a room with kids from Oakland, and they play together simply fine. Only as nature's hormones kick in, as boys' voices drop, and as girls' T-shirts protrude do things change. This is one of life's most tenuous times. Adolescents categorize themselves and others into social strata according to looks, clothes, and personality—jock, nerd, and so on. Teenagers think all parents have the plague and are to be avoided at all costs (except when the car or money is needed). They see no world other than the teen's friends, passions, and activities—that is all that matters; that is all that exists. Human emotionalism peaks during these years, when the needle on a teen's self- esteem meter bounces all over the place as they are just walking down a high school hallway, and unlike preteens, adolescents in Walnut Creek and Oakland probably only play with each other on the football field or basketball court. The dualistic principles of win/lose and them versus us are firmly implanted into their minds by the middle school and high school years.

America's performance in trying to provide the best education for its children generates mixed results. Because rich neighborhoods usually have better schools than poor ones, kids in the rich schools usually do better on the SATs/ACTs, with more graduating college. Poor kids stop caring about education earlier than rich kids because they have not enjoyed the taming forces and comforts enjoyed by the middle and upper classes. *Homo impotents* kids tend to drop out of school and get into more trouble. Why? Because poor families have fewer options than richer ones to deal with dualistic and differentiated realities. Poor kids fall hard for the allure of the ethereal world, the easy drug money, the exciting gangsta/pimp model, the "cool" gonna-make-it-big-on-my-own-so-fuck-you fantasy. Nature, science, business, technology—that's all waste-of-time bullshit to them. "I ain't deferring no gratification, baby. I want it all right now!" these teens say. *Homo impotents* parents have a tough time countering this thinking because they usually don't personify human-made world achievement. They're not rich, they're not exceptional, and they have little experience with a better material life except in their imaginations.

Having been a poor-kid adolescent, I can attest to the attraction of the dropout lifestyle. The major social distinction among adolescents when I was a teen was being either a cat or a frat. Cats wore leather jackets, had the pomaded duck's-ass hair, and sported denim and motorcycle boots. Frats were the clean-cut, madras-shirt, penny-loafer types. One of the cats in my seventh-grade class was eighteen years old—interesting guy, very Fonzie like, slick but very stupid. Cats mooched off their parents, rode motorcycles, and got into trouble with the law. Their low aspirations and hedonism were not strong enough to seduce me off the education track, and I'm glad about that, but I could understand the pull this kind of life had on strong young studs who didn't think much beyond their next pint of whiskey or piece of ass. The dualistic choices available to today's youth seem essentially the same—take the path of least resistance by dropping out of school and getting your jollies now or stick with the education/career track and see how far it takes you.

Here's the most dualistic statement you'll find in this book: ignorance is our species' and the planet's greatest enemy. Even in the United States, one of the richest countries in the world, educating kids and keeping them in school remains a significant national challenge. All kinds of arguments can be made as to the okay-ness or not of the American educational system. What is important today for America and every other nation is the extreme to which governments will go to provide basic education, job training/retraining, and higher education to the youth. What leaders will do or sacrifice to accommodate educational needs and what changes they will make in wasteful government habits (like excessive defense expenditures) to enlighten their youthful citizenry are indicators of a nation's moral health. Kids in poor areas should have the same opportunities, the same equipment, and the same quality of teaching as the kids in more affluent neighborhoods. You never know where genius/innovation/high achievers will blossom, but you can pretty well predict where these possibilities haven't got much of a chance.

Politicians grapple with many choices: bombs and bullets, infrastructure projects, or providing the highest level of education possible. Which of these should have top priority in a nation's long-term plan? What investment of public funds will yield the best return? What impact will a better-educated youth have on teenage pregnancy, drug abuse, and crime statistics? There are so many issues to consider for a nation's youth and future and so many other areas clamoring for the same budget dollars. **From a tri-worlds point of view, education should not even be in the same category with issues subject to compromise; supporting equal education for all should be in a category of its own.**

Beyond the politics of education lie the deeper issues of poverty, dysfunctional families, and social stigmas. Here are some elements of living at the poorer end of the human bell curve:

- Homelessness
- Living in a car or "the projects"
- Joblessness or leeching off relatives/friends
- Depending on welfare, workers' comp, food stamps, or unemployment benefits long term
- Refusing to work at all because menial/dirty/uncomfortable jobs are beneath you
- Pimping, pushing, panhandling
- Committing crimes
- Whoring, drugging, drunkenness
- Low/no self-esteem, giving up on life, sociopathic/hurtful/ aggressive behaviors
- Children having babies
- Gangbanging
- Irresponsibility, immaturity, pettiness
- Always blaming someone else for your problems/situation

People who live this way live the American Nightmare, not the American Dream. How much of their circumstances stem from their own instincts, values, and faiths depends on each individual's story. It's likely that these people have little education and don't understand their instincts, they may have no or low moral standards, and they probably have faith only in their own fantasies and illusions. They have little understanding or respect for the common-citizen bulge or the high end of the human bell curve, or just the opposite could be true—we common citizens don't pay much attention to the low end of the human bell curve, so we don't really know much about these folks. The truth is we are pretty ignorant (and uncaring) about their reality.

Middle-class citizens and elites in America have no right to criticize or condemn *Homo impotens* until the educational opportunities presented to the poor are the same as those enjoyed by those in other classes. Once the disparities are eliminated, once the playing field is leveled, once sane and educated people choose to remain indolent and live low-end lives, only then is it reasonable to say that they deserve what they get. Of course, America remains far from the ideal of equal opportunity despite all the progress made over the last fifty-plus years in race relations. The usual villains of greed, dualism, and status also play their parts in deep-seated, institutionalized class and race disparities. We have a long way to go as a nation before everyone has boots, much less bootstraps to pull up.

The simplest and most direct way to make progress in equal-opportunity endeavors is to accept the idea of species sameness. Optimism replaces skepticism and racism when everyone involved in the political and educational processes accepts their own humanity. All children have equal value; all children have the same needs, curiosities, and potential in the eyes of legislators, administrators, and teachers. "More idealism," you say. Absolutely! Also, why not base curricula on understanding the human paradox and the tri-worlds model while we're at it? Promote reality through schooling—how's that for a novel idea? The natural world includes biology, chemistry, physics, and other sciences. The human-made world includes languages, math, computers, economics, and industrial arts. The ethereal world includes philosophy, religion, and art. Teaching kids to appreciate the three worlds of reality will help diminish dualism as the basis for human understanding and interaction. Let dualism thrive primarily within the gates of athletic fields, where competitive instincts, young energy, and enthusiasm can be expended in relative safety.

Another aspect of poverty is time. Poor folks think in short time frames. They live paycheck to paycheck, rent payment to rent payment. Sustenance dominates poor people's agendas. Poverty consists of an everyday struggle to get money and food. Assets are few, while liabilities loom large. Unexpected expenses can be ruinous. Stealing/cheating/breaking the law to survive become an option.

Personal security for the poor consists of window shades, door locks, and prayers. Fear often stalks community streets or resides within a restless, confused, and frustrated teenager. Unappreciated children can be a constant bother. Comfort usually comes from booze or television escapism. Stress, depression, and potential financial ruin make drugs an alluring temptation. The act of surviving day to day in poor communities overpowers planning for long-term life improvement. Hope springs eternal through kids who stay in school, but troubles come aplenty from those who drop out. Individual integrity and high moral stances become difficult to maintain on an empty stomach. **Dignity, self-esteem, and optimism wane without unending, hopeful personal determination. Being respectable and self-loving in an environment of poverty requires extraordinary character, family support, and resolve.**

No single generation can solve the problem of poverty—especially in today's dualistic, zero-sum human-made world—but one generation can begin to chip away at the challenge. Perhaps the best place to start is with what we've been talking about—improving schools in poor communities. Work in that direction is already underway, but we need a national commitment to equitable educational opportunity. Experts on the details need to present their arguments for and against the policies/challenges/costs that such a national priority would require. Money now going for corporate welfare, stupid wars, and excessive defense can be diverted to this national priority. This shift will provide a much higher return for America's future than channeling money into the already fat and happy balance sheets of the rich end of the bell curve. Also, we need a tighter focus on the root causes of criminality and how to deal with mental illness.

"Wouldn't it be great if we could get a big comb, run it through our society, and groom out all the bad guys and the crazy people? We could lock up all the criminals and let them lift weights until they get a parole or die. We'll have to lock up some of the worst nut jobs too. The rest of the mentally ill, we can medicate so they don't bother us sane folks. That work for everybody? Okay, let's do it!"

There's probably never been a discussion like this by America's leaders, but there might as well have been because that's where we are with criminals and the mentally ill. If perception equals reality, then the comb's not big enough, and it's got a few teeth missing. Middle-class citizens see law-and-order shows almost constantly on TV, and the nightly news inevitably features murders, drug busts, and other criminal acts. You can't walk down an urban thoroughfare without rubbing elbows with a panhandler or a dazed-looking outcast pushing a packed-to-the-gills grocery cart. Society's current solutions and social conscience come up way short in dealing with these "losers."

Like poverty, there are no easy answers here. As we have already discussed, there's a connection among poverty, poor education, and criminality. Most prison inmates aren't Richie Rich or Einstein; they're arrogant, ignorant, or deranged. Mentally disturbed folks suffer from brain chemical or psychiatric problems that our species is just beginning to understand and treat. Neither criminals nor the mentally ill meet the criteria for positive contributors to the economy, general security, or social betterment. These people frighten us common citizens, they divert positive energy away from the mainstream, and they are liabilities with few offsetting assets. However, just like the inevitability of elites, civilized society will always have to deal with them.

Boys and girls grow up to be criminals because of the things we've been talking about. Poverty, lousy schools, broken families, low/no moral framework, inadequate self-love, physical and mental abuse—on and on, it goes. Does money from government "war-on" programs get deep enough to nip these problems in the bud? Not really. Instead of trying to tackle a resultant problem by declaring war on it, why not deal with the causative problems that lead to poverty and criminality in the first place? Why not identify mental problems sooner rather than later, probably by counseling professionals in schools, community mental health centers, and educated/caring parents? These problems aren't too big if you chip away at them incrementally. Why not institutionalize "family" in the federal cabinet somewhere—a new "Department of Family" or "Department of Health, Human, and Family Services"? Include Department of Education functions into the Department of Family or vice versa. We need some way for public dollars to officially recognize and begin dealing with the causative problems of poverty and criminality rather than so much emphasis on resultant behaviors, which are always more expensive, time consuming, and difficult to reverse.

The throats of political conservatives close up and blood drains from their heads when the idea of another federal department gets suggested. They say family issues should be solved at the family level by developing a strong religious foundation for a child and by proximity to good role models. Maybe that's true in an ideal state that resides in the heads of squeaky-clean suburban moralists, but it has little to do with the nitty-gritty, stressful, and frightening world of the needful. Everybody knows how to make a baby; fewer of us know how or are willing to nurture and tend to a child's growth and long-term needs. Everybody knows how to spend money; not everybody knows how to make and budget it. Everybody knows that smoking, booze, and drugs provide short-term escapist highs; not everyone understands their addictive/destructive/family-destroying chemistry.

Unless political conservatives are willing to build concentration camps for the needy to keep them away from common citizens and elites or rid society of them some other way, they have to recognize the human sameness of these folks and help provide more ways to educate and assist them. **Only when unfortunate individuals can clearly define the terms "initiative," "determination," and "self-esteem" can they begin to personalize these values for themselves. Self-respect and respect for others won't come from a populace that gets no respect from those with money and power.** Using public dollars to further the profits of private entities that already have these values manifests hypocrisy, greed, and anti-species behavior; it generates no return for society in general and just tends to make the already secure more secure and the already comfortable more comfortable.

Poor/sick/old people, the mentally disturbed, and criminals won't go away if we click our heels three times. Every human being gets sick and ages, every human being is a little crazy now and then, and we all have committed crimes, even if we don't want to admit it. Because we all know these things to be true, we humans tend to have some degree of empathy for those who suffer.

Families are expected to help other family members survive, and most do. Governments are expected to provide safety nets through food stamps, welfare, and so on. Public monies can and should do more to raise the floor for poor people rather than raising the ceiling even higher for the privileged few. Growth for the middle class will come more from the unfortunates' side of the human bell curve moving up rather than elites stepping backward. The hopefulness inherent in upward mobility comprises the ultimate magnetism of the American Dream and should be attended to by more public funds in addition to private philanthropy.

Unfortunates also represent major frontiers of exploration and reformative discovery for social scientists, neuroscience researchers, and other specialists. Add to this list our veterans, and you have the complement of those America needs to attend to. Elites and others at the high end of the human bell curve can find their own ways to fame and fortune without the help of tax dollars. Now is the time to begin helping the needful find their way out of poverty, the means to get medicines and the assistance needed for physical and mental health, and ways to unveil the secrets of self-esteem and economic usefulness.

Leaders and Followers

The power and responsibilities of leaders within the human-made world separate them from the rest of us no matter what our social or economic class. Leaders are supposed to be better at solving complex problems and making difficult decisions than us followers. But once a crown sits upon royal locks, corporate reins rest in a new CEO's hands, or a president-elect swears the oath of office, leaders change. What they change into becomes the concern for all social and economic classes—that's the point where we followers hold our breath.

Leaders attend to the interests of a nation, business, religion, or other pod, while we followers go about our daily lives. We trust them to improve our sustenance, security, and comfort; that's why we support them. Through the application of their vast experience, energy, and knowledge, leaders can be a source of immense pride for followers as their actions validate the confidence and trust their followers bestow upon them, or they can be a source of disappointment or shame if performance falls short of expectations. When we get good leadership, we regale them for their efforts and accomplishments. When leaders disappoint, we question both them and us. What went wrong? How did we get so far off track? What can we do to make things "right"?

The rarified air of leadership contains gases that may or may not agree with the physiology and temperament of the natural beings who lead us. Some leaders thrive in a high-pressure environment as they apply their wherewithal to solve problems. Others simply maintain the status quo and bring about little change. Some spray their musk on their pod and soar or stumble during their tenure. A few are outright failures, while fewer still make significant changes that last.

Followers often become disenchanted with leaders because leaders aren't supernatural beings. Ego-laden leaders may have hyped their way into a leadership position by making promises and pretending to be omniscient, but they often struggle to deliver because they're not really as smart, determined, or wise as they thought they were. Another reason for disappointment may be that leaders don't know about human sameness or how to leverage it. **Leaders get so obsessed with their pod's highly differentiated mission and goals that they forget that their followers are human beings who have the same basic needs and wants and who just want some respect, dignity, and control in their lives.** The worst leaders are outright thieves and tyrants who want the reins of power so they can enrich themselves, actualize an exceptionalist ideology, or attempt to realize personal fantasies—and they're usually so hard to get rid of (Bashar al-Assad, Kim Jong Un, Vladimir Putin, and "the Donald").

We followers share blame for crestfallen leaders because we often expect too much from them; we really believe leaders can achieve extraordinary results for us. Rather than accept species-focused leadership that works openly and incrementally over time, we followers create in our minds images of how a leader might, overnight, create better circumstances for our particular interest pod, how the leader will pave the streets with gold, how the leader will validate our exceptional expectations.

In American politics, when Republicans win, the elites get happy; when Democrats win, the middle class and poor get a break. Back and forth, the ball bounces one cycle to the next, with relentless dualism being the underlying continuity between political competitions. When one party wins, the other party suffers; when the other party wins, the losers have to lick their wounds and heal themselves before the next political battle. Back and forth, this contest goes, as if, in reality, this were the best way for a government to serve its citizenry. Political dualism denies species and planetary problem solving and replaces it primarily with hubris-infused, time-and-energy-consuming game playing and name-calling.

By empowering leaders, we followers end up as subjects to the instincts, values, and faiths within leaders' minds. Leaders make decisions based on the experiences of their own individual and political selves, the goals of their party/corporation/pod, and the information available at the time a decision has to be made. In both the public and private sectors, followers empower leaders, and leaders tend to empower themselves.

The leader–follower relationship seems natural to human beings because "that's the way things have always been"—top down, the best and the brightest, the few leading the many. Nature seems to affirm this leader–follower model because many species in the wild follow the lead of one among them, usually an alpha male. In the ethereal world, God/Allah/Yahweh serves as the alpha male who makes life's rules and guides and teaches his mortal flock. Many ask, "Why should the human-made world be any different?" Answer: it isn't and never will be. Varying levels of human intelligence, personality, ambition, and individual integrity assure that our species will always have those who lead and those who follow. Also, by now, hopefully, we're smart enough to realize that in the human-made world, an alpha female can lead as well as an alpha male.

Humans have adapted to the leader–follower model for millennia. Written history gives leaders top billing and doesn't focus much attention on followers who often had short lives filled with Hobbesian drudgery and toil. However, the ideas that led to modernity and progress—the Reformation, the Enlightenment, the Industrial Age, the Information Age, high tech/biotech—came mostly from the common ranks, not from leaders. Inventions, great art and music, scientific discoveries, and business/finance/commercial practices came from those who had to work with their hands and apply their minds and talents to obtain life's basics. Mozart, Darwin, Edison, and thousands of others applied their genius to their specialties so they could provide life's basics for themselves and their families. Royalty, aristocrats, or other elites may have commissioned the creators, but they did not personally provide the genius, talent, and dedication to produce the ends they patronized.

There's a rhythm between leader and follower that determines the consonance or dissonance of the relationship. Frankly, we middle-class citizens in America don't pay much attention to what our leaders do every day; we're too busy with our own concerns. At our jobs, it's when we're *un*-busy that we start to worry and look to our bosses to find out why business has slowed down. On the political scene, we're usually blasé about daily political happenings because we trust that the American system of governance functions well enough without us fretting over it every second. It's when, in our subjective opinion, the wrong political cord gets struck, a crisis develops, or when we hear a misplayed note from our leaders that our ears perk up and we start asking questions. In the church, temple, or mosque, it's when the cleric begins to wax political or translates scripture that contravenes our personal beliefs that we entertain slivers of doubt about the holy messenger's relevance to our lives.

A leader's power includes the components of knowledge, wisdom, judgment, and follower trust. Followers believe their leaders can elevate them by relieving fears, improving life conditions, and providing new directions. Virtually all leaders surround themselves with an inner circle of advisors and confidants who provide information and who serve as sounding boards. These people are supposedly more expert in specific areas of concern than the leader and provide guidance and direction for the leader, who must make the final decisions. Ultimately, no matter how much input the leader receives from others, it is only the leader's intelligence, experience, morality, and ethics that determine the effectiveness of decisions he or she makes. The leader usually bears the final burden of responsibility for decisions made regardless of whether the leader truly deserves full credit/ blame or not.

Deference represents a particular challenge for leaders and the species. **All cultures support some level of deferring to the judgments of leaders. Human nature supports respect for leaders who make decisions that affect the lives of their followers.** Ethereal religion includes deference in the first, and fourth ommandments: "Thou shalt have no other gods before me"; and "Remember the sabbath and keep it holy". Of concern with our leaders—let's call them *Homo globalus*—is the corrupting side of deference, the perfidious type of deference that may surround the few who guide the many. It's this type of deference that facilitates absolute power that can corrupt absolutely.

Under the subspecies *Homo globalus* resides the sub-subspecies *Homo smarmus*. These are the puppeteers pulling the strings of the powerful, the ones with proximity to the decision makers, the whisperers or shouters of idealistic purism, the true believers and power grubbers who act behind the scenes. **In America, voters elect a president and vice president, senators,**

and congresspersons, but we have no say about who counsels and advises our leaders. Senators approve cabinet members and federal judges, but the inner-circle staff and others around the president and vice president are personal hires, as are staff members in the congress and the courts. Only after a new administration takes office do the *Homo smarmus* players become apparent, and only then does the public find out more about them.

Presidents Kennedy and Johnson had McGeorge Bundy and Walt Rostow guiding and influencing their decisions. President Nixon had Henry Kissinger, Robert Haldeman, and John Erlichman. President George W. Bush had Karl Rove, Douglas Feith, Stephen Hadley, Richard Perle, and Eliot Abrams. Clinton, Obama, and Trump also had their devotees. Every one of these men, it turns out, including the presidents themselves, maintained thought processes that functioned in differentiating and dualistic ways, inclinations that led America down the cul-de-sac of long/ pointless wars and divisive partisanship. In a political world based on every form of dualism and differentiation imaginable, what else could we citizens expect?

In fairness, there are many brilliant and selfless advisors with access to our leaders and countless devoted civil servants, but the smarmy ones tend to have the most power, or, conversely, the ones with the most power tend to become smarmy. This is so because of their seemingly selfless dedication to the leader or their friendship, intelligence, long-time allegiance, or tact in dealing with positional superiors and underlings. Leaders demand loyalty, and they usually get it from the in-crowd.

Homo smarmus advisers seem willing to do virtually anything to retain nearness to power. Their roles are so ego gratifying, so enhancing to their personal worth, prestige, and reputation that they "empretzel" their minds and souls into practically any shape that maintains proximity to leadership. The primary goals for *Homo smarmus* practitioners are to keep the boss happy/stimulated/revered, to enhance their own professional and personal reputations, and to position themselves for retention and advancement— and to outthink and stay one step ahead of perceived opponents. Also, many *Homo smarmus* types believe they are just as smart as, if not smarter than, their leader.

History overflows with examples of kings, emperors, dictators, popes, and other leaders who believed in their own superiority and special purpose in life. Sycophants and other loyal handlers reinforced this highness and facilitated their leader's role no matter how beneficial or cruel the rulers were to their followers. Deference often means control and influence that serve no one's best interest except that of the influencer. "I'd rather be kingmaker than king," many of them say. Even in constitutional republics like the United States, which established the rule of law and balance of powers to eliminate this type of corruption, leaders and their hacks try to rule by imperial dictate. The presidency of Donald J. Trump along with his vast army of smarmy loyalists evidence that.

History shows clearly that many political leaders in the past were criminals and megalomaniacs (Hitler, Stalin, Mao Tse-tung, Saddam Hussein, Putin) who loved power more than their followers. These men weren't gods or holy beings; they were just humans like everyone else, yet they became powerful leaders by wrapping themselves in doctrines and propaganda that their uncritical, fear-filled, and credulous followers were naive enough to believe and by using brute force to gain and retain dominance. These embodiments of anti-species values leveraged the human-made and ethereal worlds to their advantage; they became myths unto themselves. **They created pseudo religions with themselves as God; they lived in a world of promises, false vision, lies, intimidation, and murder.** Their *Homo smarmus* lieutenants would do anything—yes, anything—to keep their bosses in power.

The fact that there are still places on the planet where these conditions exist highlights another weakness in our species—that is, how non-species focused some leaders are and how easily manipulated and influenced they can be by their own vanities that their loyalists constantly reinforce. **Pitifully, we humans have not demanded that our leaders put species and natural interests before those of nation, self, or other special interests that can be so differentiating and corrupting.** We need to make the axiom "divide and conquer" obsolete; our species and planet can no longer afford such a moss-covered idea.

Any serious reader of history will tell you that *Homo smarmus* deference often subsidizes incompetent and malleable leaders. Leaders whose egos are attended to by endless pomp, circumstance, and constant brown nosing come to believe they are what their tenders feign them to be—unique, top-of-the pyramid, infallible, loved by all, incapable of error, all knowing, and all powerful, anything but a normal human being. Rather than laughing off this fantasy talk, the leader dissembles to his handlers and becomes their gilded-cage captive. As history has shown repeatedly, nothing good for the species comes out of this type of leadership, especially when followers are ignorant, apathetic, or swept up in the propagandized fantasy of their leader's superiority. Rather, **once individual human beings accept and believe in their basic sameness and the importance of that sameness, then the right to demand acceptance and belief of species primacy from our leaders becomes clear.** We common people, we citizens, we voters would like a little species humility from our leaders, please—or we'd like you to step down (or be brought down).

It's true that there's nothing easy about leadership; being in charge of any pod requires knowledge, energy, and commitment. Leadership can be a very demanding and painful assignment. The quandary most leaders find themselves in today, as in the past, boils down to natural, technical, financial, and human resources. What are our goals? Do we have sufficient resources to meet our goals? What do we need more of? Where are we going to get what we need? How can available resources be apportioned to best serve national/corporate/clan interests? On and on, the thousands upon thousands of leadership questions and challenges go.

In the past, war was a common option available for tribes, city-states, and nations to obtain needed resources (why pay for needed resources when you can just take them?). Egotistical, aggressive male leaders dominate the pages of world history with their authoritarianism and determination. These men had strong wills and godly sanctioned titles. They were not afraid to fight and lead others to their deaths; they were determined dualists with no comprehension of the species. (Note: we cannot fault past leaders for their actions because they neither knew nor cared about anything but their own cause célèbre. Followers of these leaders also bear responsibility for their loyalties, but again, nothing can be gained from historic revisionism.) During their times, war was always an option; fighting was a relatively easy choice to make when arms and fighters were at hand. Male instincts ached to fight when men were fired up by a leader's promise of a better life, fulfilling God's holy mission, or revenging a perceived wrong (or loot).

Empires in the past rose and fell because leaders acted without asking human paradox or tri-world questions; they didn't need to. They acknowledged no higher power on Earth than themselves and their cause, they didn't give nature a second thought, and of course, their ethereal God/gods were always on their side. Aggressive, megalomaniac leaders believed their dualist messages that often relied on long-told legends of exceptional glory and virtue. Each leader believed he personified all the traditions and nobility that elevated a nation-state, clan, or religion to extra-special status. These leaders knew that those who believed these enshrined myths also demanded the same loyalties from others within the ranks. Differentiated and ethereal ideals were their primary bond and motivation; leader adulation, hatred of enemies, and common cause strengthened esprit de corps.

Even in the modern world, dualism still loves unique imbalances. Here's a classic quote about Adolf Hitler and the psychology of Nazi propaganda: "Never allow the public to cool off. Never admit a fault or wrong. Never concede that there may be some good in your enemy. Never leave room for alternatives. Never accept blame. Concentrate on one enemy at a time and blame him for everything that goes wrong. People will believe a big lie sooner than a little one, and if you repeat it frequently enough, people will sooner or later believe it."[38]

Today's leaders of nations follow many paths to obtain and hold onto power. Some are autocrats or tyrants. They make the law as they see fit; they rule by fiat. Some abide by control documents like a constitution, while others dilute or distort those same documents to fit their predispositions or pod politics, or they simply ignore them altogether. In addition to the furtherance of democracy, the last century also saw numerous anti-democratic regimes led by totalitarian dictators who killed millions of their own citizens in paranoid purges or racist/ethnic/religious pogroms along with millions of others in cataclysmic world wars that did absolutely nothing to benefit the species. In the modern, interconnected, globalized economy of today, does such a traditional leader–follower model still hold? Will it work for twenty-first-century humans?

No, not in its present configuration of power concentration, dualistic-thought processes, lies, distortions, and leadership thrall. Contemporary leaders have no basis to claim ignorance about nature's limits, to support beliefs that one race or polity flies above others, or to claim that God chooses only some of his creations and leaves others behind. That's all worn out dualism and differentiation that seeks to promote one partiality over another, each one aimed at making followers and leaders feel special, superior, and chosen. These antiquated approaches to leadership provide no benefit for those of us alive on the planet today, for coming generations, or for the planet itself.

What the world needs now is national leaders who share common values based on reality (acceptance of the human paradox, the three worlds, life's basics, peace, economic sustainability, human sameness, and nature's limits). World leaders need to acknowledge universal species primacy and then place species/planetary issues atop every nation's priority list. Species sameness recognition, species survival, and planetary integrity should provide the basis from which national, economic, and faith-based goals are set. No single nation or religious agenda has higher priority than that of the species. **Yes, this is a call for creating species and planetary sovereignty above nationhood or any religious doctrine or ideology, a sovereignty that elevates human concerns and actions to the species and planetary level.** For sane and responsible leaders and followers, there's every reason to strive in this direction and no realistic reason not to.

Agreement and adherence to species-level thinking will give leaders a unified higher authority they now lack and reasons for them to work together while providing followers a way to gauge their performance. As long as national/religious leaders and their *Homo smarmus* advisors continue what they're currently doing—that is, believing they have no higher priority than their own differentiated stances—the planet we inhabit will never change, and leaders will lead us to more conflicts, degraded natural environments, and possible extinction. We followers don't want that; we want to survive, we want our progeny and our planet to survive, and we want peace so we can pursue life's basics in a sustainable, healthful fashion.

Ego-driven leaders of highly differentiated nations and religions will fight and denigrate the idea of species sovereignty even though they may

understand (and even believe) its ultimate worth. They will do so because species sovereignty dilutes their differentiated power; it waters down their ability to spread their glorious munificence onto a national or a religious pod's activities and history, or they may be afraid to be the first one to step toward species-level thinking because it upsets the current global leadership paradigm and seems so difficult to achieve. To require that a king/president/ayatollah adhere to some power higher than a dynastic rite, constitution, or deity offends their sense of importance and their righteousness. "An overriding obligation to the species? That's ridiculous! It's not possible!" they'll say.

Cynically, what these leaders are really saying is that to dilute their own power with species goals and priorities takes the challenge and glory out of being a leader; it undermines the *Homo smarmus* and follower hype that makes the leader so outstanding, so irreplaceable, and so magnificently special, and it takes away the sweetness of dualistic political victory and delicious ego revenge that winners enjoy over losers. Also, it means that leaders truly have to act in service to their citizens, an idea many leaders never seem to accept. Short-circuiting nationhood and religious bliss in favor of the species seems to wreck a traditional leader's worldview when, in fact, it does just the opposite by providing a platform consistent with what citizens want from life (life's basics, sustainable development, planetary integrity, peace).

Until there's a shift to a unified higher purpose for global leaders, we followers will be trapped by leadership that values dualism (win/lose, black/white) and differentiation (Republican/Democrat) and forces us to choose within these contexts. The fact that we citizen followers want sustenance, security and comfort, peace, and a survivable and sustainable world for ourselves and our offspring gets buried by Machiavellian-type leaders, short-term economics, status concerns of elites, and religious exceptionalism.

Here's an option for America: create a third political party based on acceptance and understanding of the human paradox and on tri-worlds issues/priorities, a party broader than but including green priorities. Better option: have both existing major parties accept the human paradox, tri-worlds reality, and human sameness as the immutable canvas upon which political differences can be expressed and include this message in their leadership platforms. The ultimate goal: have every nation and religion on the planet include species sovereignty and planetary integrity into their guiding documents/policies/directives through inclusion of the idea of species sameness, the primacy of life's basics, sustainable development, and the need to peacefully sustain our species and the planet.

World leaders on the heels of massively destructive World War II took the first step to recognizing species sameness and the importance of species issues when they established the United Nations in 1945, passed the Universal Declaration of Human Rights in 1948, and conducted World War II war crime trials that established crimes against humanity. These events helped establish an international community—something that had never existed before. Now we have an interdependent, global economy that ties together and affects virtually every nation and inhabitant in the world but no effective species-centered political consensus in which to conduct human affairs. **How bizarre that we members of the same species, who depend on one another for life's basics, continue to value allegiances to the dead and the past and to keep perpetuating traditions, dogmas, and other big lies that serve to divide rather than to unite!**

Traditional national leaders are adventurers at heart, as evidenced by the power position they hold; becoming a leader was itself a huge adventure for them. To give these individuals imprimatur to do whatever they think best can be extremely risky for followers because the leader has no higher loyalty than to that society's traditional instincts, values, and faiths. With 195 sovereign nations in the world, how can the species come together to survive and sustain itself and nature if each national leader thinks he or she can act without any accountability to the rest of the species or the planet?

The United States can provide a new model for leadership beyond a mighty military and hubris-infected exceptionalism. The idea of America broke the trend of differentiated, conservative, proud nationhood when it opened its doors to "give me your tired, your poor, your huddled masses yearning to breathe free." What America has been telling the rest of the world for more than two centuries is that Old World traditions and "us" parochialisms don't hold long-term worth for species survival, whereas sameness recognition, fulfilling life's basics, and preserving and restoring the planet do.

Every country needs to become a great melting pot like America—a planet where the 0.1 percent physical differences and local loyalties among humans don't matter as much as the accomplishment of life's basics for more and more living creatures, where economic interests row together in sustainable directions, where natural limits get recognized and respected, and where the paradox of being the same but that each one is unique is understood and holds sway.

One of the strongest polarizing forces within our dualistic world has to be the tug-of-war between the rights of the individual and those of the species (the common good). We humans struggle mightily with this issue. Now is the time to face it and act. Democracy and capitalism side with the individual; socialism/communism often represent the species in this dichotomy. Neither side openly recognizes that both the individual and species already exist one within the other—the paradoxical nature of our existence. Rather than applying human intelligence to finding a suitable mix of the two realities (we're all the same, yet each one is unique), exceptionalist societies during the twentieth century dug in their heels and decided to contest their dualistic/differentiated issues through hot wars and a nuclear cold one.

Rather than take a world leadership position that acknowledged human sameness, the need for sustainability, and natural integrity, post–Cold-War leadership in America played by the old rules of nationalism, saber rattling, military intimidation, imperialism, and idealistic political purity. **Is it not apparent to all Americans now that we cannot afford to be the world's policeman, we cannot sustain our open society by borrowing our way into endless prosperity, and we cannot build a future based on exceptionalist myths?**

Ironically, probably the only way America can be exceptional in the world from this point forward is to accept the human paradox and to assume a tri-worlds outlook by doing the following: (a) striving to achieve life's basics for as many members of the species as possible through increased unit productivity, biomimicry, and the preservation and extension of natural integrity; (b) carrying out this mission through realistically modified democratic and capitalist institutions; and (c) accomplishing this goal within the context of a primary commitment to human sameness, a recognition of the persistence of paradox, irony, and contradiction (mistakes will be made), and a willingness to refocus more energy and public funds on systemic issues like natural integrity, physical and mental health care, poverty alleviation, education, crime prevention, and criminal rehabilitation. We need to give up the idea that we need to dominate other nations and the planet; that's a national will America can happily live without. Rather, let's lead by example, a skill at which America can excel.

When given deep thought by common-citizen voters, the reality of the human paradox, tri-worlds, life's basics, human sameness, peace, and natural integrity offer a common set of goals between traditional dualistic political choices colored either red or blue. How so? By focusing on the essentials of reality on today's planet: again, sustainable development, peace, a focus on life's basics, human sameness recognition, and natural integrity. These goals are what human politics should be addressing because they are fundamental and vital to species and planetary survival. The problem for most individuals is that we haven't given these ideas much thought yet. Okay, that's too generous—we haven't given them virtually *any* thought at all. Instead of looking forward, our tendency is to look back and build upon our pride, our past accomplishments, and then cast our votes based on these differentiated values' supposed worth. Our allegiances are short-sighted. They're more local than inclusive of the species and the planet; they lack vision, breadth, and vitality. They lag today's reality.

Leaders in America who continue labeling others as enemies, whose leadership power depends on frightening the citizenry, who emphasize every differentiation angle they can think of to get a political edge, who create the American version of a big lie—these people paradoxically play right into the hands of the barbarians at the gate that their imaginations envision, and they push the country into massive debt as they pursue the evildoers. America can no longer afford, morally or financially, to pursue dualistic, highly differentiated/exceptionalist policies that deny human sameness and planetary limits. That's a recipe for America's undoing.

Paradox-understanding and tri-worlds thought focus on attaining sustenance, security, and comfort for every nation's citizens. That's priority number one. Leaders should be judged on their abilities to provide and enhance citizen status in these areas and to do so without raping nature in the process. These are the things citizens everywhere want. Why can't you, Mr./Ms. Leader, provide them? You have life's basics—why can't you provide them for your people? Every citizen in every country has the right, the duty, to ask this question. What are you doing, Mr./Ms. Leader, that's more important than providing means for your citizens to achieve sustenance, security, and comfort? Making war? Kowtowing to mono-world clerics and established elites? Wasting time fighting wasteful political/military/religious battles? If you have more resources than you need, why aren't you finding ways to share them with those who struggle?

Some leaders measure themselves against other leaders, other political systems, and cultural and historical imperatives, not the needs and wants of their citizenry. Since national leaders acknowledge little or no higher power than themselves, they feel sanctioned to follow their own political inclinations and egotistical drives; they feel empowered by "the people," who often become a malleable abstraction in their minds. The power game among leaders becomes more important than true leadership that yields measurable results for a citizenry.

Here's a simple political expectation to which every world leader should aspire: leadership rewards will be tied to the health and welfare of your citizenry. No sustenance for them, no support for you. No security for them, no support for you. No comfort for them, no support for you. Is this book fomenting rebellion? No. Rather, it attempts to set new standards of performance that are easy for both leaders and followers to understand and track. Improvements in these areas can bring a leader adoration and respect; the lack of progress in these areas will bring a leader ignominy, disdain, and loss of power. Bottom line: we'll respect you, Mr./Ms. Leader, as long as you respect us and prove it. That's not anarchy; that's democracy in action. That's putting power back in the hands of the people from whom a leader's power is ultimately derived. Of course, individual citizens must take advantage of the educational opportunities and economic systems that allow them to achieve life's basics; leaders can only provide the pathways to life's basics, while actually walking these pathways must come from each individual's energies, focus, and determination. Every able member of the species is responsible for his or her own fate, especially where democratic and capitalistic systems exist to support individual initiative.

Leaders also control agents of violence; armed action or reaction is the political ace up every leader's sleeve. Military and police forces have the official sanction within every country to possess weapons, to train in their use, and to employ them when necessary. American military and police forces work within strict command and control structures that limit access to and use of force; there's little fear among the citizenry about coups d'état or massive criminal conflagrations within U.S. borders. Even after the brazen attack on the U.S. Capitol by Trump supporters on January 6, 2021, the institutional strength of the federal government proved resilient.

That's not true in other parts of the world where militias, insurgents, and other militant groups obtain weapons and then wield them unilaterally. A highly weaponized world puts fire power behind mono- and bi-world ideologies that seek to retain or expand their non-species–focused agendas. Without enforceable political agreements to quell impassioned instincts and to advance peaceful species-focused behaviors, highly differentiated and dualistic doctrines will continue to infect the global political agenda, and aggressive options will remain easy for leaders to implement. Dealing with and overcoming weaponized mindsets like these remains a high hurdle for human paradox and tri-worlds realists to overcome.

American leadership's belief that it has to be the preeminent military power ready to fight all kinds of conventional and unconventional wars leads to massive outlays of tax dollars and deprives citizens of other services that support life's basics and sustain life on the planet. From a species-wide point of view, huge outlays of this sort indicate a failure of leadership—the inability/reluctance of American leaders to maintain peaceful relations with other countries and cultures because of tradition-bound, ideological differences, and a lack of recognition of human sameness.

Male instincts and bellicose tendencies play a big role in a nation's security. While women have made in-roads within military and police forces, it's undeniable that most fingers on the world's triggers belong to men. Male competitiveness and the deep-seated and widely held belief that patriotism yields personal worth makes males especially susceptible to dualism's call to arms. The adventure, action, and potential to become a medal-laden hero outweigh just about every other sensibility young men have when they don a uniform. Being a team member whose mission is saving freedom, defeating an enemy, or spreading democracy lifts a soldier to a level of personal significance unattainable in civilian life. The expectations for each combatant are clear and simple: obey orders and ably implement training. For that, he will be respected and rewarded. As long as male soldiers/marines/sailors/airmen focus on the who, what, where, when, and how of fighting, dualistic leadership will continue to obtain their loyalty. Only when soldiers start questioning the "why" of their mission do leaders get anxious. Justifying war, especially during a protracted ill-defined conflict, like Iraq and Afghanistan, can become a daunting leadership task even with an all-volunteer force.

For some developing and Third World nations, well-armed police and military become an extension of their leader's mental health. With no sovereignty higher than their own self-interests, leaders can spawn internecine conflicts that often have soldiers confronting or killing members of their own tribes, neighboring clans, or families. For such leaders, internal power squabbles, mob control, and the protection of elite interests become more important than the concerns of citizens who get semantically transformed into troublemakers or rabble. Internal enemies can vastly outnumber external ones, especially in the minds of pliable, *Homo smarmus*–infected leaders. The military may have been trained to confront external enemies, but the likelihood of brother-versus-brother conflict has a much higher likelihood the more life's basics are denied to a citizenry. Without individual understanding of universal species sovereignty and responsibility for natural integrity, along with governmental recognition of these priorities, this tyrannical mode of governance will continue unabated. The ignorance, dualism, and blind adulation of a leader never serve to benefit the common good and will continue to keep these nations in their own political, economic, and social backwaters.

Diplomacy remains a great hope in the leadership world. At present, diplomacy functions only within the terms defined by the participants; it considers no other issues that it does not acknowledge as relevant at the time, and virtually all diplomatic corps recommendations are subject to overrides by leadership. Since species sovereignty has not been acknowledged by nations, there is no commonality among diplomats that runs deeper than their side's issues. Everyone at a diplomatic negotiating table is playing for dualistic advantage and/or to establish or save face; all negotiations are based on differentiation, with little recognition for species sameness, life's basics, or nature's limits, unless they're on the agenda. The danger of inculcating species recognition and natural world integrity into a nation's diplomatic vision is that it will be an admission of human sameness, a loss of differentiated status, and an open door to establishing species sovereignty.

With each nation on the planet obsessed with its own autonomy, security, and dignity, diplomatic negotiations to resolve problems between countries rely on the aims of each leader or convening authority rather than considerations of the species or planet. Nations today have no higher goals than their own survival and prosperity, which usually includes diplomatic negotiations based on self-serving strategies. Without the consideration or inclusion of species-wide and/or natural limitations in diplomatic agreements, these resolutions work to no higher end than their limited focus. That may be entirely appropriate in many instances but not all.

American diplomats need to consider broadening their negotiations to include the elements of reality discussed here (the human paradox, life's basics, limited resources, planet and species sustainability) to help build a more universal, species-focused base for diplomacy. If not in a formal setting, these ideas can be discussed informally. We human beings are all the same, yet each nation is unique; each nation deserves respect and hearing because its citizens are the same as everyone else on Earth, yet each country has specific challenges in fulfilling life's basics. Such diplomatic equanimity will set the tone for others to observe and to follow and will help American diplomacy be a more effective alternative to political bluster or military sanguinity. However, this strategy may be particularly difficult for the United States to implement now since many nations have felt the sting of America's past imperialism/intelligence/military policies and covert activities—transgressions not easily forgotten or forgiven.

Force of personality, local knowledge and identity, and the ability to inspire others can enhance a leader's power. What's going on inside the leader's head may be something else altogether. Idi Amin came to power in Uganda as the jovial, loyal soldier looked up to as "one of us" by fellow Ugandans. Only after his ignorance, incompetence, and paranoia completely ruined the Ugandan economy and killed tens of thousands of his fellow countrymen was he driven from power. Joseph Mobutu dragged the Congo/Zaire into poverty and revolution over a thirty-year period (with CIA backing) as he pocketed billions of dollars by exploiting the nation's natural resources. The great liberator of Zimbabwe, Robert Mugabe, stooped so low as to intercept international food-aid shipments to citizens who might vote for his opponent in a 2008 runoff election. Before they were deposed, Mubarak in Egypt, Ben-Ali in Tunisia, and Muammar Gaddafi in Libya repressed their citizens for decades and stole billions of dollars from them. Need I mention Hitler, Stalin, Mao, and others who slaughtered millions of their own citizens rather than serve them? The world no longer needs or can tolerate leaders like this. The species can no longer afford leaders who define power through subjectively defined goals, who impose massive ethereal fictions and bellicose destruction on the human-made and natural worlds, and who avoid rather than accept responsibility for the welfare of their citizenry and the planet.

Eliminating political ignorance will be a key element to breaking this cycle of archaic leadership. Crowds of adoring, cheering followers chanting the leader's name, their smiling faces all uplifted to see and hear the human legend—please, spare me. The leader is simply another human being with a tough job, one for which he or she should receive respect if he or she is serving the citizenry. But to love, to worship, and to deify a leader requires an individual citizen to suppress tri-worlds reality, to elevate ethereal and dualistic fantasies ahead of reality, and to accede to spin-machine distractions created by *Homo smarmus* power huggers. Leaders who regale in and depend on this type of adoration are simply avoiding their responsibility to help their constituents improve their lives and to treat the earth respectfully; these leaders should be stripped of power and treated with the shame and rejection they deserve.

Countless millions have died prematurely because they venerated their leaders without question. These followers believed what their leaders told them, and they obeyed their leaders' commands. Millions upon millions of followers have died to advance the goals of their masters' wills or in a quest for glory, loot, or heavenly sanction. This means that people who are 99.9 percent biologically the same killed others who were only 0.1 percent different. Of course, these people didn't know intellectually, morally, or scientifically about their sameness, and oral or written histories/traditions didn't help because they emphasized differences not sameness. What past leaders did was perpetuate their own big lie that their pod's exceptional sense was greater than its common sense and that there was no natural sameness with the rest of the species, especially perceived enemies, and vain/ignorant/obedient followers bought into these prideful differentiations and died protecting them.

Times have changed. **We citizens of the world are too intertwined with one another now, we know too much about one another, and we have come to know and respect one another too much to play exceptionalist games. Species survival and planetary integrity now need to become the overriding higher powers to which all leaders aspire and to which followers hold leaders accountable.** Perhaps the greatest threats to this aspiration come, again, from human ignorance and the vast arsenal of weapons available to highly differentiated, dualistic leaders now running national governments.

Any leader today who keeps his or her finger on the trigger personifies outdated, anti-species leadership. These leaders are copping out on their responsibilities, they're playing to a loyalist audience and exploiting their followers' ignorance and fears, and they're building their case on dualistic/differentiated/anti-species rhetoric. These leaders are adventurers and gamblers; they aren't looking out for any nation's best interests, especially their own. They're putting abstract, simplistic, big-lie, flag-waving idealism ahead of the expense, pain, and hell their war will have on their country and those who have to fight it. Of course, in the process, they'll try to make sure most of their citizens aren't economically inconvenienced or their patriotic illusions aren't betrayed, just as Bush-the-younger did during the Iraq debacle ("Everyone should just go shopping"). Or when Putin kept his citizens in the dark when he invaded Ukraine.

Leaders obsess over differentiation while they ignore and deny human sameness. Why? Because the universally understood common sense of human sameness dilutes their arguments. Hitler would never have gotten away with war and the Holocaust if there had been a cultural principal of human sameness within German society. Instead of acknowledging the sameness of human beings (Jews, Poles, Slavs, Germans), the Nazi Party of the 1930s focused on propagandized differences and created racist laws to affirm these distinctions. As the world's greatest personification of evil, Hitler's antipathy toward human sameness was the taproot of his hate. He conned the German people with his propaganda by appealing to their ethereal exceptional sense; he took human differentiation to its most illogical, deadly extreme. That was evil then, and racism of any sort is evil now.

Sameness can also be taken to illogical extremes. Karl Marx tried to eliminate differentiation among individual laborers/owners/aristocrats and replace it with a property-less and egalitarian society—capitalism and private property would eventually evolve into socialism and then communism, he believed. Soviet communism in practice failed because it stomped on the basic paradox inherent with sameness: that **we common citizens recognize differences in intelligence, ambition, and motivation among individuals and we respect those differences and believe they should be rewarded.** There's no reason why someone who works harder and is smarter shouldn't have more money, property, status, or power than someone who does not possess those qualities or is not willing to perform. The smartest, most experienced, and most decent among us should be our leaders. Communism's ideal of "from each according to his ability, to each according to his need"[39] ran counter to human nature; therefore, it fizzled out. Soviet communism proved to be nothing but a noble sentiment exploited by mono-world and bi-world dualists who established a totalitarian dictatorship that couldn't actualize their big lies.

Why has the world ended up with so many megalomaniacs, kooks, and hand puppets for leaders? Because we have created a dualistic and differentiated world where the staircase to power ends at a chair too large for one sane individual to fill. Of course, the people who sit in this big power chair won't admit this; they think they're very comfortable and deserving and sane. The problem is that they are just human beings like you and me. There's nothing superhuman about our leaders. It's virtually impossible for one human being, no matter how smart he or she is, to know all that needs to be known to make decisions that prove wise over time. Nation-states are too complex; nature's too unpredictable. There's too much information to weigh and refine; there are too many uncontrollable changes and shocks. This has been true ever since tribes, city-states, and nations began to form.

Many human governance problems stem from leaders' limited grasp of circumstances and the willingness of followers to obey orders anyway. Most leaders attain power primarily by force of will rather than wisdom or genius. Bureaucracies of experts and policymakers exist to fill the information voids in leaders' minds and to help with decision making and policy implementation, yet now even they struggle to stay current with all the information volume and dynamics within their own areas of responsibility, and no one can see the future. **Without some agreed-to species-wide goals, dualism and differentiation will continue to dominate political leadership decision making and will continue to fracture the species.**

Do leaders listen to what their experts and policymakers recommend? Yes and no. Since voters have empowered them to do what they think best, that's what leaders do. Their best effort may or may not be what's consistent with the law or with recommendations made by those with more expertise about an issue, however. The leaders have been elected or took power, and now by God or in spite of him, they're going to exercise their power and rule. Because we common citizens grant them power, either through our vote or our apathy, leaders become emboldened, pampered, and often isolated. If they have an internal megalomaniac switch, it gets flipped on soon after they sit in the big power chair.

Because leaders are physically constructed like the rest of us, they get tired, they get grouchy, and they burn out. Sometimes they just enjoy the adventure ride up to the big power chair and really don't like the job once they get it. Disagreements with other world leaders can result in personal antipathies among national leaders, and they may waste time obsessing about these affronts. *Homo smarmus* sycophants around the leader may be helpful or harmful in their recommendations; they're human beings too, with all the concomitant strengths and weaknesses of our species.

The media don't help as they hang on to and amplify every word out of a leader's mouth, often shading it with one dualistic/differentiated slant or another. Personal and political affinities or animosities sidetrack what should be matters of national and international concern. Leaders can spend a lot of time not getting much accomplished for their citizenry because political falderal, vanity, and elite accommodation overwhelm clear focus and action.

Most leaders have to struggle so hard and so long to get power, they will do anything to retain it. In our dualistic and differentiated world, there's usually no place to go but down for the powerful. Tyrants, dictators, prime ministers, presidents—they all love that big plush power chair even when it gets lumpy and uncomfortable. The reality is that leaders make decisions with the information they've got available at the time, their own experience, and with the support or cautions of those near them. Predisposed to dualistic thinking and not having any basic value structure larger than the one in which they already believe, all national leaders govern with blinders on. They've made no commitment to the continuation of the human species (except their own "us" citizens). They're only going to protect the earth as much as the law requires (they don't want to alienate campaign donors who make huge profits by exploiting natural bounty). They'll continue to work along the political continuum they inherited (to do otherwise would belie their conventional leadership role), and they'll honor God and acknowledge their fealty to him (yet they know God won't do anything to stop them from implementing their earthly powers). Still, another paradox: national leaders deal with issues and problems that affect species survival and natural integrity, yet they do so outside a species-wide survival and natural consciousness context.

Why do leaders do destructive and deceptive things? Because they make mistakes yet don't want to lose face, because they are ego and pod centric, and because they love power and don't want to lose kinship with those they lead. They don't focus on the species or the planet because that's territory that's way outside their authority—or so they believe. Leaders are totally dependent on citizens in their pods following their lead and, in democracies, being empowered by them, but disquiet hovers like pollen in the springtime air. Leaders don't give up power easily; relinquishing power disrupts their physical, emotional, or psychological needs along with the follower adulation that sustains their self-worth. When leaders feel threatened, they dualistically identify or magnify the threat of an enemy or devil or competitor that needs to be overcome.

Human-paradox and tri-worlds political leaders differ from traditional dualists in that they appeal to our species-wide identity in their endeavors to provide institutions, systems, and processes to enhance the sustenance, security, and comfort of constituents while renewing planetary integrity. These leaders recognize that nothing, *nothing*, NOTHING rises above these priorities. We followers need to remember that it's our individual responsibility to provide for our own sustenance, security, and comfort as much as possible; even with this new leadership model, individuals will still have to compete to ascend specialization pyramids to achieve personal goals.

The government's primary responsibility is as follows: (a) to provide services that individuals/private-sector pods cannot provide economically for themselves, such as national defense and various social/health/ education services; (b) to stay out of the way of private endeavors that support sustenance, security, and comfort as much as possible yet defend the common good against private-sector excess; (c) to provide safety nets for citizens unable to sustain and secure themselves; and (d) to protect common/natural assets for their own sakes and for posterity. In a perfect, glistening paradigm of social harmony, private enterprise would develop products and services in competitive markets, while the government would provide the rest, along with creating/enforcing laws, focusing on the common good, and providing national defense—an overly simplistic model, I know, but that's a lowest common denominator virtually everyone can understand.

Every leader needs to develop, manage, and modify ways to provide for the sustenance, security, and comfort of the species within his or her jurisdiction along with maintaining the integrity of the planet upon which our species depends. That's a tremendously challenging full-time job in itself. All leaders worldwide in all areas should aspire to this simple vision because it's what their citizens want; it's what we humans can control for our own and nature's best interests. A vision of commonly shared reality needs to guide all world leaders, not separateness, superiority delusions, or some other fantasized exceptional status, and of course, citizens need to hold leaders accountable through motivated and participative citizenship.

America can provide the model to redefine both leading and following if it chooses. America has the potential to act with significant authority in redefining leadership and political power away from dualistic thinking, bellicosity, and intolerance and toward a sustainable future for nature and humankind. This can be done while respecting local moral/ethical/ religious codes that encourage peaceful coexistence among the species. Because paradox, contradiction, and irony will remain persistent as long as humans walk the earth, consistency in applying human sameness and tri-worlds principles must remain default assumptions over time. In other words, the realistic core values of individuals need to be amplified as the core values of each nation. Thanks to the founding fathers' wisdom and the sound organizing and controlling documents they created, this has largely been done in America. Now the hard work of actualizing "all men are created equal"[40] and "secure(ing) the blessings of liberty to ourselves and our posterity"[41] needs to be made real throughout a planet with physical limits. As we should have learned by now, this won't ever happen in an environment of dualistic, polarized, back-stabbing politics, voracious economic greed, social polarization, and natural diminishment.

America's future power lies in enlightened reality, pervasive practicality, and conscionable individuality oriented toward species and planet survival, not continued dualism and differentiated exceptionalism. The future of America as a world leader depends on the ability of its citizens to recognize human sameness, life's basics, peaceful coexistence, the planet's limitations, the need to address problems stemming from basic underpinnings of our society (such as racism, endless economic growth, and monopolistic capital accumulation), and the importance of loving faiths rather than exceptional faiths.

A lot of ethereal fantasies need to be deemphasized within the public forum to make room for plans and actions as to how we and others in our species can best achieve sustenance, security, and comfort for all citizens and to let everyone in the world know these are America's goals. Life's basics are something everyone in the species understands; they are the source of a new and renewed political power and global influence and credibility.

Preserving and restoring nature are the contexts in which this social progress will be made. These ideas make so much more sense for investing our nation's energies than any other political platform. Also, establishing and implementing this platform from a position of reasonable military strength, which will still be needed, will help other nations understand, identify, and trust that this is America's unified vision.

Enlightened reality means we believe what's proven. If thousands of scientists have spent tens of thousands of career years studying global warming and climate change and their data say it's real, then it's real—end of debate. Natural evidence proven by objective science trumps any baseless ethereal claim or biased economic or political concern spouted by short-term mono- or bi-world thinkers. Also, another example—common sense says that no one is putting petroleum back into the ground for us to discover later on, so oil *is* a finite natural resource, and there is no scientific validity that, as some kook activists claim, there's an oil generator at the center of the earth generating endless petroleum supply. Without doubt, oil demand will outstrip supply within the twenty-first century if we don't go electric. We must develop energy alternatives now for the human-made world, not when the wells run dry. Coal remains a cheap and plentiful resource, yet it exacerbates the condition of the air, which every human being depends on for life; reliance on it should be reduced and/or eliminated, not increased, if its deleterious effects cannot be contained. These are not just political and economic issues; these are provable species-wide realities that require corrective action rather than more partisan debate and political procrastination.

Pervasive practicality means developing ideas into actions that improve the sustainability of life on this planet. Significant progress is already underway with enlightened capitalists, government/international agencies, and social entrepreneurs through their nongovernmental organizations (NGOs). New technology from the private sector will be a big help in reducing carbon footprints and creating more biomimicry systems that translate into sustainable sustenance, security, and comfort. Governmental research at such places as the National Renewable Energy Laboratory in Golden, Colorado, the Lawrence Livermore National Laboratory in Livermore, California, and many other government-run research facilities and research universities provide a foundation of data/ideas/proof that the private sector can build upon to bring sustainable ideas to commercial scale. Thousands of private-sector startup companies, along with the expanded interest of corporations into natural capitalism–type endeavors, shore up the trend toward more sustainable productivity. Organizations like Hernando de Soto's Institute for Liberty and Democracy prove that NGOs can have a deciding impact upon a nation's future by showing the effectiveness that formal title to property can have in offsetting poverty and outwitting terrorism. Also, the Grameen Bank stands out for its success in making micro loans mostly to women in Third World countries so they can start up entrepreneurial endeavors in their villages. (Conjecture: women who have a purpose in life other than childbearing will have fewer children.) While none of these things individually will be a saving grace, collectively, they constitute the beginning of tri-worlds momentum in the area of pervasive practicality.

Conscionable individuality means thinking and living beyond "local." Wherever you are, whatever you do, you're a player in the planet's future because you make decisions, consume resources, and generate wastes. There's much more to life than the small kingdom of "me or us." The bumper sticker says, Think Globally, Act Locally. Life enrichment comes in large part from learning what's beyond your reach and what's outside the 'hood as well as giving new ideas consideration and thought as they may apply to everyday life. Having informed opinions doesn't cost much, if anything, and it enriches every life. You can self-isolate if you choose to, and you can probably get away with it, but oh, what a pity for you because fear, insularity, and habit will dominate your life! Just about everyone who thinks locally and acts locally eventually becomes bored with themselves and those around them; big fish in little ponds slowly suffocate, float to the top, and stink. Why? Because local is mostly a mono- or bi-world, one not inclusive of the universalities of life. Being strictly local is often filled with hubris about exceptional local qualities that do not enhance species survival or planetary integrity. What's unconscionable? Denying your species sameness and dissociating yourself from nature and life's diverse forms of mental and spiritual introspection.

Globally, a problem for many nations remains power in the hands of local-obsessed, patriarchal, and well-armed leaders who do not acknowledge human sameness and who ignore their leadership responsibility to provide pathways to life's basics for their citizenry. These big-chair egotists will continue to practice old tactics of fear, exceptionalism, and bellicosity rather than accept responsibility for the more difficult challenges of improving their citizens' lives. *Homo smarmus* lieutenants who benefit from old ways will continue their whisperings of tradition, honor, patriotism, and clannish dualisms that ultimately benefit the few at the expense of the many.

Of course, it is not solely leaders themselves who assure political troubles but also the propagandized mono- and bi-world cultures and populations that support them. Without a wide understanding, acceptance, and elevation of species sameness among populations and sincere support of this reality by individuals and political/religious institutions, highly differentiated thinking will continue its ruinous ways.

The way forward for the species needs to include the dilution and then elimination of the traditional concepts of power, leadership, and nationalism. **Leaders need to publicly swear that attending to reality will guide their use of political power and that reality creates the bounds of their power, not some mono-world or bi-world of differentiated dualism that claims exceptional status.** Reality includes recognition of the human paradox, tri-worlds reality, species sameness, the importance of life's basics, and the need for peace and natural integrity. All of the leader's decisions will focus on sustaining human life along with the planet that supports it. These policies will provide an adequate framework so individuals can pursue in sustainable fashion their self-interests and thus attain sustenance, security, and comfort in their lives.

It's time to call the bluff of current leaders at all levels. How do their stances and policies advance species and planetary survival? What are they doing that's so important that they can't attend to life's basics for their citizens? If leaders are so great/outstanding/powerful, why are there still hungry, poor, and ignorant people in their nations? Where's all the tax money going—to meet basic human and planetary needs or to appease powerful elites? How many more bombs and missiles do we need? Why can't leaders agree that human beings are the same species wide and that we have the same needs and wants? Why can't leaders commit to unified global endeavors that benefit the species? Lots of angry and not-so-angry questions have yet to be answered by the powerful, and yes, lots of questions have yet to be asked.

The concept of nationalism stands in the way of truthful responses to these questions. Nations are not organic, but the species is. Nations are contrivances of the human-made world. National identities obscure human sameness, as do all other identities that differentiate humans from one another. Again, inevitably, every human being will identify himself or herself through their nationality, race, religious affiliation (or not), political party, state/city/school/team, and so forth. This helps us become unique individuals. At the same time, the human paradox says we're all the same no matter how unique we believe we are. National boundaries don't make us physically different; nor does our status as a Catholic, Caucasian, or Californian. Because humans believe differentiation makes individuals more personally interesting, the fact of our species' physical, emotional, and psychological sameness gets little attention and little unified support, and this has been our species' Achilles' heel until now.

The moment is at hand for America's political leaders to begin transitioning away from species self-destruction to modes of species self-care. Ethereal fantasies, parsed belief systems, and narrow dogmas need to be de-emphasized, denied, or rejected so enlightened reality, pervasive practicality, and conscionable individuality can get a foothold and grow. The natural world needs attending to to assure human and other species survival. The human-made world needs to recognize human sameness and nature's primacy and to change its ways in sustainable fashion. The ethereal world needs to reorient its messages to the benefit of humanity alive on this earth at this moment.

Who will lead the way?

Purposeful Women

Males of our species dominate the pages of human history because they were the adventurers, the brave warriors, the risk takers, and the chroniclers. They found their way into the big chairs of power by birthright, brute force, or cunning. Literature and drama (and comedy) thrive on the adventures of willful males who manifest every conceivable facet of beneficent and corrupt behavior. Women have always been a presence in historical annals, but relatively few had the lead.

As in the past, many male leaders today incline toward ideologies or cronyism at the expense of agreed-to governance or business principles, they expediently appease followers for a short-term financial or political gain, or they turn into brutal tyrants who thrive on violence to assure regime legitimacy. Males like to manage within defined boundaries such as a nation's borders, a corporation's vision/goals/objectives, or a religion's tenets.

However, once men master one domain, their ethereal minds reach out for something *more*—conquest of other nations, diversification into new markets, proselytizing heathens, or growing their flock of devout followers. Vladimir Putin's unprovoked attack on Ukraine in 2022 is a primary example of this male tendency. This is the point where male leadership falters, where their adventures go off track, where primary interests become simply a cash cow in service to the new passion. Virtually none of a male leader's new ambition is driven by species survival or planetary integrity. If a male leader can't control an endeavor, if it gets too big for him to manipulate, then it is inherently *un*manageable; ergo, it is not worthy to pursue, unless passion overwhelms reason (which it did with Putin in Ukraine). Women think differently; that's why their role in tri-worlds leadership becomes so critical, why now is their time.

Female stereotypes of envious, untrusting, lustful sex objects can only be replaced by women willing to speak up whose intelligence, sound decision making, and articulation make gender irrelevant. Women have tended to be the stewards of moral sentiment and social values in local communities; this has given them power and influence in the past. There's no reason they can't exhibit these strengths, among many others, at the national and international levels. Three women shared the Nobel Peace Prize in 2011 because they actualized their beliefs in the rough-and-tumble human-made world. Hillary Clinton did an admirable job as U.S. secretary of state, as did Madeline Albright. Kamala Harris is vice president of the United States. Nancy Pelosi gets things done in the House. Angela Merkel was the de facto leader of the European Union for more than a decade. Janet Yellen heads the Department of the Treasury after serving as chairwoman of the Federal Reserve Bank. Mary Barra worked her way to the top at General Motors. Jacinda Ardern, is prime minister of New Zealand. These women display qualities most consistent with what this book espouses. Fiona

Hill stood up to the Trump administration with her articulate testimony before Congress. A majority of college graduates now are women; they will become CEOs, mayors, governors, senators, cabinet secretaries, prime ministers, and, someday, president of the United States.

Human-paradox understanding and tri-worlds progress will be made on the gender-neutral ground between male and female. This is a place where family, business, government, and religious interests advance because intelligence, planning, and conscientious resource management replace testosterone-laden ambition. Practical matters, the basics, the important issues within sustenance and security need to be attended to by both men and women with equal input and vigor before there's any focusing on affordable frivolities and lavish comforts. Women who relegate their interests and energy only to the latter and forgo the former do themselves and humankind a disservice.

When I look at historical photographs of an old textile factory with dozens of women attending loom spindles or an old telephone switchboard operated by a long row of women in high-neck shirtwaists, I can see my mother's face. She had several wheel–cog jobs like these; she was one of numerous women in a large room sitting at adding machines punching in numbers and running tallies for a department store in New Orleans. Her post-Victorian world offered few opportunities to advance beyond this level; after my father died in 1958, she worked because she had to, strictly for life's basics rather than any affinity for work itself. Her career ambitions were nonexistent; she was reared to be a Southern belle, a polite and genteel woman who raised well-mannered children. Her role as a woman came to be known primarily by her association with her husband. Thirty years after my father died, my mother was still signing her checks as Mrs. Harold J. Mulley.

Women today don't tend to lose their identities to their husbands this way, but it still happens. Victorian values in a post, post, post-Victorian era die hard. Too many women still want men to take care of them; they want to be "kept." Too many women still depend on their big breasts or their sexy legs or their "flirtus maximus" skills to land a mate. Too many women still think getting married and having children is all there is to life. Too many are shy, passive, and easily intimidated. Too many are unwilling to do anything about male excesses or dualistic antagonisms; after all, it's still "a man's world," they say.

Also, some women in cultures outside of America are completely overwhelmed by legal, religious, or cultural constraints that don't even allow them to show their faces or ankles in public; some of these women even find these constraints comfortable. Women in male-dominant cultures are often belittled by physical female castration or fear of death at the hands of husbands, fathers, or other males. All of these things and more frustrate women's abilities to get to a neutral ground with men. **Guess what, ma'am? Whoever you are, wherever you are, you're just as valuable to the species as any man who has ever walked the earth, and so are your daughters!** For the sake of the planet and humankind, please internalize this fact and use it to build self-confidence and political bravura.

Role redefinition can come with recognition of the human paradox, tri-worlds reality, and planetary needs. That's true for both women and men. When every human being accepts that we live in all three worlds all the time, regardless of gender, and that we're all cut from the same genetic cloth, then sameness gains ground, and many gender-specific role assignments can be reevaluated. That's already occurring in many parts of the modern world. Women are sometimes the breadwinners in Western societies; men stay home and care for the kids. Women business executives, prime ministers, senators, governors, and mayors—these are all major steps toward the neutering of traditional male domination. Neutering doesn't mean castration; it simply means female perspectives find their way into decision making and planning just as male perspectives do. The likelihood of optimum political decisions for the species increases when all concerned parties, regardless of gender, have their say in decision making. That goes for the workplace too.

To deny deserving women status and responsibility is to deny the species half of the world's brain power (only men could think of that!). It makes no sense from a species perspective to inhibit/restrain/discourage that much gray matter, not to mention the immorality of denigrating fellow human beings. With the planet facing an extraordinary array of complex challenges, it's time to liberate women beyond reproduction and distaff responsibilities. Where could we be in pursuit of sustenance, security, and comfort if we doubled our potential for ideas? How much better off could we be if we unleashed so much energy and creative potential? How could future generations benefit from the liberation of nearly four billion minds from traditional constraints and stifling role assignments?

Because nothing changes quickly in tradition-bound cultures, there will continue to be male chauvinism, female oppression, and the denial of equal rights. Those who accept the human paradox and tri-world realists will eventually attain political power that will lead to sustainable economic development and technical superiority over bi-world and mono-world ideologues. Why will this happen? Because women will be included in decision making and because women will be allowed to contribute ideas, leadership, and energy that more retrograde societies will squander. **Sustainable development, species integrity, human sameness, natural integrity, and peace will all advance with the advice/counsel/experience and wisdom of women and men working through the details together.**

CHAPTER 5

Ethereal World

Think left and think right and think low and think
high. Oh, the thinks you can think up if only you try![42]
— Theodor Geisel, *Dr. Seuss*

Dualists got one thing right: we human beings live an outer life for others to see and an inner life that others cannot see. The real me, the composite individual, the thinking and feeling entity that makes me unique spends most of its time engaging itself through head chatter, visualization, and emotions; it's my own very special world that shares itself with others only with my willing permission or by an occasional Freudian slip.

This ethereal world inside my skull hosts my arena for thinking, fears, and various forms of mood along with endless questions, thoughts, and musings. It is also the launching pad for my ambitions, humor, and dreams as well as the place where I wallow in my heartbreak and despair. **This ethereal microcosm in my head serves as my mainframe computer, my multiplex theater, my act-out kid zone, and my dank dungeon where I keep anger and lust chained to the walls of self-restraint and social conditioning.**

Of course, there's a paradox here too. The human brain and the human mind are the same thing, yet they seem different somehow. Where does a brain end and a mind begin? A human mind seems more than just gooey brain tissue, chemicals, and firing synapses—or is it simply all this stuff working together? Do I really make my own decisions, or am I just a slave to my biochemical processors and electricity? What about the soul? Where in the mind-brain does it reside? Issues of the heart—aren't they really issues of the mind or brain? Where do all the crazy/fantastic dreams come from? My mind? My brain? (My acid-reflux stomach?)

While science works to answer mind-brain questions, conventional wisdom says the brain serves as the central processing unit and storage device that does all the electro-chemical processing, whereas the mind includes the software and output the brain produces. The mind stands superior to the brain in this depiction; the mind is more esoteric and refined than a neurological organ that looks like a big walnut. All natural, human-made world, and ethereal thoughts stay stored within our brain until our mind chooses to formulate and express them or to repress or delete them.

The most intriguing aspect of any mind-brain is the ethereal world of thought, emotion, and memory that is singular to each human being. This fascinating mental domain includes each person's exclusive mental territory that is configured from the same brain matter that we all share as a species. This mental sphere is our heavenly acreage, our utilitarian workspace, our virgin pastures of pure imagination, along with our Gordian knot of stress, fear, and earthly hell.

Each highly customized ethereal world in our head sculpts the unique individual within us, the personal interpreter of natural and human-made world reality, the ultimate, differentiated human being that gives each of us a singular personality. This ethereal world houses our exceptional sense about ourselves that drives our vanity and desires and adapts our various identities to situations and circumstances in the natural and human-made worlds.

Only one species, *Homo sapiens*, has developed and sanctified a complex ethereal world. There is no ethereal world without the presence of human beings; as we go, so goes the ethereal. This world exists solely because we do; it has no importance, none, until we think, believe, and then act upon it. Other thinking/learning organisms may conjure up mental alternatives to their circumstances, even create their own group cultures, but they usually don't have the physical ability or mental resources to willfully alter their fates. Also, for virtually all species in the natural world, instincts have more value for their survival than reflections, feelings, or memories that may cross their mind-brains.

Interestingly, a thing called proof has the greatest weight in the natural and human-made worlds, but proof may have little to no value in the ethereal world, where personal empowerment and ego often brush aside bothersome truths. How we consciously and subconsciously configure our ethereal world, how we proceed outwardly based on our mind-brain content, how we manage our motivations and constraints, how we let the ethereal world of powerful individuals influence and lead us—these are the factors that will ultimately influence our individual fates and impact the future of the species and planet.

Humanity now needs to break the bounds of dualism and differentiated historical precedent that dominates so many retrograde American mind-brains. By acknowledging and understanding the human paradox, we can greenlight a new ethereal vision of species sameness, human creativity motivated by nature's limits, and leadership that evidences the human-caring value. **We need to replace history with "ourstory"—a contrived word that defines the purposeful achievement of life's basics through sustainable development, natural integrity, and peace.** Ourstory provides an ethereal vision that unites rather than divides and focuses attention and energy on human reality for the current and future generations. Ourstory lets us, as a species, take control of our fate. The paradox, of course, will be that each of us will have *his*-story or *her*-story for us as individuals and our pods, yet we'll also share in ourstory because of our indisputable human commonalities and our mutual desire to fulfill life's basics and sustain the planet.

Utopia? No, just a hopeful, manageable direction.

Creating "My" World

The process of building a personal ethereal world starts early as parents embed dos, don'ts, and fantasies into children's heads. Children may not care much for the parental discipline, but they eat up the fantasy. Enchanted cottages, good and bad witches, unicorns, youthful wizards, angels, Prince Charming, superheroes, a pot of gold at the end of the rainbow—some images inspire, others fade, and others linger for a lifetime. We humans adore the fantastic mental terrain of this ethereal world because its contents involve and enthrall us. We love the topography of this world's soaring high peaks, its lush landscapes, and the mighty rivers of thought and emotion that run through it. Oh, how time flies! Oh, how we relish the lightness of perfection! Oh, how much security and comfort exists in welcoming and loving arms!

As we mature, this ethereal world becomes our most private retreat. Within this inner world, we imagine the company of anyone we want at any time we want: "I know he/she could love me because I'm so, so special!" Not just any*one* but any*thing* can be had within our ethereal mind: "When I get this job, I'll work my way up to CEO and get that new Lexus!"

However, as we all know, the ethereal world also harbors the darker contrarians of disappointment, anger, and fear. We're all a little crazy or overwhelmed by the demons of frustration, anxiety, or hate during various stages of life. Sometimes these mental flares last just a few seconds. Sometimes they rage into all-consuming bonfires. Most often they simply smolder for a while, soon to be replaced by more immediate concerns and passions.

In a highly differentiated and dualistic society like America's, we oftentimes have to retreat to our ethereal world just to keep our sanity. Along with our culture's dualism and differentiation comes polarity, a tugging of emotion and thought that pulls the mind-brain in conflicting directions. The human tendency is to withdraw into our private mental world first to seek safe harbor from life's threats; we try to figure out what's upsetting us, and then we conjure up ways to get relief. Our motivations, values, and principles reside within our ethereal world along with our coping mechanisms and passions. The constant tugging and delving into our mental recesses for situational resolve consume extreme amounts of mind-brain energy. We Americans can easily exhaust ourselves without doing any physical work at all; we're awfully good at burning mental incense at the altars of dualism and differentiation.

Common traits of the ethereal world include perfection and its dear cousin—escape. Charismatic entertainers enlighten our imaginations with stories/movies/music/games that always seem better than in-the-flesh reality, or we mentally conjure up our own alternative life scenarios that make us feel secure and comfortable. **There's no world more perfect than the one inside our skulls.** Escaping the mundane natural and human-made worlds to the perfection of our ethereal world provides daily refuge for every human being on the planet. Mental dreamscapes, a hoped-for relationship with a new love, quiet sexual arousals, the lotto win, an ice pick in the boss's neck, God's eternal love—how much time of each person's day gets spent traveling among these mental oases?

No living human being on the planet can claim disinterest in perfection and escape because these are primary ingredients of hope. Hope buoys us when the natural and human-made worlds evidence their harshness. The ethereal world serves as the only place we can retreat to where there's little to no downside. Everything plays out perfectly in our backyard of rationalization, imagination, and dreams, where we are understood, loved, and the hero of every plot. If for no other reasons than these—hope and a mental safe haven—the ethereal world can claim a significant portion of every human being's lifetime.

While this ethereal inner world may bring us solace and inspire our lives, its vastness serves as fertile ground for mono- and bi-worlders to implant traditions, doctrines, and conjured fantasies into our malleable mind-brains, especially during our youth. Within the ethereal world, everything appears possible; there are no boundaries, no constraints to impede either glorious or malevolent intent. The hard work of achieving sustenance, security, and comfort gets demoted to lower levels of concern as family/teachers/preachers/politicians/movies/video games/TV implant ethereal seeds into our heads and then water them into flowering illusions of love, adventure, power, salvation, heroism, wealth, and happy endings.

Every generation has its own models of the perfect family, job, and mate. Every generation has its own superheroes that can fly, lift locomotives, and save the damsel in distress. Every generation uses ethereal ideals to motivate itself in the quest for life's basics, to right the world's wrongs, or to conquer it. Also, every generation includes within itself the religiously faithful for whom a heavenly paradise can be achieved through obedience and good deeds. Fantasy, inspiration, and faith look ahead toward worlds yet to be, often at the expense of worlds that are. The uncomfortable realities of the natural and human-made worlds always come in second place within the ethereal world.

Humans with a bias to the ethereal world often let others do their thinking for them. They're easily guided out of the other two worlds into an alternative consciousness where daily human concerns like food and shelter and the laws of nature fade into the background. For humans with a more balanced disposition, an occasional escape into a surreal alternative can be a lot of fun, inspirational, or exciting; **it's when people get hooked on ethereal offerings and when they believe these alternatives have more importance than natural and human-made reality that individual lives and societies go awry.**

In the worst instance, humans with a strong bias to the ethereal world become irrational, delusional, or obsessed. They become convinced they are sanctioned and protected by an invisible force or being, some power outside the natural and human-made worlds that strengthens and shields them. Somehow this special and blessed status makes them different from mere mortals around them. Somehow the bounds of healthy skepticism get crossed. Somehow their irrational state becomes ultra-virtuous, and they act out alone or link up with others of similar stripe. Disrupted relationships, psychoses, and criminality in the human-made world often result from such exceptional, mono-world ethereal mindsets. Terrorists, for example, devote their minds and bodies to the purity and perfection of their ethereal-world visions; they become enamored with their devotion to their cause and often die in its name.

In the best instance, humans with a tilt to the ethereal world question their head theater, include the other two worlds in their thinking, and develop realistic perspectives. After thought and reflection, the ethereal experience becomes an ideal, a goal, a vision. The individual knows the vision cannot be achieved fully, but even partial realization thereof will result in achievement and reward for him- or herself and others. Nations also build identities inspired by ethereal ideals like liberty, freedom, and justice for all or the perfect socialist state where everyone's taken care of.

Progress, change, and a better life for individuals and nations can come from a shared ethereal spirit and the motivation that that spirit inspires.

Inside every human mind-brain, the boundary between rational thought and behavior and irrational thought and behavior can be just a hairline or an ocean of seemingly impenetrable undercurrents, eddies, and mists. Because no natural or human-made place may hold an allure as perfect as an individual's ethereal ideal, other humans outside this dreamed-of world may struggle to understand or abide it.

Compromises within families, businesses, and nations ultimately result from the goals of ethereal inspiration subdued by the limits of the natural and human-made worlds. Progress is often the nexus of natural and human-made world potential meeting with ethereal inspiration. Antisocial behavior and crime may come from an ethereal obsession operating without constraint in the human-made and natural worlds. **All ethereal-world outputs, especially political claims, need to be filtered through natural and human-made world reality for them to have worth for our species' survival.** Good thoughts and high intentions themselves won't shelter us or feed, clothe, or comfort us.

Some etherealists create fantasy worlds we humans love to visit from childhood until death. Bedtime stories, folklore, myths, allegories, *Alice in Wonderland*, Star Wars, the Rapture—we humans eat this stuff up and beg for more. We love escaping the boundaries set by the burdensome natural and human-made worlds. We adore characters with whom our ethereal hopes can identify. We love fantasizing that we can function beyond the laws of physics or have a movie star fall in love with us or obtain eternal life after death. However, we never really question the effect of ethereal constructs on our behaviors in the other two worlds; we assume others in our species can tell the difference between realities and make-believe. Most of us can; some cannot.

The insane are more devout to their ethereal world than those of us who claim sanity. We sane ones believe we can filter out the best aspects of ethereal fantasies and fulfill at least a few of them in the human-made world or use them to provide a benefit to the natural world in some way. We sane people realize flights of fancy for what they are—just dreamy passing thoughts, imagined happenings beyond reach, or just a new/fun/creative idea. Those among us who are irrationally enamored with the ethereal can't easily distinguish fantasy from fact; the insane, naïfs, and fanatics among us believe perfection or escape can actually be achieved through devotion, duty, sacrifice, terrorism, suicide bombing, or other dramatic actions here on Earth.

Most folks can go to a movie, watch the film, and walk out of the theater without being proselytized. We like the film or not, enjoy its humor/drama, or write it off as a dog. Most of us forget the experience fairly quickly. American culture recognizes the possible impact of films and television shows on young minds by rating systems that, although imperfect, help parents steer children toward or away from certain offerings. At the same time, parents acculturate all sorts of ethereal fantasies into their children's minds during the child-rearing years; the only rating system at work here is the parent's.

To protect childhood innocence, virtually every culture respects parental controls and encourages them as part of healthy interaction between parent and child; virtually every civilization defers to the parents' best judgments because, supposedly, no one cares more for a child than its parents. Bedtime storytelling leads to heavy eyelids on a child and eventual sleep (the parent's reward) while letting the child know the parent cares for them via the act of storytelling (the child's reward). What's not readily apparent in this transaction is the weight of the content, the imprint of ethereal fantasies on the child's mind, and the cumulative effects of ethereal fantasies over time.

The joy of childhood comes from being loved and overcoming fears and powerlessness by slowly expanding life into the worlds of natural and human-made reality. Learning progresses under the primary tutelage of parental love and oversight. Without parental unrequited love, patience, and support, the ability of a child to discern earthly realities breaks down. Their ability to learn and care about others gets hindered. Adolescence can be a troublesome time because teenage years bridge childhood fantasies with the limits and demands of the natural and human-made worlds.

Teenagers don't like to give up their childhood fantasies; they do so reluctantly and often with a fight. Throw in a surfeit of hormones, and it's not hard to see why adolescents and young adults often have tumultuous years on their road to self-knowledge and self-esteem. Teenagers try to make their ethereal constructs real by imposing them onto the natural and human-made worlds. As they mature, they discover that natural and human-made world puzzles rarely accommodate their subjective ethereal pieces.

Religion

For many adults, religion comprises the mainstay of ethereal activity—mosque on Friday, tabernacle on Saturday, or church on Sunday. Many Americans attend their respective houses of worship on a regular basis where they pray, enjoy familiar rituals, and feel safe. Ethereal faith is the motivator of religious commitment.

The number of people who go to religious services and are true believers is not known and not knowable. Every person of faith may be 100 percent dedicated to the teachings and practices of their faith; I don't really know. I do know anecdotally that many Americans just go through the motions and answer yes when asked if they're religious; they at least go to services regularly. Many have their personal doubts about the grand claims made by religion. They attend services as much for social, community, or business reasons as religious ones. Many go simply because it's an established part of life's routines, they enjoy the music and ambiance, and it's a mark of good character in local society.

Religion's hopefulness has great magnetism and personal worth for many individuals. It's, in many ways, invaluable for civilization because it provides content and order to ethereal thoughts and feelings. We humans enjoy the comfort/security of believing that a father-like figure will love us and take care of us for eternity, and even if we truly don't believe this to be life's outcome, it's still great imagery. Beautiful stories of revelation and miracles open doors to possibilities we wouldn't dream up on our own.

Religion provides moral values and structure for individuals and families. It generates and reinforces warm and familial feelings; it builds a sense of community that appeals to our social instincts. The act of going to religious services gives a family reason to do something together, to give youngsters exposure to people they would otherwise never meet, and for everyone to build relationships with others outside the bounds of school, work, or home.

Also, religion provides a foundation for constructing an ethereal world. It provides structure to feed our innate curiosities along with direction to live moral lives; it provides the mental repository of intangibles (morals, ideals) that help us live and function in the other two worlds. Religion can provide great value for community stability and can help still the passions and disappointments of everyday survival.

Art, music, and architecture are rife with religious themes; many of these works serve as standards of beauty in their disciplines. Houses of worship are often the only places we allow caring for other human beings to extend beyond the closely held boundaries of family, friends, and selves. Women and children generally feel safe in religion's social milieu. Many people regard members of their house of worship as family.

Religion's ultimate value for our living species comes from its socializing functions, its claimed universalistic mutual respect for others, and its emphasis on personal introspection. "Love one another," "every man is my brother," "forgive and forget"—these and hundreds of other homilies help broaden our selfish natures to include consideration and caring for other human beings, other living creatures, and God's Earth. Religion's message that one has to open one's heart to the potential worth of other people/creatures/things has valuable potential for the species' future.

However, because religion is based on faith and faith lacks proof, there's always a gap between faith and reason in the minds of many congregants. This quiet skepticism, believers keep to themselves. Not all religion makes sense because every religion tends to deny the importance of the other two worlds. Organized religion claims preeminence over the natural and the human-made worlds yet doesn't offer living human beings the really big rewards it promises the dead. Whether organized religion today brings living members of the species closer together or pushes them further apart remains highly debatable.

Another point: religion that resides in any individual's mind-brain may not be as differentiated or dualistic as that of the formal faith to which he or she belongs. Esoteric, personal religious faith can get buried beneath the dictates of doctrine and tradition that all organized religion requires of itself. Major religions preach human sameness but depend on differentiation to assure their organizational survival. Individual religious belief and organized religion coexist like tri-worlds reality. There's a lot of overlap, questions, and muddle that each person must work out for him- or herself, or a religious follower may believe in the other extreme—that the creed/dogma of his or her faith is all there is to life. Every word in a holy book must be followed without question. Mindlessly (or brainlessly) following the dictates of an organized religion tends to separate rather than unite the species because of its claims of uniqueness.

Today's paradox for organized religion stems from its tendencies toward self-absorption—from ignoring or downplaying the importance of the other two worlds. As kids with a religious foundation grow, they discover that despite God's love for them, God won't put bread in their mouths or coins in their pockets. God may get credit once the bread is being eaten or the coins jingle in the pocket, but some action within the human-made world using natural resources brought about these results. God did not make the bread or mint the coins; other humans did. God did not grow the wheat for the bread, bake it, and sell it; he did not mine the metal, smelt it, and send the ingots to the mint. Other humans did these things. Children learn as they mature how the human-made world works and how nature provides. Children learn that bread and money come from their own labors, the generosity of family, or the largesse of persons or institutions more fortunate than a single individual; these things do not come directly from God.

For the natural and human-made worlds, the main problem with organized religion comes from the wide variety of ethereal foundations that natural instincts and human-made values are supposed to build upon. Religion generates feelings, not facts. Success in the human-made world requires knowledge and understanding of nature's resources, forces, and processes; useful skills come from knowledge, talent, and experience, not emotions. Like other aspects of the ethereal world, religion is catalytic, not substantive; it can provide vision, inspiration, and spiritual union with others but virtually nothing tangible for a living species dependent on the natural and human-made worlds for its survival.

Organized religion also causes confusion. Muslims say Islam is perfect and the entire world should be Muslim (*umma*), Christians say you can't go to heaven without knowing Jesus, and Jews say Jesus wasn't the Christ and that the Messiah has yet to reveal himself—and all these religions worship the same God. Each religion claims exclusive righteousness for its orthodoxy and some variant of "chosen" status for its people; each differentiates itself from the other two in numerous and often antagonistic ways. These monotheistic faiths have basic tenets from which variations of the tenets have been extruded into elaborate belief structures and mandated conformities. None of them will admit that God did not create the differences among Christians, Muslims, and Jews; nor will they admit that human beings created these variations for differentiation purposes. It's doubtful that any of these religions would concede that individuals of one faith probably would feel just as emotionally comfortable under a different faith if that's how they had been raised. All religions promise some degree of emotional peace yet among them create considerable, seemingly irreconcilable friction.

No organized religion can afford to say that humanity created God and religion for its own ends. Admissions like these would undermine the leap-of-faith base upon which each religion's credibility depends. Organized religions have created huge time-, energy-, and resource-consuming domains for themselves that, ironically, keep the species apart and that politicize arcane differences and subsidize dualism and differentiation. **Paradox: organized religion aims to unify humankind to reach noble ends but does so by claiming exclusive means that parse the species into sanctimonious pods, pods often antagonistic toward one another, pods that keep a truly species-wide vision of humanity beyond reach.**

Interestingly, the same innate curiosity in human beings that led to the development of science was applied to the ethereal world early on but without any uniform intellectual protocol such as the scientific method to test it. Simple and similar ethereal ideas of spirituality within human mind-brains got differentiated over time into the thousands of sects, cults, denominations, philosophies, and organized religions that we have today, all without much questioning or analysis. Most followers in the past were too afraid of God/gods and their agents to ask questions or to express doubts.

The species-enhancing tenets of most organized religions contain remarkably similar elements (love, family, sharing with the poor, fealty to a higher power, and so forth), yet the cumulative dicta and dogma that govern religious organizations oftentimes overshadow these basics. Humans have muddied up religious waters through bureaucratization of them and through sanctification and glorification of the resultant differences. Also, human politics now get mixed in with religious messages to add even more confusion and emotion to religious biases, thus deepening separations within the species.

In some countries, the importance of the natural and human-made worlds to an individual are afterthoughts to religious dogma. Rather than recognizing the need to partition part of the foundation of an individual's mind to the natural and human-made worlds, religionists attempt to capture, hold, and dominate the entire mind-brain function for itself. Organized religions can be very greedy in this way. No organized religion seems willing to design its ethereal foundation to accommodate essential elements found in the other two worlds. A few elements they may adapt to, maybe—all of them, never. If religionists compromise their unique concepts of perfection and safe haven, what's left for them?

Preachers, priests, rabbis, and imams must lock themselves into their faith's brand to maintain credibility. They may exhibit tolerance for other faiths or not, but their main commitment, their primary obligation, is to follow their particular set of beliefs, to observe its differentiating practices, and to personify its claimed virtues. While every religious believer has a mentor/friend/ideal that fits the entrusted paterfamilias religious role model, arrogance and intransigence can also be problems with the self-righteous, especially religious fundamentalists. These clerics' fire-and-brimstone, hellfire attitudes cower those they say they love; their sermons tend to separate parishioners from the rest of humanity while claiming to include them in it. At some point in a domineering holy man's career, he becomes the shepherd, and the parishioners become sheep. They become things, not people. They become units, percentages, and digits. Religion becomes a competitive business seeking to retain its existing customer base while adding new ones. The house of worship may grow into a massive building with a gym, bowling alleys, and refreshment centers. Proselytizers become salespeople trying to expand the religion's territory and increase its cash flow. Simple messages like love of self, love of others, and love of Earth get buried beneath the demands of a religious pod's corporate survival; *Homo smarmus* influences begin to take hold. The purity, simplicity, and loving aspects of religion become commodities useful for differentiating sermons, marketing campaigns, and growth; religion becomes competitive and commercial, just like the human-made world that it claims to rise above.

Clergy often live rewarding but tortured lives. Being loved, respected, or feared is just a side benefit to saving souls. Feeling responsible for an ethereal belief structure and the behavior of congregants can rest heavily upon spiritual leaders' minds. Clerics are human beings too; they have strengths, weaknesses, passions, and doubts just like the rest of us. By the nature of their work, they commit their lives to a specific set of beliefs that they are bound to espouse and live by; they are both supported by and captive of these beliefs. They are expected to behave in certain ways, to do some things and not do others. Their work isn't nine to five; the role they play requires a near total commitment of time and energy. They spend little time out of character. They know that parishioners can sense their sincerity and commitment or lack thereof and, hence, their credibility.

Through contemplation of a specific doctrine along with increasing comfort with its messages and success in its propagation, the clergy develop a deep sense of confidence about and a dependency upon their brand of faith. They deal with intellectual challenges to their faith based on the certitude their beliefs provide them. In their minds, they've worked through many of the contradictions and paradoxes that their belief structure may include; they've developed talking points around most of them. The more certain they become about their faith, the more others listen to, trust in, and believe in them. The best clerics become true purveyors and personifications of their creed the deeper their personal commitment to and dependence on it become. For every question or challenge to the faith, the outward face of the cleric has an answer, yet the inner face, the one parishioners do not see, has doubts of its own. Knowing the doctrine as well as they do, they can see holes in it; they have questions about it for which they have no answers, questions they keep to themselves. Changing times reveal that their precepts may not be so relevant after all. They develop doubts about the doctrine and their role in purveying it.

On the other hand, many of the feelings of completeness and elevation emanating from religionists come from the moral superiority of their faith's stories. Holy books are brilliant documents in that they address virtually every moral situation an individual human being can envision. Prescriptions for a highly moral and possibly contented life are spelled out literally in chapter and verse; followers can find a historical prescription to resolve almost any moral or ethical quandary. You don't need to think much to find answers in these religious books; you just need to learn, believe, and follow the wisdom prescribed.

Despite their good intentions, the Pentateuch/Bible and Koran don't truly emphasize human sameness because each has been translated by human differentiators to become a tool for advocating salvation if certain beliefs are taken or foresworn. Each book sets prescribed conducts to follow, with each supported by an organizational structure of men and women who've committed their lives to keeping supplicants on a particular version of a straight and narrow path, a path that clerics can control, a path distinct from other religions. Also, there are so many ways to interpret the holy words; the same passages can be used to validate various points at various times depending on the sermonizer's needs.

Because organized religions tend to overpromise and under-deliver for living human beings, a lot of damaging things can happen in their name. Through exclusive promises of salvation and by implicitly or explicitly downplaying the value of the human-made and natural worlds, religionists often create an aura of moral superiority and differentiation over those who are not like them.

The Crusades lasted three hundred years, killed hundreds of thousands of people, all inspired by a quest for regaining and holding the Christian Holy Lands. Today's Muslim extremists contort the teachings of the Koran to kill thousands of innocents through terrorism, all in the name of moving the world back in time to an imagined bliss of the seventh century under

Mahdi rule—all a betrayal of the religion's basic peaceful/loving/sharing intent. The stubbornness of Jews in sticking with exclusionist, isolationist, and chosen traditions along with a Zionist obsession to return to their sacred homeland has led people to hating them and initiating pogroms to kill them. Causes for each one of these motivations stem from self-righteousness and man hating man, direct contradictions of each religion's basic teachings.

A smart religion would step back and admit that God can't get credit for all the good in the world yet not get any splash back from the bad. Why does God need to be perfect? God can't claim realm over mankind and all of nature without responsibility for flaws in his designs or limits to his powers that lead to wars, killer earthquakes, and terrorism. Believers know that God may play a spiritual role in their lives, but he won't feed them, finance them, or protect them from nature's elements. God's great, but he's not that great, or maybe he's just moved on to bigger and better things somewhere out there in the cosmos and left humans to their own devices. He obviously expects human beings to take care of themselves and the planet they inhabit. If he didn't, why did he give *Homo sapiens* big mind-brains, ambition, free will, muscles, and thumbs?

For the sake of humankind and the earth God created, religionists now need to emphasize the value of individual morals, personal responsibility, and spiritual union for *living* people here on Earth and to deemphasize the glories and rewards in the afterlife that often require archaic notions of strict obedience, self-sacrifice, and martyrdom. Isn't living a healthful, moral, and responsible life here on Earth, one that accepts others and supports life and the planet, good enough to get you into heaven? Isn't that a message all religions that espouse an afterlife can teach in good conscience? Isn't getting along with one another, prospering and honoring God's Earth, a responsible enough path? Why all the drama, prostration, and sacrifice? Haven't we outgrown these clichés? Why can't organized religions come together to emphasize our ability to coexist peacefully—to honor God's human and earthly creations? Organized religions need to recast their messages to more wholly embrace human sameness, life's basics, and the importance of planetary integrity.

There's little reason for optimism in this area. The throw weight of tradition and the supposed sacredness of differentiated religious beliefs will defy unifying changes, as will the lack of courage among religious leaders to initiate new ideas. It's simply not in the best interests of each differentiated religion to step back and to take a more universalistic position or to admit that their doctrine, which they've been espousing for hundreds of years, could have flaws or need updating. "Why fix what's working?" they ask.

Catering to the social conservatism and harmony of a congregation is much easier than challenging it, and there's another issue: the patriarchal management model. Who's going to be the first to give up religion's proven command and control tools? The Pope? An ayatollah? Your rabbi? Not likely any of these because it might affect their own life's basics and threaten their leadership role. Plus, who among the movers and shakers in the religious communities would be willing to acknowledge and include the other two worlds as equal in importance to their ethereal constructs? That's *way* too threatening to the promise of perfection they proffer.

While reality recognition by organized religion would be more than welcome, it's much more likely that eternal paradises will never yield to mere mundane concerns like saving the earth and true peace among humankind. **Because salvation and/or doctrinal integrity are the most likely top priorities for leaders of organized religion, it becomes incumbent upon thinking *individuals* to assert the relevance of the natural and human-made worlds into the realm of organized religion.**

Individual human beings need to identify religion's intransigence for what it is—a denial of reality, a mono-world chauvinism that encourages obedience and subservience to aged doctrines, a retirement subsidy for an intransigent patriarchy. It's time to put away all the holy armor, swords, and shields along with the fantasies of being the chosen ones, the blessed few, or God's soldiers. God needs to be a unifier and builder, not a dualistic and sanctimonious differentiator, as many religious traditionalists espouse.

Perhaps an opening into organized religion's fortresses of self-interest can be found among its wonderful stories. None of the great religious books has been updated in centuries because they don't need to be, religionists say; the stories they tell are ageless. The stories' messages help shape the moral bounds of followers, and it's up to each religion's clergy to have those boundaries adhere to doctrinal specifications. Because these stories are dated, the clergy must translate them or update them in their sermons to fit into today's world. Whether the words out of the mouths of today's clergy conform to a backward-looking orthodox creed or to a more contemporary, heterodoxic view constitutes the tri-worlds question mark. As centuries past have proven, many brave and realistic religious leaders were burned at the stake for their reform ideas, while orthodox conformists survived and prospered under the conservative wing of their doctrine. Espousing the human paradox, tri-worlds reality, and planetary integrity in a religious setting will take guts.

While the faithful may not get all their questions answered by the clerics, the power of the stories, the power of their presentation, the beauty of the music and sanctuary, and the ambiance of a religion's community create a domain of comfort and righteousness within an individual that satisfies many spiritual needs. Old, orthodox messages usually cause more dozing than dazzlement within this domain, however. Without a personal touch from the cleric, some humor, and some updating, the holy book stories don't communicate as well as they did in bygone days (assuming those folks were awake).

With the earth beginning to struggle with human-made demands on it, religious stories also come up short because they never anticipated such a circumstance. Nowhere in the Bible or Koran are the issues of climate change, the depletion of natural resources, or human-made catastrophic forces like nuclear proliferation addressed. With today's Internet systems allowing instant access to historical and scientific information, many religious stories can be scrutinized from more than one direction, and they usually don't fare too well in the process. Provable archeological or other scientific data tends to invalidate rather than shore up claims made in the holy books. For instance, dedicated historical scholars of the New Testament have found thousands upon thousands of textual mistakes, revisions, and additions made over the centuries in the historical manuscripts of the Gospels; they've discovered more errata than the total number of words these four books of the Bible contain.[43] Also, none of the New Testament Gospels (Matthew, Mark, Luke, and John), were written by the disciples they're named after; the true authors of these writings are unknown.[44]

If you put on your natural-world or human-made world thinking cap, lots of questions about religious stories pop up. Here's one: what's most ironic about the Ten Commandments? Answer: they're unnatural. Not one commandment has to do with protection or stewardship of the natural world. Nothing in these dicta mentions the responsibility of human beings to take care of the earth and its creatures that God spent six days creating, tiring him so much, he had to rest on the seventh. Doesn't it make sense that God would have included a commandment about caring for the earth he worked so hard to build? Why didn't he? Perhaps he didn't because the Ten Commandments were written by human beings (men) for the purpose of controlling other human beings. These ten life imperatives are a great management tool to keep obedient humans in line and wayward humans anxious. Patriarchal leaders over the centuries believed they needed all the help they could get, and these commandments have proven an effective management tool in Judeo-Christian-Muslim populations. At the time they were written, there was no concept of the earth and the cosmos as we have today. It was beyond the scope of human imagination to envision humans having any real impact on the earth itself; the earth was something to be used solely to advance the goals of humans and the gods.

God spent six days creating heaven and earth tiring himself so much he had to rest on the seventh. Why isn't there a commandment to steward the natural world he worked so hard to create?

Another irreverent question has to do with sex. Why are 20 percent of the Ten Commandments concerned with sex? Perhaps because pious/ frustrated men wrote the commandments, not God. God gave humans sexual organs so we could, like other species, reproduce. In the process, humans discovered that there was more to sex than having babies, so we partook simply because it gave us pleasure, which (oops) generated more babies. Too much extracurricular sex by men lusting for the girl next door undermined patriarchal authority, so adultery and coveting thy neighbor's wife (or the patriarch's daughter) had to be added to the thou-shalt-not list.

Also, why don't the Ten Commandments have restrictions on homosexual or other non-heterosexual activity if God doesn't approve of them? Why restrict just marital infidelities? Why no commandment about prohibiting abortion? Why no commandment to love and honor thy children? Because the authors of the commandments weren't concerned about these issues at the time the commandments were written; these issues simply weren't within their span of concern.

One of the most interesting points about organized religion beyond its stories and dictates has to be its deep-seated patriarchal nature. Christianity, Islam, and Judaism base their teachings around a backbone of fatherly love, judgment, and moral supervision. God/Allah/Yahweh oversees from a mystical high place all the activities of every human being on Earth every moment of their lives. Each religion has rules and strictures that require certain types of behavior, some degree of sacrifice and reverence, and a propagation of the faith to be "in" with the man upstairs.

While God/Allah/Yahweh works in mysterious ways (earthquakes, disease, and so forth), organized religion tends only to emphasize his love for his creations, his forgiveness, and his promise of eternal life (if one plays by the rules) or his wrath upon those who defy or betray him. Isn't there a clear parallel between a heavenly father and a traditional human-world father's control and influence over his family, a clan leader over his clan, or a government leader over his citizens? Isn't it possible that religion grew out of the need for men to add ethereal powers to their tool belt of management controls?

Over the span of history combining dominance in the human-made world with dominance in the ethereal world via religion created a male power package nonpareil. What else would a king or emperor need on his side beyond human-made power (weapons, money, soldiers) and ethereal power (God, clergy, holy books) for political rule over a largely illiterate flock? Again, the natural world got left out of this scenario because none of the gear shifters in history gave the natural world much thought; nature just existed to be used and exploited to enhance human and God-given rights.

Perfecting the religious patriarchal management model in the human-made world required creative thinking. To assure that control over the afterlife was never ceded to any but the clergy, avid religionists created some awesome control techniques.

Sin and salvation have to be the most powerful and enduring concepts yet developed by religion. Sin is dualism at its finest: right or wrong, black or white. Salvation runs a close second. Being delivered away from the pain of sin, being redeemed and included in the reign of God—wow! What an extraordinarily creative idea that sin can be forgiven, that there can be life beyond death, and that it might be a place of plenty where all souls live comfortably in peace and the soul is freed of ego—all available by adhering to religious patriarchal direction and dogma!

Especially creative was the image of the afterlife being a transfiguration of life here on Earth, with the newly dead being reunited with departed loved ones, of getting to sit on a cloud next to God/Jesus/Allah, or of acceptance into heaven by walking through the pearly gates—all ways to make individuals feel special, loved, and cared for. Especially alluring was not having to work anymore, no more stresses, fatigue, or pain from the human-made world, no more obstacles, limits, and heartbreaks from nature, no more feeling old or sick—and all of this cakewalk for eternity! Absolutely brilliant imagery to fill the screens of each believer's ethereal-world theater!

Also on this side of the religionists' coin is God's love. God loves every human being, especially those who play by the rules as stated in the holy books and as expounded by clerics. For those who have strayed from these teachings, there may still be hope for their souls because of God's willingness to forgive. Being liberated from past sins by a forgiving father figure touches the heart of all human beings who have ever been forgiven by their earthly father for a transgression. We all know how good it feels to be in our father's/mother's good graces.

On the flip side of the God coin is what religionists expect from God's children in the way of performance, obedience, and submission. The idea of blasphemy proved a powerful way for patriarchal religionists to intimidate the ignorant and fearful. An individual human being can only attain salvation and its rewards by adhering to the teachings and rules of the doctrine (and by giving tithes). Saying anything profane or sacrilegious about the doctrine might get a follower ostracized, excommunicated, or set alight. Blasphemy—what a powerful tool for intimidation!

Heresy was another tool that swept even the unfaithful and uncaring into the grasp of religious control, particularly during inquisitions when all nonconformists and freethinkers were guilty until proven innocent. The various inquisitions conducted by the Catholic Church in Europe over several centuries encouraged individuals to spy on neighbors, to inform inquisitors about observed behaviors, and to make up sins about others for purposes of settling a personal score or taking over a neighbor's property. Ironically, the inquisitors depended on the sinful behaviors of accusers to maintain control over their more obedient and doctrinally pure flock once an inquisition got underway and after it was concluded.[45]

Chastity vows elevated the chaste above the impure by separating clergy from their natural inclinations, thus making them holier than lustful mortals. As time has proven, religious humans in estrus with no way to find sexual release can do hurtful things to others. In the Catholic Church, these frustrations have manifested themselves through deceiving parishioners and youth and then molesting or raping them, which is not just a modern-day phenomenon. To protect their status, the offending clergy implant fear into their victims' minds and then order them to stay mute about their now mutually shared sin. Talk about evil!

Enter the devil, the anti-Christ, Lucifer and his pals. What a utilitarian contrivance this crew continues to be for clerics! The devil provides a bottomless pit of blame for all things bad while concomitantly providing cover for God, who gets credit for all things good. Talk about dualism!

As every adult knows, natural instincts make human beings hungry, thirsty, randy, curious, aggressive/passive, brave/cowardly—that is, vulnerable to evil choices. The human-made world provides ways for humans to satisfy their sustenance, security, and comfort needs through human ingenuity and social/economic systems, yet it also provides ways to fulfill evil desires. Ethereal religion says the devil pollutes human activity through the seven deadly sins and other transgressions, while God forgives us, loves us, and accepts us into eternity if we reject the devil's seductions and we follow God's rules. What a stressful, dualistic pressure cooker this is! What a time- and resource-consuming diversion away from natural and human-made world survival concerns! What an emotional, troublemaking, time-consuming cauldron as one religion pits its sanctity against others!

Throughout history, every religious tenet gave mainly religious *men* control. These men were recognized agents of God who had the knowledge of other worldly states and the sanction to save souls. They were literate in times when the ability to read and write was a powerful tool for social control. The clergy understood how hard life could be on this temptation-ridden, dangerous planet. Their ethereal vision of perfected reality provided the comfort and solace the natural and human-made worlds lacked, and it provided life's basics for themselves. Their empathy, guidance, and love were sometimes the only counterpoise to the harsh trials and tribulations of daily life. They could usually be trusted to help and listen to individuals when others would not; they were often positioned as the good guys in the community. What the clergy asked in return was submission/obedience/ commitment (and tithes). Despite religious pretensions, men of the cloth were still men—human beings with hungers, emotions, and instincts. Many of them played their roles well by living what they espoused. Others were mediocre, bored, or confused; some exploited and defiled. Exemplars, functionaries, and rogues—clerics over time have proven not so morally different from men in other lines of endeavor.

Physically, men, on average, are about 30 percent stronger than women. Men have been exploiting this advantage since we dragged our knuckles across African savannahs. Gender role assignments, contributions to societies and cultures, economic and political developments over the ages have all been affected by this basic natural fact. Men performed certain functions because they were more physically able; women did the rest. Assignments for the heavy lifting of sustenance and security fell mainly on men's laps, along with a bit of comfort for kith and kin; women helped with sustenance, provided comfort for men and feelings of security for children. It's still "a man's world" because these age-old role assignments still hold sway even though the 30 percent strength advantage really doesn't make much difference in modern societies.

How have men fared in their dominant historical roles? Sometimes great, sometimes good, sometimes not so good. Men tend to forget they are just human beings and begin to believe in their own ethereal deification. In ancient times, they actually did proclaim themselves gods; today we elect them president, promote them to CEO/chairman, or award them gaudy rings for sports championships. Being both a man and a god can be a confusing assignment for an individual male, especially when the stress of leading armies, facilitating production and trade, feeding the populace, or keeping sports fans happy are role demands. Having a host of *Homo smarmus* types around to suck up is nice, but it doesn't resolve challenges that seemingly never end.

The burdens of dominance are lessened somewhat when a man starts to believe he's godlike and can do whatever he likes with impunity. This is very seductive territory for a man. Being treated godlike lets him think big, make big plans, take on the world, or at least make part of it abide his will. He believes others will support his endeavors to fulfill his ethereal goals (because he's so special!). Favoritism/corruption/megalomania often accompanies this he-god scenario. The added corruption of *Homo smarmus* sycophants reinforcing his fantasy begins to have its effect. Religion tries to offset some of these pressures by stressing a higher power and an afterlife to which the he-god can defer. Religion also provides the model of hierarchy, obedience to a higher power here on Earth, and the demoted status of being mortal and sinful. "I'm just following God's will," says the leader ever so modestly. Organized religion plays right into the job description of a he-god power broker.

The patriarchal model of leadership remains pervasive in organized religions and in much of the human-made world because males created them in their own image; they believed no other worthy image was available (surely not women!). Men with different perspectives developed different religions based on their local circumstances and their ethereal or human-world political experiences and fantasies. Having God or the devil handy to thank or blame for good or bad times helped compensate for the variables they themselves could not anticipate. Disasters, bad harvests, and military defeats could be explained away by bringing the ethereal into play: "It was God's will," "God works in mysterious ways," and "This is the devil's work" were common refrains. "We won this war because our cause was just, and God was on our side." The arbitrary use of God's imprimatur to justify a belief or action still gets play with some politicians and clerics. Male egos that follow the patriarchal management model know no limits when it comes to exploiting every resource available to exonerate themselves from troubles and to exalt their magnificence; anything seems fair to them to retain power and influence.

Today the dependence of interest pods on their leaders, still mostly men, to make guiding decisions for both the long and short term has risen to extreme heights, especially at the level of nations. Habits of obedience, loyalty, and trust engrained into cultures around the world obligate citizens to support national leaders whose dispositions usually align more with the he-god prototype and dualism than species sameness and tri-worlds reality. It takes a large ego to become a national leader, and for most leaders, that ego will not be denied. These men were empowered to espouse and advance a nation's interests, and because the leader is he-god like, he relies on his own mind-brain interpretations of issues to govern. Good, bad, and indifferent decisions result as citizens cheer, curse, or shrug about the leader's performance, but the dependence on and acceptance of the he-god model still prevails.

In America, an unwavering point within the citizenry about the success or failure of leaders is the underlying sense of unity within the citizenry that stems from faith in "one nation, under God." Whereas individual leaders rise and fall, America's democracy has survived so far because of its tested and proven foundational strengths (three branches of government, checks and balances, rule of law). Another of these political strengths, according to the religious, is faith in God, who will see us through our hardships—an obvious tactic to differentiate Americans from the rest of humankind and to make Americans feel special.

An argument can be made that the religiously faithful in America are missing the point. **Perhaps Americans and the rest of humanity have outgrown the need for such a deeply embedded archetype as a patriarchal God in human politics. The founders separated church and state for a reason. Reliance on religion to help solve problems we humans created for ourselves doesn't make much sense today or seem in any way fair to the deity.** Perhaps the burden to solve these problems should be put squarely on our shoulders instead of expecting God to bail us out. Perhaps what God would like to see more of is human self-reliance. Perhaps that's why he's so aloof, why he works in such mysterious ways.

The danger for humanity in religion today comes from organized religion's seductiveness and its own self-sustaining ambitions. As mentioned earlier, Islam aspires to rule every aspect of daily life for every human being on Earth; Islam believes there is nothing beyond Islam. Christianity is not quite that aggressive but, like Islam, offers a model of reward for obedience and self-sacrifice as a prerequisite for eternal happiness. Judaism claims to be both a religion and a race of God's chosen children that, basically, just wants to be left alone. Both Islam and Christianity depend heavily on after-life promises of blissful eternity to attract and hold followers, Judaism not so much. All three religions, like others on our dualistic planet, believe that they are the right and true path. How can one religion be right and every other religion wrong? Isn't that just slicing and dicing ethereal mind-brains within the species and threatening future conflict based on dualism and differentiation?

Another problem with organized religion, from a species perspective, gets down to the nature of adherents. Faith defies reason and natural considerations in many of their minds. The seduction of the message, the oh-so-special differentiated value of each follower, and his/her faith become more important than anything in the other two worlds; emotion and devotion to intangible perfection displace earthly sensibilities and commitments. It's all so easy; all you have to do is believe, obey, and follow, and all the promises of religion will supposedly come true. Becoming one of the chosen, the blessed few, becomes more important to true believers than the basics of life, their sameness with other members of the species, or any acknowledgment of their basic dependence on nature. They believe they're so special, so above it all, so securely in God's embrace that life on Earth becomes trivial, a trial one must endure prior to eternal rewards.

Did it ever occur to religionists that God may be disappointed in our species because we can't come together to understand our human paradox and to accept our three worlds? He created the paradox and gave us these three worlds, didn't he? Maybe he doesn't really want to interact with us until we get our act together; maybe that's why he keeps his distance. Maybe we're on our own until we prove to God that we can live peacefully together and can, at least, obey the simple golden rule. Maybe that will trigger the second coming or some other redeeming or uplifting revelation. Obviously, our inability to treat others as we would like to be treated ourselves makes hypocrisy another deep and pervasive species-wide problem.

Maybe it's our turn to prove to God that we're listening to him, that we're appreciative of his direction and gifts. Maybe we need to show God that we've got some initiative and can take care of ourselves. All the supplication, praying, and other forms of subservience and groveling are selfish and obsolete ways of behaving in today's world. People hoping to take the quick route to heaven manifest this behavior in excess and often to the detriment of life here on Earth. Blind obedience, unquestioning supplication, and thoughtless conformity are greedy behaviors when you think about them. Subservient belief exists more to assure obedience to organized religion's traditions and patriarchal management model than to obtain God's good graces or to benefit the natural world and humankind he created.

Religion's value today comes from its alignment with peaceful and civilizing inclinations and its ability to inspire individuals to think and act collectively. Paradox: organized religious activity that intends to unite humanity instead divides the species through its highly splintered, prideful identities. "Yes, I'm a member of the Southern Presbyterian United Reorganized Brotherhood Universalistic Reformed Day Church & Fellowship Inc. and mighty proud of it!" How silly we've become about our innumerable differentiated identities and prides!

Call it a paradigm shift, a revelation, a reformation, whatever you like—the human species needs to redefine organized religions so they become a much more enhancing force for humankind and the earth. Recognition and emphasis of better living here on Earth are the pathways to heaven, not divisiveness, claims of exclusivity, and duality. Every religion can't be right, every denomination can't be the exclusive path to salvation, and every religious advocate can't be the true mouthpiece for God no matter how much believers like and respect their clerics and holy books. **The hypocrisy and self-interest inherent in each differentiated faith's teachings need to be stripped out, leaving only a simple moral creed to which all religions can adhere (and humans can understand).** That single creed should focus on love, family, peace, nature, humility, empathy, sharing, tolerance, and moderation—elements many faiths now claim as part of their exclusive spiritual domain.

If science can prove that humans are a species whose members are remarkably similar in physical makeup, sensibilities, needs, and behaviors, why can't different religions come together to identify those common elements that affirm our species' basic spiritual needs? What are religious leaders doing that's more important than uniting humankind? Why can't leaders of the world's religions come together in a grand convocation to define and link their teachings so we can get on with an updated mission: proving to God we are all his children, that we can live together peacefully, and that we respect the gifts he's given us? Perhaps then he will reveal more of himself to us.

Belligerence

War is etherealism acted out. From the big power chair of a nation's leader down to the lowliest foot soldier slogging through the mud, war's seduction begins with ideals, fantasies, and emotions resident within dualistic and differentiated mind-brains. **All war, ultimately, is a clash of political wills, each side believing fervently its special righteousness and its willingness to risk all by fighting for some exceptional purpose.**

Name a century when there was no war on this planet. Okay, how about a decade? A year? A month? A day? Suffice it to say there have been more days with hostilities since civilization began than days without it. Is it not clear that conflicts result from anti-species behavior, from ethereally sanctified differences rather than an emphasis on human sameness, from dualistic and glorified fantasies instead of an understanding of others' instincts, values, and faiths? You'd think we humans would have grown tired of all the carnage and waste by now. You'd think we would have tried harder to coexist. You'd think we would have recognized higher priorities. But we haven't because we're still locked into exceptionalist sentiments and pod-centric obsessions; **we still have wars because we haven't accepted the reality of species-wide human sameness.**

Our species remains deficient in this area because of the usual suspects of dualism, differentiation, and exceptionalism but also because, ironically, most human lives go unmolested by war. Paradox: American democracy opts for war via support of a majority in Congress whose members do not have and never will have first-hand experience with war itself. (In the 117th Congress, only 74 of the 435 members of the House are veterans, 17 of 100 senators.) American Congressional leaders don't *really* know what they're getting into. They may think they know, but they really have no clue because they've never been through the process themselves; they just deal with abstract descriptions of war and vicarious storytelling, not the gut-level memory of the experience itself.

War is not real to most modern humans because it's an ethereal experience lived out through others and through media; its rigors are completely distant and vicarious for most citizens. War remains odorless and tasteless and forgettable except for the few who do the fighting and suffering. **War's harsh reality lies far distant for most American politicians and civilians, yet the concept of war rests comfortably within their political bag of options.** War remains a valid tool for collective action because the differentiated sectors of the species place no higher priority above it. Americans are insincere about giving up war because we really don't value all human life; we're still stuck on dualistic thinking that values *our* lives more than *their* lives.

Most women don't go to war. Most men don't go to war nowadays either. Very few Americans make direct contact with an enemy and fire their weapon at another human being. Ironically, most armed services personnel don't see combat either; most are support specialists. For most noncombatants, war's something to fear at a distance, to read about in history books, or to watch on TV. It's a terrible thing but paradoxically exciting at the same time. Boys still play at war, Hollywood still cranks out war movies, and ethereal game players spend endless hours anesthetizing their mind-brains to violence as they blast away cyber villains.

We humans rationalize war as a natural activity because of our instinctive behavior to compete for limited resources, to act out a fear or hatred, or to fulfill a learned/cultural/patriotic duty. "We're all animals," we say. "We all fight to survive. Our confrontational nature is immutable. We'll always have war."

War's just another item on the thought agenda for most citizens and its way down on the priority list because it's not a factor in the day-to-day pursuit of life's basics. We rationalize that war's not an action item for civilians because there's not much an individual citizen can do about it. Most Americans have no realistic concept of war because it simply rests as one option among many within a wide array of political choices. We common citizens give in to war, support it, or oppose it with lip service. We never question war's essential character because we really don't know much about it, and we're pretty sure its privations will never touch us directly, which is just how things play out for the vast majority of Americans.

When American war drums start beating, most citizens follow leaders' decisions either faithfully, skeptically, or apathetically. We say hooray for our side and boo on the bad guys. We draw lines in the sand. We're sure we'll win any fight because we're do-good Americans. The ethereal concepts of American righteousness and purity of purpose affirm our support, however strident or dilute that support may be. We always give the president/Congress/military the benefit of the doubt at the start of a conflict. War is a leadership tool. Our prideful culture spurs on male combative instincts, plays to warrior-like vanities, and promises above-average status when fighters return home alive, wounded or dead.

The lead-up to war includes a host of rationales and high spiritedness justifying one pod's martial action against another. Pro-war politicians proselytize citizens through fear, propaganda, and repetition. The excited warrior's cry drowns out peaceful perspectives and the common values all humans share. Personal fears yield to the seduction of pod-biased dualisms, adventurism, and ideological sanctimony. Differences between one pod's willfulness and that of another spur others to defy and confront it. He-god leaders and *Homo smarmus* compatriots validate each side's purity of purpose and the righteousness of aggressive action. Respect for others in the species gets put on hold as soldiers leave home to fight others who are the same yet different.

Young men and women must fight old men's wars because traditional values and national security demand it. During wartime, the virtues of duty, honor, and country come before young citizens' sustenance, security, and comfort because "every generation has to shoulder its share of the burdens." Young minds are the only ones malleable enough to shape into a fervent warrior stature, and young bodies are the only ones durable enough to stand the physical demands and psychological torments that come with war. The youth can abide what age cannot, so young citizens get tapped to dance to the martial music the politically empowered play. The youth are the ones who will do their jobs and not question authority. They're the ones who'll stand in the line of fire and die, especially male youths who are adventuresome, excitable, and naive. Some youths seem politically expendable to sustain America's oh-so-unique exceptionalism and premier world status, and that's okay for most average citizens who have no personal scars or remembrances of war's grim realities.

To compensate for the lack of direct war experience, we Americans celebrate with patriotic ardor our youthful soldiers, sailors, airmen, and marines whose minds initially house virtually nothing but ethereal ideals, curiosities, and fears about their military duty. Some among us put magnetic ribbons on our cars, hang the flag in front of our house, and honor the uniform when we see it. America's war culture promises that the loving arms of the nation will welcome home heroes who have selflessly given life, limb, and sanity to serve the greater cause.

There are more just wars and good wars than "oops" wars according to America's war justifiers. Scales continue to tip toward war as an option for human behavior because most American citizens can't imagine a world without it. It's such a powerful and potentially decisive option, and it's worked for our nation in the past, and because we're such an upright people, we believe our nation only engages in honorable wars. Americans also tend to war because we know we've always got the upper hand; we know we've got that giant military fly swatter and that stockpile of nuclear insecticide handy to wipe out anyone who bugs us.

I don't think there's ever been a second in my life when there wasn't war going on somewhere on the planet. My mother gave birth to me in 1945 during the ending months of World War II. Underlying my lifetime was America's Cold War with the USSR/communism and this conflict's pervasive nuclear threats and fears. One of my sisters dated a veteran of the Korean Conflict whom I silently looked down on because, in my youthful mind, America lost that war. Vietnam, my war, seemed to last forever, and then along came Kuwait, Afghanistan, and Iraq. America's invasions of Panama, Grenada, and Cuba are hardly worth mentioning because of their small scale, not to mention CIA insertions into the Dominican Republic, Chile, El Salvador, Haiti, Guatemala, and Nicaragua. We still have troops in Bosnia, Germany, Japan, Korea, and dozens of other countries all over the planet. The sun never sets on America's military outposts.

Why does any nation go to war?

- Attacked by another country
- Treaty/pact commitments
- Hate/holy inspiration/political expediency
- Leadership megalomania/fantasies/psychopathy
- Ethnic reunification (irredentism)
- Recover lost territory/acquire new territory
- Historical grievance
- Hierarchical/dictatorial survival
- Natural resources envy
- Political survival
- Lack of energy/imagination/resolve by leaders to find peaceful alternatives

Ethnic, racial, and cultural differences often play a role in war. Every nation believes it's special in some way and that the enemy is deeply flawed, threatening, and evil. Of course, there are more nuanced reasons for fighting and lots more stupid ones, none of which—I repeat, NONE of which—make any sense from a species-survival perspective.

Wars get positioned by those who politically benefit from them as the ultimate national, religious, or human experience. Wars are brutal and expensive, but once a war ends, the self-vindicating winner dominates the loser, and the winner's special way of life gets preserved. That's all that matters to dualists and political differentiators who've never given the species' best interests a second thought.

America's most persistent excuse for fighting on some foreign shore is that it's in the country's national interests to do so. Would that still be true if America led the world in species sameness recognition? Would that be true if American leadership dedicated itself to sustainable sustenance, security, and comfort for its citizens and urged others to follow its lead? Regrettably, yes, but to a much lesser degree than now because national antagonisms would be less ominous.

All the justifications for a strong defense will persist in the future because American leaders will never reject the possibility of war— because they cannot. They can't because different peoples around the world will accept some version of human paradox understanding, tri-worlds reality, and human sameness at their own pace, or they may reject these ideas entirely. Other countries/cultures/faiths may choose to go down fighting in defense of their own mono- or bi-world views. There's too much nationalism, global uncertainty, and ignorance not to have a strong but reasonable defense. Also, it seems American leaders will always be able to convince us fear-ridden common citizens and especially us testosterone-laden, adventure-loving males that each fight is for a just and worthy cause.

The impact of warfare never truly hit me until January 1969, when I was in a jeep driving north to Cu Chi from Long Binh, a U.S. military base in Saigon (now Ho Chi Minh City). I had been in Vietnam three days and was ordered to serve as an individual replacement officer in a signal battalion supporting the Twenty-Fifth Infantry Division. As the traffic noise and the sultry air engulfed my senses, my mind began to grasp where I was. Anyone on this busy roadway could pull out a gun and blow me away simply because I was wearing green fatigues. *While I'm in this country, I'm no longer me. I'm a thing, a target, an object for the locals to detest/admire/fear and to shoot at*, I thought. *I'm a statistic in waiting.*

This realization transported me from a state of mind where I was in charge of my life to one where the outside world controlled me; I was trapped in life's ultimate dualistic experience. Every action I contemplated had to take account of where I was, what my uniform represented, and how a local person might perceive our differences. I had become a tiny speck of dust in a hostile, volatile universe, and there was no way out.

Every soldier in a combat zone lives in the bowels of dualism. Surviving in a war zone requires all soldiers to identify with "us" and to not fully trust "them" no matter who *they* may be. **War *is* instinctual, it *is* primitive, and it *is* dualism at its most basic. It's also inherently inhumane because it goes against the positive value teachings of the human-made and ethereal worlds.**

All that Sunday school talk about loving thy enemy as thyself—*poof!* It's gone once the bullets start flying. To have to degrade and hate other human beings, to feel mortally threatened by them, to maim and kill them demeans every sane human being. "Him versus me," "kill or be killed," "I haven't got anything against these people," "What am I doing here?" "What would Jesus do?"—confused thoughts and questions like these run through every combatant's mind-brain. Ironically, soldiers on the other side are likely experiencing similar fears and confusion.

Once a combatant accepts where he is and what he represents, his world gets reduced even further. Relationships with those closest to him, his squad or platoon members, become the only important thing. Who's got the dominant mindset in this unit? Who's the wimp/loser? Who's the gung ho, gonna-get-me-killed lifer? Who's smart? Who's stupid? Who's the clown? Is our leader cool or a fool?

Every soldier evaluates himself and others nearest him relative to the dynamics of each personality and each situation. Who can be trusted to perform when the shit hits the fan? Who can't handle being a speck of dust? Each squad or platoon becomes a pod of mono-worlders looking out for themselves yet, paradoxically, a cohesive, functioning unit that has to maintain symbiosis for survival's sake. Individuals with separate identities must surrender their own exceptional worlds to the dynamics of the group for everyone/most/some to go home breathing.

War is a maturing and warping machine that has no sympathy for individual human beings. It's maturing because youthful exuberance and curiosity have few options for release in a war zone. Young soldiers can't choose to do this whimsical activity or that frivolous one as they might at home; they must follow orders and do what's required of them. Sure, soldiers horse around and have fun, but it's not like home fun. If youthful self-indulgences continue in a military setting, the young soldier gets reprimanded, court-martialed, or kicked out of the service. Also, within this maturation rests the sense of duty that involves the essence of warfare: destroying enemy assets and killing the enemy when required. No matter what gloss a back-home patriot or politician puts on military service, the essential job of a combatant is mission fulfillment; inherent therein rests the potential use of deadly force.

Every member of the military has a high- or low-tech role to play leading to the elimination of enemy assets and personnel. Those in the military who are distant from the blood and guts usually suffer low to moderate warp compared to those who see it up close. Warp consists of the mental and emotional conflict between learned familial/religious/moral teachings and the reality of killing and destroying, the guilt and anger of having to put a callous over your brain to dull the pain of zapping other human beings and wasting their property, and the psychological burden of returning home to loved ones a different, stranger person from the one who departed. Personal secrets and repressed experiences within a combatant's mind-brain add to the warp; fighters often don't want to admit to themselves or others their part in war's harsh realities. They don't like to admit that all screens in their mind-brain's multiplex theater show the same combat reels repeatedly; they don't like to admit that they can't forget. There's no service ribbon for post-traumatic stress disorder (PTSD).

Generals, admirals, and rah-rah politicians will support the continuance of a strong defense ethic because it serves their interests; they're just doing their jobs. The grunts, trigger pullers, artillerymen, and tankers who saw the shit go down hardly ever get to testify before Congress. They don't get public attention because noncombatant home citizens don't want to hear testimony that runs counter to their patriotic/dualistic/differentiating pod purity. They don't want to hear ideas that might dilute the concept of war as a viable option in support of their oh-so-exceptional/patriotic/fervent beliefs, and ironically, most veterans don't want to resurrect old memories and talk about them anyway.

Perceptions of noncombatant civilians, America's majority, matter more to politicians than those who know war's filth, cruelty, and senselessness. There are veterans out there who will speak up if asked, but they hardly ever are; their perspectives go unappreciated. Virtually all the testimony Congress hears comes from senior commanders who always buffer war's painful realities. The paradox for America continues to be that those with the political power to declare and fund war are those with the least first-hand experience of it (including presidents). That point was proven most clearly by the noncombatant ideologues who dreamed up justifications and support for Vietnam, Iraq, and the twenty-year presence in Afghanistan.

The defense industry in America has become so large, so institutionalized, and so resource consuming that the likelihood that the country will demote war's status anytime soon seems remote. War may get pushed to the back of the planning table, but it will never go away. So many high-paying common citizens' jobs depend on the defense industry that any transition away from it will take tremendous political will, planning, and persistence. President Obama and his secretary of defense chipped away at the defense establishment, but President Trump just built it back up again. President Biden will be tested by the need to be a stalwart NATO partner after the Ukrainian invasion.

The Pentagon budget pendulum has swung between 3 percent to nearly 9.5 percent of the GDP from FY 1961 to FY 2022—up in war years, down in years with low action. In 1969, when I was in Vietnam, the DOD budget was $84.99 billion; for FY 2022, it is projected to be $715 billion. While the DOD budget grew in leaps and bounds, budgets for other federal departments barely kept up with inflation during the same period. Maintaining America's nuclear arsenal of over 6,800 warheads and their delivery systems costs billions of dollars each year to maintain. Why do we need so many weapons? We could easily destroy the entire planet, including ourselves, before we would use them all up.

Then there's the ethereal, techno-whiz-bang aspect of defense expenditures. Long-term military plans to provide real-time information to soldiers on the ground so they can always have the advantage run into the hundreds of millions of dollars each year. Prototypes of the futuristic infantryman like the army's Future Warrior 2020 builds on the Future Force Warrior 2010 program that makes soldiers look more like robots than human beings. Also, essentially, that's what they are—human–electronic weapons platforms with sufficient intelligence to successfully outwit and out-fire enemy combatants in a hostile environment. The 2020 program focuses on nanotechnology for extremely small systems, devices, and materials for the infantryman.

Inside all the futuristic gear of a homo-robo warrior, however, there still will be a young person who is physically the same as others in his unit and as the enemy being fought. Unless taught species sameness beforehand, this fighter will only discover human sameness traumatically when he looks at the bodies of those he's destroyed in the latest firefight. His eyes and his brain will tell him that the blood and guts he's seeing are the same blood and guts inside him. He may get a headache, and his ears may ring; as he gets a whiff of a corpse, his lunch may revisit his throat.

Whatever he feels, he keeps his mouth shut because he has no option but to stay within the confines of his mono-world and the good graces of his speck-of-dust buddies. To stay functional in his unit, he must attend to the differences between himself and the dead enemy, that now lifeless object. He has to stay silent or be macho; he can't think about the fly-infested corpse having a wife, parents, and kids. Any regrets he may feel about killing other human beings gets stowed away in his Pandora's box. "Better him than me," the grunt says as he hoofs off to the next assignment, unaware that his memory box won't open until he gets home.

Soldiers talk to one another. It's mostly quips, comradely kidding, and bullshit. Occasionally, there's some serious talk about why they're fighting and who they're fighting. In Vietnam, these talks keyed on keeping communism from engulfing all of Southeast Asia, showing Communist countries that the United States could stand up and fight, and giving Vietnam a chance to become a democracy. CIA operatives and special forces who entered Afghanistan right after 9/11 had a strong revenge motivation to keep them pumped up, and they eventually got Osama bin Laden. After expenditures between $1 trillion to $2 trillion over nearly two decades, U.S. forces left the country in 2021 to stew in Taliban juices.

In Iraq, when no weapons of mass destruction were found, the inspirational rug for that war got pulled out, and the overall military mission had to be shifted to finding and fighting terrorists, giving Iraqi politicians more time to legislate, or some other cause de jour. Bush's political mission shifting must have been a morale funk for our in-country troops and, I assume, led to endless trash talk within the ranks about politicians and senior commanders who had to conjure up "stay" rationales. No one in the Bush camp realized that it was the values gap between modern/sophisticated America and local/tribal Iraq that led to so much heartache. Simple people concerned with the struggle for their own living space and life's basics can't be expected to welcome and understand the motives of a confused leviathan; nor should they be asked to. Fucked up beyond all recognition (FUBAR)—a worthy moniker for all of America's latest conflicts.

American combatants know when they're involved in a senseless war. Vietnam, Afghanistan, and Iraq all proved excessive because the United States had little to gain and much to lose with these conflicts. These wars exhibit innumerable political leadership and *Homo smarmus* failures.

What exactly was to be gained by fighting in Vietnam? Containing communism? Stopping the falling dominoes? We "lost" in Vietnam, and global communism took a nosedive anyway; winning in Vietnam wouldn't have contributed one iota of difference to Soviet communism's ultimate failure, but bellicose war hawks surely would have claimed that it did. A strong foothold for democracy in Vietnam? That wouldn't have ever happened because of the deep-seated corruption among South Vietnam's leaders, who didn't really understand democracy and who enjoyed smoking their heroin wrapped in $100 bills. Exclusive commercial contracts for rice, rubber, or bamboo? That's about all this poor agrarian nation had to offer and surely wasn't worth losing more than fifty-eight thousand dead Americans and more than five times that number wounded or maimed.

The Iraq war turned out to be even more ludicrous than Vietnam because it diverted resources away from Afghanistan, where America's 9/11 enemies were. The shameless run-up to the Iraq war was based on faulty intelligence, neo-con *Homo smarmus* influence, a hand-puppet president, leadership deceptions and lies, an anxious-to-prove-itself military, and roll-over media—all of which neglected the instincts, values, and faiths of the Iraqi and U.S. populations. Gung-ho, flag-waving non-veteran politicians plunged America into a stinking morass of Iraqi quicksand that will indebt the United States to foreign creditors for decades. Corporate media sold out their objectivity because it was their chance to cover a big conflict and to report on a for-sure victory. They never pressed Bush and his crew for proof of their ridiculous WMD claims. (Question: exactly how was Saddam Hussein going to get his reputed weapons of mass destruction to the United States? On SCUDs? On Iraq's nonexistent fleet of Polaris-like submarines?)

Wars today are leaders' wars, not peoples' wars, each conflict proving to be another arrow in the quiver of dualistic/differentiated political thinking carried forward for no species-advancing or planetary enhancing purpose. There are no clear-cut military victories anymore because human sameness cannot be explained away as easily as in the past. Most American veterans struggle to articulate how their service was important to the nation except to regurgitate stock phrases like "We were fighting to stop the spread of communism" or "We wanted to give Afghanistan and Iraq a chance to stand on their own two feet." We citizens need to realize that fighting leaders' wars only pays homage to outdated models of leadership and to exceptionalist fantasies.

Every culture has its own mix of the ethereal and human-made worlds, its own heroes and traitors. While every nation says it wants peace, most cultures glorify war and warriors and seek to dualistically inspire those in their pod to take up arms when needed. Paradoxically and mostly unnoticed, every culture during war time also continues its efforts to move toward sustenance, security, and comfort for its civilian citizens. However, wars significantly interrupt these basic endeavors, push them aside, and, once the conflict ends, leave the widows and survivors to wonder why the wars were fought in the first place.

The sense justifying a war is often hard to find after the fact. Historians still don't agree as to what caused World War I. Class? Race? Empire? Elite egos? Ethnicity? A bit of each? Harsh reality replaced grand illusions when Gavrilo Princip fired his pistol and killed the Archduke Franz Ferdinand and his wife Sophie on June 28, 1914. Treaties, allegiances, aristocracies, monarchies, hubris extraordinaire, and deep-seated ethnic hatreds, along with dreams of expanded empires and fatter treasuries, spurred along this war's dualistic game. Families on all sides of this conflict sent off their young men at the train station, waving flags and blowing kisses as brass bands blared a patriotic march. Every participant nation was convinced of its righteousness and took comfort in God's sanction to defeat the heathens, rapists, and baby killers on the other side. Individual fighters entered the fray believing the heroic war stories their grandfathers had told them. They believed their chance for personal glory was at hand; this was their opportunity to be recognized by nation, peers, and family alike. It'll be just a few months away and then back home again. War was their window to ultimate adventure and male self-validation.

By the end of World War I, instead of clarity and values reassurance, nations and survivors found only depletion, exhaustion, and grief. Some eighteen to twenty million people died in the conflict; many millions more were injured and maimed. Monarchies, aristocracies, and governments fell. The "war to end all wars" became a stepping-stone to more conflict as fascism, Nazism, and militarism got a foothold on the world stage. No one really won World War I because it led to World War II.

World War II, the world's most massive conflagration ever, was so widespread, it affected virtually every nation and individual on the planet in some way. Racist, egomaniac, he-god leaders tried to expand their empires in the Pacific and Europe ostensibly because of Japan's need for oil/territory/laborers and Germany's need for growing room and racial purity. The idea of human sameness never crossed Emperor Hirohito's or Adolf Hitler's mind.

These aggressors believed their superior homogeneous nations would stomp inferior societies into submission. In their minds, racially mixed lower cultures could never attain the same cultural/economic/military heights as those of pure blood and purpose. The deified Japanese emperor, the all-powerful führer, the shogun-warrior spirit, Aryanism, Lebensraum—on and on, their utopian-inspired, fantasy-driven ideologies pushed to achieve ethereal destinies.

They were defeated because the Allies had more war materials and more soldiers, sailors, and marines and because the Allies were angry and determined to stop these metastasizing cancers. World War II cost humanity an estimated forty-eight to sixty million lives, with tens of millions more wounded or crippled, and it also gave civilization its nadir: the Holocaust. It also bequeathed to humanity the ultimate step in anti-species militarism: nuclear weapons, which, ironically, helped cap even grander-scale aggressions.

Rather than elevating the basics of reality (that is, human sameness, the three worlds, life's basics, natural integrity) to a status commensurate with their value, aggressive leaders in historic war periods donned the old mantles of cultural superiority and exceptionalism, national/racial uniqueness, territorial expansion, or the simple "we are better than they are" theme. Only after the conflicts ended did the combatants discover that what remained were corpses, ruins, debt, and new hatreds; only then were thoughtful reflections and a renewal of interest in life's basics resurrected.

If there's any optimism to be had from these conflicts, it is that World War I was the first giant step toward the need to acknowledge human commonalities and needs; World War II was the second. Both wars proved the weakness of aggressive, exceptionalist arguments and within their outcomes provided the grist for breaking down these arguments' rationales.

Obviously, subsequent wars since World War II indicate the reluctance of nations to accept the human-sameness principle. The continuation of belief in differentiation and unique purpose/status still takes lives and impedes species progress, as so amply demonstrated in, for example, the Bosnian War and the Rwandan genocide. **The question for a civilized world in the twenty-first century becomes the following: why not forgo**

the fighting, recognize our species sameness, concentrate our political energies on reality's basics, and focus on sustaining life on this beautiful but limited planet? A simple question like this won't get a simple answer from today's political leaders. "Life's too complicated," they'll say. They'll mock and degrade the question before they'll answer it. If they do answer it, each and every word they say should be regarded as empty homage until their policies and actions respond to the question's premise of peace and species-planetary focus.

Problem: there's so much equity and momentum built into national and cultural differentiation, religious differentiation, and elite influence and posturing that a set of straightforward, common goals for all of humanity rubs against almost everything to which leaders and patriotic nationalists aspire. Why carry on this ruse anymore? How can we, as a species, consider these politicians true leaders when they don't lead us anywhere except to old timeworn paths that keep us apart?

Current world leaders struggle to reach accommodations among themselves because of a paucity of mutual goals. Each nation feels sanctioned in its own view of how its citizens should live their lives, but local priorities often deny universal truths. Because leadership has not accepted the human paradox, because leadership has not stated openly that life's basics (sustenance, security, comfort) for the citizenry are their top priorities, and because leadership has not acknowledged that the physical planet cannot sustain endless growth, they focus on national issues that they believe they can control and resolve. Rather than leading their nations, they're simply riding the coattails of tradition and precedence. They're denying true reality while pretending to manage it. They're not focusing on their own nation's and the species' best long-term interests, which should be one and the same.

Understanding the human paradox and applying tri-worlds reality (human sameness, life's basics, sustainability, natural integrity) to individual mindsets and future relations among nations provides a common base for potential understanding and problem solving that might avert war. Acknowledging that all human beings are essentially the same allows principles to be established that put potential mutual benefit or reasonable compromises ahead of the impacts of incessant dualism, differentiation, antagonisms, and male-driven belligerence.

Holding all world leaders responsible for the sustenance, security, and comfort of their citizens as a top priority empowers citizens; they can judge their leaders' performance and hold their feet to the fire for issues constituents genuinely care about. He-god, dualistic leaders and their differentiated prides need to be identified and exposed to shame and rejection for their irrational bellicosity that wastes human and natural resources. **There is no higher priority for national leaders than life's basics, human sameness recognition, sustainability, and natural integrity—priorities shared species wide.** These peaceful rationales stand head and shoulders above any aggressive bellicose reason to spend lives and treasures on another war whose outcome would achieve little for the nations involved and nothing for the species and planet.

New human-paradox understanding and tri-world ideas are all worth a try as America repositions itself as a world leader. To downplay the importance of sustainable sustenance, security, and comfort, to advocate endless consumerism and resource depletion, to place ethereal, religious belief ahead of natural and human-made concerns, and to posture as an aggressive, belligerent superpower reveals a nation in denial of reality and disunion with humankind. Narrow self-concepts of superiority and uniqueness cannot be sustained by earthly reality.

Transitioning to a more peaceful and sustainable future isn't just a leadership challenge. Common citizens' acceptance of our own basic sameness with everyone else on the planet will be a difficult pill to swallow. Who knows how many generations and sets of dated beliefs need to be exorcised before the species willingly accepts the basic sameness of its instincts, values, and faiths and the need to address any differences peacefully? Unfortunately, we may need to choke on our own wastes and have a few more world wars before the sensibility and inevitability of making these changes takes hold. Hopefully, we're smarter than that.

America holds the key to changing its ways and possibly leading the world to a more peaceful state of coexistence. Opposing this shift in policy stands an armada of self-interests: huge standing arsenals and powerful weapon makers, a politically influential military, economic growth dependent on defense and carbon-based systems, conservative national hubris, an economy obsessed with short-term growth and profits, a fearful/selfish electorate, *Homo smarmus* infected politicians, and leaders willing to exploit superpower status in chauvinistic ways.

These self-serving forces will mock and resist the idea of America becoming a model for species sameness, peace, planetary care, and the responsible advancement of life's basics. Ironically, only America can take on such a leadership role now because of its huge military and weapons arsenal, which could help persuade other countries to follow suit in sameness recognition and peaceful species survival, many of which, I believe, would do so enthusiastically even if America didn't have such a big defense cudgel.

America needs to begin to lead other nations beyond the strictures of nationhood to a more species-based focus. Power does have its privileges and influences, especially when these energies are directed at universally comprehended goals. America simply hasn't come to the realization of this new purpose yet. Question: can other nations be trusted to accept tri-world goals? Sure, if America exhibits its trustworthiness and sincerity and, as Ronald Reagan said, we trust but verify.

The possibility that America will take the lead here and that all the countries in the world would sign up for true peaceful coexistence defies imagination; it's pure ethereal idealism on the part of human paradox and tri-worlds thinkers. There's too much ignorance, mono-world religiosity, and dualistic national pride out there. There are too many jobs, too much investment, and too many belief systems that rely on differentiation and warfare for these systems to make concessions to the species. Nothing in the history of humankind suggests even remotely that such an outcome might be possible. If that's true, then apparently, we humans truly haven't learned much from our past mistakes since we just keep repeating them. Regrettably, it's possible we never will, but we should try.

The optimum solution? Beyond nations and their leaders, *individual* species- and planet-oriented political thinkers need to serve as counterpoise to divisiveness and propagandized exceptionalism; that's how a human-paradox understanding and tri-worlds groundswell needs to start.

Only as individuals begin to live as principled members of one species, only as individuals teach their progeny that they live constantly in three worlds, only as individuals accept that others want sustenance, security, and comfort just as they do, only as individuals decry differentiation as it separates, demeans, and dehumanizes other members of the species, only as individuals balance the considerations of the natural, human-made, and ethereal worlds, only as individuals accept that paradox, contradiction, and irony are always present in life, and only as individuals live their loving faiths day to day will the hope that nations can change their ways become more real.

Trumpism

I went to Vietnam; Donald J. Trump went to Club 54. Honestly, I would have gone to the club with him if I'd had the chance, but he was the playboy with money and connections, while I was the lower-middle-class guy who barely had carfare. Now I'm happy living in the mountains in Colorado, and he is a wounded narcissist stuck in a big-lie fantasy he can't let go of. I hope he can snap out of it and find some peace and happiness for his remaining years, but I think it's too late for that.

Donald, the man, is an abandoned campfire. His rageful, smoldering embers could flare up again, but Republicans may be ready to move on by 2024. It's his political legacy that's most worrisome. **His mythology will live on for many years, and every second of it will deny the human paradox and tri-worlds reality. His mythos is the antithesis of what this book is all about.** His ethereal fantasies will still cast their spells even after his passing.

Trump's base, the 35 percent or so of the U.S. voters who stuck with him through thick and thin—the non–college educated, neglected, angry working class that listened to him ramble on and on and on about their grievances (and his); the Women for Trump admirers, the rally groupies, the swag sellers, the flag wavers, and the Fox addicts who had to get their daily/hourly/minute-by-minute Trump fix; the Second Amendment zealots and fundamentalist Christians, the Proud Boys, the 3 percenters, the KKK, the neo-Nazis, QAnon fantasists, and every other far-right-wing fringer who found their "guy" in Donald; the elected Republicans who kowtowed to His Highness out of fear they might get hate-tweeted; the corporate types who believed he could strengthen their bottom line with someone who understood business in power; the billionaires who chuckled as they signed campaign checks that would shore up their/his class—all these Trump basers and more are testament to how weighted the human paradox scale in America is tilted toward individualism at the expense of the species and planet. Seventy-four million people voted for Trump in the 2020 election, each vote a testament to mythic individualism, ethereal obsessions, die-hard dualism, and differentiation.

Does anyone in Trumpland have any concept of the human paradox or human sameness? Do these fellow human beings understand that we all live in three worlds our entire lives? Why does being enthralled with one man have more political value than the species and planet? Can't his loyalists see that he's led them up a blind alley?

Obviously, these folks prefer the me/us end of the human-paradox spectrum over the species and planet; each Trumper believes that he or she is exceptional, blessed, and unique in some very special way because Donald made them feel that way. A superior salesman, Donald convinced his disciples that he personified the Ayn Rand, "Go west, young man," John Wayne, rugged individualist. He was the valorous hero flying in his 767 to a rally near you. He alone made his fortune, he alone became president, he alone can fix it, and you too can rise above others if you trust him and follow his lead—Trump the god, you the demigod (if you believe and follow).

Trump reinforced over and over his ethereal, exceptionalist mindset and topped it off with his favorite adjectives: "amazing," "winning," "rich," "perfect." His followers couldn't get enough of him and his message. If you have to step over a few bodies to get what you want, well, that's the way it goes. Nature? Nature is just there for us winners to use, no problem. Ethereal beliefs? Believe what you want as long as it's Christian (with Jewish okay in election years). Nothing matters but the human-made and ethereal worlds to Trumpers, the world like Donald's: tailored suits, beautiful women, class properties, and plenty of discretionary income. Dogged determination, high energy, ego passion, and lots of lawyers will get you where you want to go—just like it did Donald! All you have to do is believe (and support MAGA)!

On the other side of Trump's hyperbolic coin are "weak," "stupid," "corrupt," "loser," "fake news," "deep state," "liar," and whatever other dig he could think of. Part of his legacy is that a highly differentiated lexicon of simple wording is sufficient for life in a complex society. Everything is black or white, good or bad, in or out. Enemies are anywhere and everywhere. Congress is a hindrance to my/our America. The judiciary is ignorable; only what I say counts. You don't need any expertise to be a champion. Just listen to my common-sense, profane, win–lose, down-to-earth reasoning, and you'll be fine. You'll come out on top; you'll realize it's all just a game. Also, it's downright fun to mock others; bashing the libs/experts/bureaucrats/pundits makes for a great hobby and makes the basher feel good inside—really good.

Trump sold a comfortable folklore to people who were not secure in their own life's basics (sustenance, security, comfort). His base was not founded on those who had fulfilled their American Dream but on those who had been denied it (and it was all the "government's" fault). No doubt they had been cheated—Donald said so; it must be true. Trump believers never recognized species sameness beyond their fellow Trump groupies because all Trumpers are an exceptional and deserving "us." Natural and common sensibilities were demoted to near nonexistence in Trump World in favor of the exceptional sense that Donald emoted and promoted. Any move toward the species end of the human paradox was labeled "democrat," "socialist," or "liberal"—all filthy pejoratives to Trumpers.

During Trump's term, a fervency of flag-hugging, emotional patriotism replaced that middle-ground mindset that traditional conservative policymakers used to accept and strive for. Trump determined with his mouth what patriotism meant for the right wing. Even high-ranking generals didn't know as much about war and peace as he did. He knew more about nuclear weapons that the physicists. Only he could solve the COVID-19 problem. Everything rolled up into Donald's omniscience, his beautiful and smart mind-brain. All hail this exceptional individual! He personified the American Dream of ultimate individualism. Follow him and reap the spoils; be superior just by believing in him! Just like Jesus does for your soul, Donald will do for your pocketbook, your farm, your job, and your family! Oppose him, and you are the devil incarnate; you will be found and dealt with.

Species-sameness denial is *the* basic tenet in Trump mythology. No social group has any worth beyond your family, your job, your church, your nation, and the Republican party. That's it; the rest is "bullshit" and should be opposed. In Trump World, life literally is black or white, for or against, in or out. Inside the Trump cocoon, you are blessed, chosen, anointed for better things; what a beautiful butterfly you will be if you stay loyal to "the Man"! You are different, unique, the ultimate individual whose righteousness cannot be questioned. If you are beyond question, then you are also above the law, as is Donald. Since there are no "facts," other than what Trump says, there is no need for deliberation and consideration of other points of view, ergo no need for democracy. Probably the only asset history will grant to the Trump administration is that his term as president was a stress test to all the institutions, laws, and norms that constitute the government of the United States of America.

As president, Trump could not escape conflict; he loved it. Not the death-and-destruction type of conflict (perhaps one of Donald's few admirable traits is his desire to avoid armed conflict)—his type of conflict is more of the drama type: the tension among individuals or political groups that keep the action ascending before it reaches a resolution that reveals a winner and a loser. His decades of television programming drilled this brand of conflict deeply into his Aryan mind. *The Apprentice* manifested his obsession with competition by vying competitors against one another for a reward of, usually, short-term employment within the Trump domain. Easy millions for him—all he had to do was look interested in the contenders, make appropriate facial expressions, and then decide like a CEO who would stay and who would go. His power over others on and off TV stems from his ability to generate conflict and then manipulate competition among the embroilers, a tactic he used daily in the White House. Power derived from dramatic conflict became behavioral heroin for an otherwise abstemious man.

Trump never had to worry about sustenance. His entire life was assured of three squares a day. Security, the financial kind, was also a slam dunk (his father, Fred, gave him $200,000 a year starting at age three; he was a millionaire when he was eight years old[46]). Comfort was also assured, so he felt free to be the incubus for beautiful women. There never was much for him to strive for, so he decided to play instead. Everything was a game: doing deals, playing golf, chasing women—and he cheated at every one of them. Lying stems from cheating or the other way around, so he mastered each game by bending or ignoring the rules; he decided early on to abandon the standards of norms, morals, and ethics—that was for suckers. He believed his years of experience in the "rock 'em, sock 'em" New York real estate market, his tabloid fame, his heart of a gambler, and his professional life spent skirting the law made him bulletproof, cool, impregnable. It worked—kind of.

His biggest ego blunder was riding down the escalator of Trump Tower to declare his candidacy for president of the United States in 2016. Any hope for happiness as an individual vanished that day. While this step too far probably fated him to a moribund and desolate personal life in his later years, his polity took the lid off the unsettled conservative millions who had quietly tolerated their own frustrated existence (which was, for sure, all the "government's" fault). Trump gave them carte blanche to wail and act out about their grievances. His broom swept in marginal right-wing elements that traditional Republican politicians abhorred. He reached out to every nook and cranny of conservative psyche he and his advisors could find. Then he hugged them, assured them of their uniqueness, and lied to them all. His ethereal world became their ethereal world, and that was enough for them and him. The irony is that in real life, he wouldn't spend a social second with any of his common-citizen followers; he knows, for sure, he's way above them in every regard.

Vassalage, fealty, omertà—devotion blind to sensibility led thousands of Trump followers to the Capitol on January 6, 2021, to stop the certification of electors making Joe Biden president. Trump fanatics assaulted police, five people died, dozens were injured, and parts of the Capitol were trashed. Trump watched it all on television, his ethereal obsession. Only after 187 minutes, when the dust settled and reality set in, did Trump's maniacs begin to evaluate their futures. He tweeted his love for them and told them to go home.

Trump's base remains viable; the memory of him is still fresh. Many in this tribe will never change their minds about him, but some might when life's basics improve for them. Time and age may mollify some of the most fervent zealots; their thrall may slowly ebb. Trump's affinity for Vladimir Putin may also cost him some political points. However, the hold of individual exceptionalism is very strong in the conservative mind; it's the foundation for every conservative's mindset. Trumpers will deny that the human paradox, species sameness, and the tri-worlds have any relevance to their own lives; that's just liberal BS, they'll say. Donald's hardcore fanatics will continue to put more faith in their exceptional sense than in their natural or common senses. They will struggle to accept human sameness, tri-worlds balance, and the need to focus on species survival and planetary integrity because these things are counter to their sacred individualism; these issues don't generate the party-like high Trumpism does.

Like all mono- and bi-world conservatives, Trumpers stopped learning at some point in their lives and became intransigent/smug/arrogant about their own truths. Most will die before the changes espoused by this book emerge, and that's just fine with them. Trumpism's problem is that it sanctions a system in which the less intelligent lead the more intelligent. It values political reliability more than innate or learned ability; it replaces the human paradox and the tri-worlds with lies, half-truths, and distortions.

Beyond their truncated and parochial views, Trump followers are still fellow human beings. One can only hope that as the world transitions to more recognition of human sameness, they will acknowledge that they too are unique but the same as the rest of us. Maybe they need their pastor to convince them of that. Accepting and understanding the human paradox might be their gateway into new insights about themselves and their loved ones. The truth that we all live in three worlds our entire lives may help them realize that their conservatism is learned, not innate. Revelation can be secular as well as religious.

It's time to trump Trumpism by accepting the human paradox, human sameness, and the universality and importance of life's basics. Reorienting America's politics to the fulfillment of life's basics for more and more people while assuring natural integrity is the only realistic path forward for our own future and that of every other living species.

Chapter 6

Wrap-Up

Nothing can bring you peace but the triumph of principles.[47]
— Ralph Waldo Emerson, *Self-Reliance*

So what now?

Our species lacks a unifying political philosophy about life. Our current state of worldly affairs is locked into historical traditions and values that deny the whole for the sake of the individual, the "local" pod, and overvalued political boundaries. We love our dichotomies, our "me/us vs. you/them" competitions, our binary ethereal programming. Our species wallows in a fickle adolescence because we refuse to elevate the ultimate issues of species sameness, species survival, and planetary integrity above nations, ethnicities, and cultures.

The primary elements of species survival include:

- Recognizing the human paradox: we're all the same, yet each one is unique.
- Accepting human commonalities—that is, we all live in three worlds every minute of our lives.
- Fulfilling life's basics (sustenance, security, comfort) for more and more fellow human beings.
- Reestablishing and maintaining planetary integrity.

- Minimizing cultural/political/religious dualism and differentiation to serve our species best interests.
- Growing human priorities beyond nationalism, elite gratification, and political ego exceptionalism.

The main components of planetary integrity include:

- Accepting humans as one species among many.
- Recognizing natural-resource and ecosystem limitations as we pursue life's basics.
- Revising democracy and capitalism to recognize Earth's limits.
- Developing human productivity that mimics natural systems.
- Taking individual responsibility for eco survival (reducing personal carbon footprints).
- Giving back more to nature as we fulfill life's basics (reducing wastes, recycling, reusing).

Modern cultures and economies thrive on political dualism and differentiation because we have been taught that competition is key to survival; we still have deep-seated win/lose tendencies that we consider normal. We kill one another in senseless wars that serve antiquated ideals spurred on by outmoded leadership. We consume more and more stuff and support ever-upward economic growth because we can't imagine any other way to sustain ourselves. We overvalue comfort. We fill our mind-brains with fantasies that make us feel exceptional, that raise our egos to Olympian heights, that shield us from all the troubles/sins that we know are "out there."

Civilization's prevailing thought modes don't openly avow a citizen's role in extending species survival and preserving natural integrity, yet ironically, and as this book espouses, this mode of political thought may provide some of life's greatest rewards for the individual, the planet, and our species. America's original sin of slavery was sanctioned by the constitution and not faced by the founders, who decided to procrastinate that issue's resolution, which resulted in the Civil War. Let's not create another mega sin with today's grand issues; we don't need to put off decisions about species survival and planetary integrity when both provide such huge opportunities for a peaceful and prosperous future. If Americans ("we the people") need a new noble image of ourselves, let it be as the world leader of a polity based on human paradox understanding and acceptance, species survival, and natural integrity—a society that has morphed into a middle path both sane and considerate to its citizens, all of humanity, and the only planet we'll ever have.

The leader–follower model needs revamping. All political leaders everywhere should, at a minimum, aspire to fulfill life's basics for their citizenry while keeping nature whole. That's where thinking, caring citizens want to be led. The era of fawning over almighty and all-powerful leaders needs to die. Traditional hero worship gets the species nowhere; there are no he- (or she-) gods. Without shared species and planetary goals, leaders of all nations will continue to fall short of citizen expectations. They will continue to make promises they can't keep; they will continue to exercise their mono- and bi-world platitudes. But with universally shared goals, leaders can address issues followers genuinely care about (species survival, sustainable economic development, human sameness recognition, peace, and planetary integrity). They can set attainable, incremental goals; they can build the Sustainability Age.

Small thinking, exceptionalist loyalties, and conflict-ridden political leadership are all behaviors our species and planet can no longer abide because of declining natural resources and ecosystem debasement. Of course, the paradox rule says we'll always have to deal with these and similar attitudes, we'll always have local identities, and we'll still value "our" prideful achievements. Yet, we billions of Earth inhabitants don't have as many options for experimentation with civic, military, and judicial order as our ancestors did. We've got to set mutually beneficial goals and then achieve them sooner rather than later. If we don't shift our priorities to a species and planet focus, we'll just continue to shred our species and planet piecemeal. Status quo politics will debase us; climate change will degrade nature and human economies. *Homo sapiens* will regress to more belligerent behaviors.

You, the species-and-planet-oriented *individual*, are the key to change.

Here are some PRINCIPLES for your consideration:

- You are a natural being. Your existence and that of your species requires a respect for natural processes and a concerted effort to emulate them in the human-made world.
- Your body sustains you; you must sustain it. Healthful foods, exercise, and behavioral moderation are your concessions to its natural requirements.
- Your dignity rests upon this simple trinity: (a) self-respect, (b) respect for others, and (c) provable reality.
- You do your best to recognize someone as special every day by loving them, sharing with them, and helping them.
- You support the species every day by (a) pursuing reasonable objectives to attain life's basics, (b) living within your means, and (c) achieving success within the bounds of your conscience.
- You grant political power to those who acknowledge primary allegiance to our species, the primacy of life's basics, peace, sustainable development, and natural system integrity and replenishment.
- Species survival and natural integrity take precedence over dualistic and differentiating ideologies that can lead to conflict.
- You believe that women on the ascendant help balance perspectives that serve the species and the planet's best interests.
- All ethereal-world content needs grounding by the natural and human-made worlds for it to have value for species survival and planetary integrity.

Remember, you are both specialist and generalist during your lifetime. You may feel an overriding duty to serve your nation, profession, or faith, but you also have commitments to your species, other living species, our atmosphere, and the planet because you make choices, consume resources, and generate wastes. You are a natural, living being just as much as you are an executive, a carpenter, a beggar, a father, a Christian, a billionaire, or a politician. Only the dead can claim to be 100 percent specialists as they have totally mastered inactivity. We are all the same, yet each person is unique.

The human paradox and our shared three worlds (natural, human-made, ethereal) compose reality and can serve as a global alternative to political structures that divide rather than unite. Remember our tagline: Human

Fulfillment on a Whole Planet. By working outwardly from a core understanding of the human paradox and the three worlds, the claims, arguments, and shouts of others can be scrutinized and evaluated based on species and planetary realities rather than a simplistic, self-serving, or fantastical spin.

Without individual and national commitments to species sameness and natural integrity, we human beings have nothing to look forward to but more self-inflicted wounds from dualism and differentiation, wounds that never completely heal and can lead to more exceptionalist rationales as to why we hate one another, all behaviors founded on base instincts and fears rather than common human values and beneficent ethereal faiths.

Here are the hard facts we now face:

1. The natural world cannot and will not change its ways while you and I are alive on this planet.
2. Within the human-made world, we humans will continue to explore and exploit nature because we have no choice; we need natural resources to attain life's basics.
3. Within our mind-brains, we humans are impatient/frustrated with the natural and human-made worlds, so we fill our heads with ethereal ideals and fantasies that give disproportionate weight to dualism, differentiation, and exceptionalism.

Conclusion: we human beings do not value our basic species sameness. We tend to value our human-made and ethereal world constructs more than nature. We focus on the short term rather than the long term because we struggle to comprehend (and care for) any time frame beyond our own lives. Also, we value our individual comfort more than the sustenance and security of others. We easily recognize individual uniqueness as manifest in elite/mentor/celebrity status while we concomitantly downplay species sameness. We are convinced that dualism and differentiation have more value than sameness even though deep within ourselves, we know that's not true. We know we're capable of political change, but we're very reluctant or afraid to act. Admitting to and then modifying these attitudes are the genesis of accepting the human paradox and tri-worlds progress in assuring species survival and planetary integrity.

Let's end with a few ACTION ITEMS to complement our principles:

- Remember every day that you are unique but the same as the rest of us.
- Feed all three worlds by overcoming ignorance wherever you find it, especially within yourself.
- Honor nature by respecting your body and nature's gifts.
- Develop your specialized skills and knowledge with vigor and commitment; aspire for excellence but disavow greed.
- Be skeptical of human-made world and ethereal world movers and shakers (everyone is selling something).
- Embrace the practical; eschew the fantastical.
- Remember that ethereal powers reside only in human mind-brains; use them to inspire and motivate, not to deceive or harm.
- If you believe in a personal god, assume that he's removed himself from human affairs. Take on the divine loving/nurturing/sustaining role yourself and act accordingly.
- Support leaders whose actions affirm a commitment to understanding and acceptance of the human paradox, life's basics, human sameness, sustainable economic development, natural integrity/restoration, and peace.
- Old sex roles—male as protector/provider, female as nurturer/homemaker—are already breaking down; do what you can to quicken the pace.
- Support politics founded on species and natural sovereignty. It's time for everyone to graduate to species-level thinking and action guided by human beings alive on this planet today.

Do what you can to create *ourstory* and do it passionately. Consider it your patriotic duty.

ENDNOTES

1 Heather McGhee, *The Sum of Us: What Racism Costs Everyone and How We Can Prosper Together*, One World, an imprint of Random House, New York, p. 273.

2 Donald J. Trump, *Think Like a Billionaire*, Ballantine Books, New York, p. xviii.

3 National Human Genome Research Institute, "Human Genetic Variation," www.genome.gov/dna-day/15 ways/human-genome-variation.

4 Henry David Thoreau, *Walden*, Quality Paperback Book Club, New York, 1997. p. 118.

5 Infoplease.com, National Center for Health Statistics, National Vital Statistics Reports, vol. 54, no. 19, June 28, 2006; NationMaster.com, various United Nations and other citings.

6 Edward O. Wilson, *The Future of Life*, Alfred A. Knopf, New York, 2002, p. 106.

7 Jared Diamond, Collapse, *How Societies Choose to Fail or Succeed*, Penguin Books, New York, 2006, p. 488.

8 Charles Darwin, *The Descent of Man*, Encyclopedia Britannica Inc., Great Books, Chicago, 1952, p. 590.

9 Thomas Malthus, *An Essay on the Principle of Population*, 6th Edition, John Murray, 1826, Book III, Chap. VI, p. 12.

10 Herbert Spencer, *Principles in Biology*, 1864.

11 Tim Flannery, "The Weather Makers," Grove Press, New York, 2005.

12 Jeffrey Moussaieff Masson and Susan McCarthy, *When Elephants Weep: The Emotional Lives of Animals*, Delta Book published by Dell Publishing, New York, 1995, p. 232.

13 Will and Ariel Durant, *The Age of Reason Begins*, Simon and Schuster, vol. VII, The Story of Civilization, p. 646.

14 Fritjof Capra, *The Turning Point: Science, Society and the Rising Culture*, a Bantam Book, published originally by Simon & Schuster, 1982, p.57.

15 Ibid., p. 59.
16 Ervin Laszlo, *The Systems View of the World*, Hampton Press, Cresskill, New Jersey, 1996, p. 11.
17 Op. Cit., Capra, p. 92.
18 Ibid., p. 87
19 Op. Cit., Laszlo, p. 10.
20 Oliver Wendell Holmes, U.S. author and physician.
21 *Oxford English Dictionary*, 2nd Edition, vol. 4, Creel–Duzepere, 1989, p. 656.
22 *Newsweek*, April 7, 2008.
23 Ronny Shaked, "The Palestinian Rothschild," Israel News (IsraelNationalNews.com), July 27, 2006, www.ynetnews.com/articles.
24 Warren Buffett Quotes, Brainy Quotes: www.brainyquote.com/quotes/authors/w/warren_buffett.html
25 Lipsey, Sparks, Steiner, *Economics*, Harper & Row, New York, 1973.
26 Edwin Mansfield, *Economics*, W. W. Norton & Co., 4th Edition, New York, 1983.
27 Geoff Dembicki, "The Case for Climate Liability," *Audubon Magazine*/Fall 2021, p. 12.
28 Herman E. Daly, *Steady-State Economics*, Island Press, Washington, D.C., p. 17.
29 Ibid., p. 18.
30 Tim Jackson, *Prosperity Without Growth: Economics for a Finite Planet*, Earthscan, London, Washington, D.C., 2009, pp. 2, 3, 141, 142.
31 Fred Krupp and Miriam Horn, *Earth: The Sequel*, copyright Environmental Defense Fund, W. W. Norton & Co., New York, 2008, p. 8.
32 Robert J. Gordon, *The Rise and Fall of American Growth*, Princeton University Press, 2016.
33 Bill Gates, *How to Avoid a Climate Disaster*, Borzoi Book, A. Knopf, 2021, pp. 59–60.
34 Klaus Schwab, with Peter Vanham, *Stakeholder Capitalism*, Wiley, 2021, p. 26.
35 Ibid. p. 249.
36 Naomi Klein, "The Bailout: Bush's Final Pillage," The Nation, November 17, 2008.
37 Hernando de Soto, *The Mystery of Capital*, Basic Books, New York, 2000.
38 Wikipedia, "Big Lie."
39 Karl Marx, *Critique of the Gotha Program*, 1875.
40 The U.S. Declaration of Independence, July 4, 1776.
41 U.S. Constitution preamble, September 17, 1787.
42 Quote DB: www.quotedb.com/quotes/675
43 Bart D. Ehrman, *Misquoting Jesus*, HarperSanFrancisco, 2005, pp. 89, 207.

44 Bart D. Ehrman, *Jesus Interrupted*, Harper Collins, New York, 2009, pp. 102–112.

45 Emmanuel LeRoy Ladurie, *Montaillou, Cathars, and Catholics in a French Village*, Editions Gallimard, 1978.

46 David Barstow, Susanne Craig, Russ Buettner, *New York Times*, October 2, 2018.

47 Ralph Waldo Emerson, *Self-Reliance.*

Index

Judaism, 227, 233

USSR. *See* Soviet Union (USSR)

V

Vatican, 44
Vietnam, xii, 95, 239–40, 243–46, 252
Vietnam War, xi, 95

W

Wallace, A. R., 72
Wall Street, 117, 128, 131
Walnut Creek, California, 164–65, 168–69
Wayne, John, 253
Weather Makers, The, 78, 265
When Elephants Weep, 80, 265
White House, U. S., 44, 127, 255
Wilson, Edward O., 66–67, 265
World Economic Forum, 126
World War I, *247–248*
World War II, *186*, *239*, *247*, 248

Y

Yahweh, 29, 178, 227
Yellen, Janet, 204